Everything
I Never
Dreamed

Everything
I Never
Dreamed

My Life Surviving
and Standing Up to
Domestic Violence

RUTH M. GLENN

ATRIA BOOKS

NEW YORK   LONDON   TORONTO   SYDNEY   NEW DELHI

An Imprint of Simon & Schuster, Inc.
1230 Avenue of the Americas
New York, NY 10020

First Atria Books hardcover edition October 2022

ATRIA B O O K S and colophon are trademarks of Simon & Schuster, Inc.

For information about special discounts for bulk purchases, please contact Simon & Schuster Special Sales at 1-866-506-1949 or business@simonandschuster.com.

The Simon & Schuster Speakers Bureau can bring authors to your live event. For more information or to book an event, contact the Simon & Schuster Speakers Bureau at 1-866-248-3049 or visit our website at www.simonspeakers.com.

Interior design by Hope Herr-Cardillo

Manufactured in the United States of America

1   3   5   7   9   10   8   6   4   2

Library of Congress Cataloging-in-Publication Data
Names: Glenn, Ruth M., author.
Title: Everything I never dreamed / Ruth M. Glenn.
Description: First Atria Books hardcover edition. | New York : Atria Books, 2022. | Includes bibliographical references and index.
Identifiers: LCCN 2022016025 (print) | LCCN 2022016026 (ebook) | ISBN 9781982196004 (hardcover) | ISBN 9781982196011 (paperback) | ISBN 9781982196028 (ebook)
Subjects: LCSH: Glenn, Ruth M. | Abused wives—United States—Biography. | Women—Abuse of—United States. | Women—Violence against—United States. | Family violence—United States. | National Coalition Against Domestic Violence (U.S.)
Classification: LCC HV6626.2 .G545 2022 (print) | LCC HV6626.2 (ebook) | DDC 362.82/92092 [B]—dc23/eng/20220613
LC record available at https://lccn.loc.gov/2022016025
LC ebook record available at https://lccn.loc.gov/2022016026

ISBN 978-1-9821-9600-4
ISBN 978-1-9821-9602-8 (ebook)

To David, my one and only,
my son, my life, whom I love fully.

And to my grandchildren—
Jordan, Josiah, Deontae, Jocelyn, Jocie, and Joseph.

And to my great-grandchildren—
Jayleen, Elena, and Ethan.

These people are the loves of my life.

And to their mothers, for the gift of them—
Danielle, Laura, Jennifer, and Darcie.

Contents

Part IV: Designing Solutions

Everything
I Never
Dreamed

Prologue

In 1992, when I was thirty-two years old and living in an apartment in Denver with my fifteen-year-old son, David, my husband kidnapped me at gunpoint. I had left Cedric a few months before, after years of physical violence and emotional abuse, and taken David with me. We had moved into the apartment on a Friday in late September. By the following Monday, Cedric had found us. A female friend of his had gotten my new address by going into my bank and pretending to be me—ID checks were a little more lax then than they are now. She'd also wiped my account clean. That morning, I had been talking on the phone with a woman from Project Safeguard, an organization that supports victims of domestic violence, through safety planning and legal advocacy, when someone started pushing the buzzer at the main door of my apartment building. I could hear it ringing through our intercom. I tried to focus on what the woman was saying. I wanted to find out about their legal clinic, I wanted information about getting a divorce. But the longer the woman and I spoke, the more she realized I was very likely in danger from Cedric. She suggested that I immediately seek an emergency protection order to keep him away from us. And then, as if on cue, I heard Cedric's voice coming through the little speaker in the hallway. David had pressed the button just to ask who it was. He knew better than to buzz his father in.

The woman from Project Safeguard called the police and said David and I should get on the floor. She kept me on the phone as Cedric demanded to be let in. By the time the police arrived, Cedric was gone, or had hidden. They escorted David and me out, and we stayed at a shelter for two nights. Shelters are invaluable to women being abused, and I'll be forever grateful for them. Everyone working there was kind and supportive. But shelters aren't the cure-all people often think they are. I felt very on edge there. I knew that going to a shelter was another layer of trauma for David, after we'd just fled the home we shared with his father. I managed to get a temporary protection order against Cedric. But it soon became clear that wasn't a cure-all either. It would protect me from nothing.

I had laid the groundwork for leaving Cedric very carefully. In a domestic abuse situation, you don't discuss it with your abuser. Saying you're leaving, or being caught trying to, can get you killed. Domestic violence is all about control; signaling you are about to assume some autonomy is very often the trigger for an escalation of violence and more desperate attempts by the abuser at controlling you.

Cedric was very explicit about the danger I was in. He used to say to me, "If you leave, even if you're in Alaska, I will find you." Sometimes he just said, "I'll kill you if you leave."

You feel damned if you do and damned if you don't. Sometimes, as strange as it sounds, the safer option for the moment is to stay.

But once I'd made the decision, I worked stealthily. I had been putting aside money for months, and had opened my own checking account. I'd hunted for an apartment in secret, and paid the deposit on it. The phone and utilities were hooked up and waiting for us. Cedric didn't know about any of it, but there was a slight change in the air. He could sense that my attitude was different. He suspected something was up, and he got a little calmer, though it wasn't a pleasant sort of calm: I could feel him observing me.

It wasn't just Cedric I kept it from. I'd told almost no one I was leaving him. I was afraid if Cedric found out someone had supported my decision, their lives would be in danger, too. I didn't even tell David we were leaving until he got home from school that day. The two of us packed up the U-Haul I'd rented and drove to the new apartment. (To protect my friends who knew, I wouldn't accept their offers of help moving.) And then I went back to the house for Cedric's 9 p.m. call. Whenever he was working double shifts at the Colorado Division of Youth Services (where I also worked), he'd call me on his break to make sure I was home. I knew that if I didn't pick up the phone that night, he'd immediately get suspicious. So I bought myself some extra time by racing back for the call.

And then I went to my new apartment, to begin the rest of my life.

I was on my own now, but I was far from free. Stalking and harassment are an abuser's way of demanding that you think about them, that you live in fear of them; it's a theft not only of your freedom of movement but also of your inner world. Over the next few months, Cedric continued to stalk and harass me. He would show up when he was drunk, or high, or agitated. He used to park in the outdoor lot or sit in the grassy yard that faced our apartment, from where he could see our balcony. He called me one day from his house and said, "You think I'm not watching you? Look out your window." There was actually a worn patch in the grass where he sat—or even slept, when he was passed out drunk.

And then came the day in 1992, when I pulled into the parking garage attached to our building. There was Cedric, standing in my assigned spot. He had a bottle of liquor in one hand; the other hand was in his pocket. As many times as I'd seen him angry, this was worse. He looked possessed. I thought, *I don't even know this person.*

He came around to the passenger side of the car and climbed in. "Drive," he said.

I said, "What's this all about, Cedric?"

"Just drive to my house."

"Where's David?" I asked.

"Listen, bitch. David's just fine."

I tried to get him to talk to me about what was going on, but then he pulled a gun out of his pocket, and said again, "Drive."

"Okay, okay," I said, "just don't hurt me."

I backed out of my spot and headed slowly toward the garage exit. There was a maintenance man at the garage door, fiddling with his toolbox but with an eye on Cedric and me. I clearly remember thinking he suspected something was wrong and was trying to figure out what was happening. I looked at him and tried to communicate that I was scared and needed help, that I was being taken against my will, but either I was being too subtle because I was terrified, or the man was too afraid to intervene.

Cedric told me to drive to his house, about six miles away, in Aurora. As we turned onto East Hampden Avenue, just a few minutes from my apartment, I was trying to figure out if I could jump out of the car. One of the things that stopped me was the fear that I could cause an accident that would leave other people injured. So I just kept driving, wondering how I was going to get out of this alive. I don't recall that we said much on the way, but at some point Cedric told me he'd been upstairs in the apartment with David. By then, our son had seen enough to know that Cedric was likely going to go after me, which was why, as we neared Cedric's house, I saw a police car flying down the road in the opposite direction, away from us: David had called them right after Cedric left our apartment, and he'd given them Cedric's home address. When they didn't find anyone there, they left for my apartment.

Cedric saw the cop car, too, and said, "You just keep driving."

Later I would think I should have flashed my headlights at them or honked or swerved off the road. But I was in a car with someone I knew might kill me, and I couldn't think straight.

Cedric lived in a split-level house in Aurora with his girlfriend. I didn't see her when we went inside. Cedric grabbed some money and the bullets that were lying on the coffee table.

Holy shit, I thought.

When you're in a relationship with a violent abuser, you learn how to manage the chaos and violence to minimize the risk of escalation and the danger to yourself and your children. You learn how to appease, how to pretend to be passive. You learn to maneuver in the presence of your abuser because your life depends on it. *Just go along with it*, I thought. *Just keep him calm.*

Cedric told me to get back in the car, and to head out 6th Avenue. He didn't say where we were going. He would only say, "Turn left here," or "Now turn right." It was clear he had a destination in mind, but was making me take a back way, on side streets, to avoid the cops. It was like being in a maze but knowing that wherever we eventually emerged would only be the beginning of another nightmare. *I'm a captive*, I thought, *and not a single person outside of this car knows where I am or what's happening to me.* Rattling around in my head that whole drive were the words *Does anybody see me? How can I get them to see?*

PART I

Before

CHAPTER 1
Somebody

The people we come from are never perfect. Many of us spend our lives trying to make peace with their flaws, or trying to shape ourselves in opposition to them.

When I think of my mother now, what comes to mind first is her strength. She possessed incredible fortitude—she wouldn't have lived through the things she did without it.

Of course, it's not that simple. I have spent my life with a set of contradictory feelings about my mother, a state of constant tension that has never resolved itself. On the one hand, there is that strength, and the admiration I feel for it. On the other, there was something about mom, the way the world had beaten her down, the way she seemed at times to inhabit the role of victim too readily, that made me determined to become the opposite. It has never been about being better than she was; it's been about not letting the world wear me down—not society, or the environment I was living in, or people who didn't want the best for me.

My mother, whose name was Bobbie, grew up in Sacramento. Her parents were white working-class people of German extraction. It was an abusive household. Her mother, Wilma, who had a job in a cannery, was a bear, a domineering woman who abused my mother physically and verbally. My mother told me a story about Wilma throwing a pair of scissors at her one day, which stuck in her leg. My grandfather, Earl, was the opposite, small and docile, an electrician, but also an alcoholic. I gather that he, too, suffered at the hands of Wilma.

Mom was a wild child, always chafing against her mother's attempts to control her. By the age of fourteen, she was pregnant. It would be the first of nine pregnancies (she would lose two of those children—a son after two days, and a daughter who lived only a few hours). Ric was her first child, born in 1952. She and Don, Ric's father, married only to give Ric a surname, but they never lived together. The marriage was annulled immediately after Ric's birth. He didn't talk to his father until just before Don died in 2008.

For the first couple of years of Ric's life, he and my mother lived with Wilma and Earl. Although she was always clashing with Wilma, my mother stayed at her parents' house until she was eighteen; Wilma had threatened to take Ric away if my mother left when she was still a minor. But once she was gone, she was *gone*; she barely spoke to her mother again. By the time Mom was out on her own, she'd met her second husband, Bill Mead, a ranch hand and rodeo rider, who had wandered into Cooper's Doughnuts on K Street, where she was working. They married and moved north to Eureka, where Mom got a job as an information operator with the phone company and Bill went to work on a ranch. Mom's second son, Will, was born soon after, and in 1958, she lost Robert, her third son. So many details of my mother's complicated history of husbands and children are murky, and I have never known the cause of Robert's death. But my mother remembered riding in the family car with Ric and her husband Bill, taking Robert's casket to the cemetery in Arcata, her neighbors having been generous in providing flowers and paying for the small grave marker.

Shortly after Robert's death, Mom and Bill separated. She was soon on her way to Reno, intent on learning how to deal cards so she could work in the casinos. My father was in the air force, stationed then at the nearby Stead Air Force Base. My mother's first two husbands had been white, as she was, but my father, David—whom everyone called David E. because his middle name was Edward—was Black. When they began seeing each other in 1959, they were subject to the usual trouble that interracial couples had then. One night out walking they were arrested and put in jail for a few hours. Their crime was "vagrancy"—a catch-all term police used if they wanted to harass people like my parents, warning them against carrying on together.

My mother got pregnant very quickly after meeting David E. They weren't together long, and though I would make contact with my father at a couple of points in my life, I never did learn much about him. For several years I actually believed that my stepfather, Alvin, was my biological father; he was Black and his name was on my birth certificate, after all.

My mother had met Alvin through a friend at a New Year's Eve party in 1959, while she was pregnant with me. Within a year of my birth we had moved to Riverside, California, and I already had a baby brother. My mother would go on to have three more sons with Alvin, as well as a daughter, Juanita, who died soon after birth.

Alvin worked off and on as a trash man and a janitor. Once in a while, he would bring something home from his trash pickups, like a tricycle. We were poor enough that even a toy taken from the trash seemed new and exciting. Mostly we were living on welfare. All of us in that household endured violence at Alvin's hands. There were times I had to protect my mother and my younger brothers from Alvin's rage. I recall one awful day when Alvin had my mother in the laundry area and was trying to put her head in the washing machine. When I realized there was nothing I could do to stop him, I got my brothers outside and safely out of Alvin's reach. (Facebook, in their infinite wisdom, recently suggested I "friend" Alvin.)

There is a photo I have of my mother with two of my brothers, Ronnie and Brady, and me. There is also a white child with us, a neighbor whose mother must have snapped the photo. I see several stories when I look at this picture. First, I notice that my mother isn't looking at the camera. She never did until she was much older. She didn't want to see herself. (I'm not looking at the camera either but in my case it may be because of my bad eyesight. I am squinting, as I always did in the years before I got glasses.) But what comes across most poignantly to me from my mother's expression, what I can see from her bowed head, is sadness. I see the sheer hopelessness and helplessness of her existence. I also see a white woman with three Black children. That alone—never mind the abuse and the poverty—must have been incredibly isolating and difficult; there just wasn't a society then that was open to her and her family.

Judging by our ages in the photos, it's a good bet my mother was pregnant when the picture was taken. I think Alvin kept my mother pregnant deliberately—what is known in the domestic violence world as "reproductive coercion," and what in those days might have been called, more crudely, "barefoot and pregnant." Gary was the last of my mother's children, and though I was only eight, I would soon be taking care of him. My mother simply wasn't able. By then she must have felt her life had spun completely out of control. Five children under the age of nine, very little money, and Alvin's constant abuse. She was also coping with the loss of Juanita, who was born in August 1963. The days around Juanita's birth and death would weigh heavily on my mother. Years later, she described to Ric how Alvin went into the funeral home to see Juanita and came out looking like he was in a state of shock. He told my mother that they had Juanita lying on the counter in a paper bag and that she should definitely not go in and look. The guy who owned the place had actually said to Alvin, "I don't know what all the fuss is about, she only lived six hours, it's not like she was a normal baby." My mother was haunted by images of how such a person would dispose of her daughter's body.

My mother had medical problems after Juanita's birth. She was in a weakened state, mentally and physically. Alvin, meanwhile, was up to his usual "ripping and running the streets," as she would say—carousing and philandering—and it was all she could do to take care of the three children she had at home. "I didn't follow through about Juanita," she told Ric. "And it really bothers me now, as do all my shortcomings when they come back to smack me in the face."

By the time my brother Gary was born, I had learned from a neighbor girl that Alvin wasn't my biological father. I was so happy I wept. It wasn't long until I decided that I had to find my father. Part of the impulse was wanting a protector, and imagining that he could be that. My mother was a little reluctant to stir anything up, but she agreed to help me. She understood how important it was to me given the life we had with Alvin, and to her credit she soon began making phone calls. She ended up tracking David E. down through the air base in Reno where he'd been stationed. By then he was living back in South Carolina. I had a vision, like any young kid whose parent has vanished, that that parent was going to swoop in and save me, but my father definitely wasn't up to the task. We did exchange a few letters—in one he enclosed a Polaroid of himself—but I was the more eager correspondent. He was undereducated, and his letters were more like notes; I can still see the few lines of chicken scratch. And then the contact abruptly ended. We would communicate just once more, in 1992, several years before he died. But by then, my father, and whatever I had dreamed he might be to me, had receded into the background of my life.

——

I have heard people say being a victim of domestic violence is akin to being a prisoner of war. I've never been a prisoner of war in the literal sense, but from what I've read of that experience, I think it's an appropriate analogy. (In the 1980s, those working in the field of trauma began to understand that the psychological syndrome seen in survivors of rape, domestic battery, and incest was essentially the same as that seen in combat veterans and survivors of war.) The impediments to your escape might not be in the form of locked doors or chains—though of course there are such instances—but they nonetheless exist, in economic, legal, and social forms, and in the form of sheer terror. When you're abused within your own home, you are always kept off-kilter; you never know what the day will bring, or what your abuser will do from one minute to the next. You just pray it's a good day, and you live your life in the grip of fear, enduring abuse that is hidden from the outside world. The way an abuser isolates you, and keeps you guessing, is part of the psychological manipulation, the exercise of control. You're constantly in reactive mode, trying to predict what will keep you safe today, or at least alive, which might be different from what kept you alive yesterday. And in the process, that person you used to be, the perspectives she had on things, the way she saw herself, slowly erodes.* It can become hard to remember the time when cruelty and violence were not the norm—to really believe that they *aren't* normal. When you think about your escape, you know that if your plan fails, or your will falters, you could wind up in a more terrifying scenario than you've ever been in before. You could even wind up dead.

I don't know what finally drove my mother to leave Alvin. She never discussed it with me, even when I was much older and leaving my own abusive husband. I know only that on the 4th of July, 1970, when I was ten years old, my brothers and I were hanging around the kitchen while my mother cooked fried chicken, and at a certain point, as though in answer to an inner voice, she looked around and said, "We're leaving."

There must have been more to the moment than that (had her sudden decisiveness followed an argument, or some particularly awful abuse?), but the fact that I remember it that way probably says something about how I felt growing up in that household: the sense of unpredictability, how I too often had no idea what was going to happen or why.

My mother loaded up the station wagon and we piled in. It wasn't an easy getaway. For whatever reason, my mother didn't wait until Alvin was out, and I recall, as though it were yesterday, the mayhem that accompanied our departure: my stepfather and uncle attempting to drag me out of the car; one of my younger brothers climbing a tree at one point to get away from Alvin. We did manage to get away, and though we were

---

* Throughout the book I have often referred to victims of domestic and sexual violence as female and abusers as male. This reflects what is most often the case but is not meant to exclude the many men and nonbinary people who are also victims of domestic and sexual violence.

terrified of him hunting us down, I only remember him showing up once at our house.

We landed on the top floor of a duplex at Park Avenue and 11th in the Eastside neighborhood of Riverside, a poor section of town where there was gang activity. Our house, which was rimmed by a chain-link fence, was dilapidated and in need of painting. No one lived on the first floor, and at night, transients and homeless people would sometimes sleep there. By then, I was accustomed to poverty and chaos.

And then I met Mrs. Malcolm. She was my fifth-grade teacher—young, energetic, and fashionable, she carried herself with an air of confidence and was very kind. In her apartment, I would discover my first oasis of calm. A few years earlier, I never would have crossed paths with her. But busing had recently begun in our school district, and so I was bused to Liberty Elementary, a majority-white school about seven miles away, in the Arlington neighborhood, where Mrs. Malcolm taught.

When people think of segregation during that period, they think mostly of the American South, but de facto segregation was the norm in California, and racial tensions were high. (Even as late as the early 1980s, the Riverside–San Bernardino arm of the KKK was the largest of its three branches in California.) In the late summer of 1965, as the Watts riots were unfolding in Los Angeles, parents of minority children in Eastside had begun to organize and speak out about inequities in the segregated local schools—substandard books, dilapidated buildings, understocked cafeterias. They were preparing to address the school board about it, but in September, just before children would return to their classrooms, an elementary school attended almost entirely by minority students was burned to the ground. Lowell School was less than ten blocks from my house. The fire was almost certainly arson, though no one has ever been arrested for setting it.

The fire, coming on the heels of the Watts riots, put people in Riverside on edge. Staff were told to visit the campus only with police escort. But the fire triggered action. Almost immediately, the school board pledged to create an integration plan within a month. By October 1965, Riverside had become the first large school district in the nation to integrate its schools without having been ordered by a court to do so.

So there I was, on the big yellow bus, headed to Mrs. Malcolm's class.

Aside from me, the "mixed-race girl," there were only two Black children in the class. Racism insinuated itself in subtle and not-so-subtle ways. When one of the girls from the more well-to-do white families got head lice, her mother went to Mrs. Malcolm and said, "The Eastside kids are giving our kids lice." The nurse came and checked all of our heads, going through our hair with her fingers. (Even Mrs. Malcolm took off her 1970s-era wig and had her own head checked.) But no one in the class except the nice white girl and her friend had lice. The Eastside kids weren't the source of the infestation after all.

At that age, I felt plain-looking—or even homely, depending on the day. I was skinny and wore the great big glasses I'd had since I was in kindergarten. But despite episodes like the head-lice accusation, I remember a feeling of safety in elementary school, and Mrs. Malcolm had a lot to do with that. I was the sort of student any teacher would love—I always had my homework done, always raised my hand, was always polite. On the playground, I could hold my own, through a toughness I learned from growing up with brothers, but in class, I was the model student.

Mrs. Malcolm was in her second year of teaching, and she picked up on my love of reading and nurtured it. There were no books in our house, so I read whatever I could find at school—*Pippi Longstocking*, *Onion John*, the Nancy Drew series. Mrs. Malcolm took me to buy books of my own, too. She encouraged me to read the Newbery Award winners, given each year to the best children's books.

Mrs. Malcolm spoke to me in a way no one ever had. She asked me questions and listened carefully to my replies, as though what I said mattered. She was the first person who made me feel I was *somebody*.

Sometimes, Mrs. Malcolm would pick me up on a Saturday and I'd stay over at her apartment. Her husband was working nights, and I'd eat dinner with the two of them and then he would go off to work. Mrs. Malcolm showed me a world I wouldn't otherwise have seen. We went to the movies. She took me to my first musical, a children's show at the Fox Theater in Riverside; we sat in the balcony, and I was mesmerized. She took me out to dinner, too, showed me how to order in a restaurant. We'd go shopping at the mall: pretty socks, colored barrettes, cookies, ice cream. My brothers wanted to know everything I'd gotten to do at Mrs. Malcolm's. They'd beg to go with us, and Mrs. Malcolm would always say, "I'm sorry, it's just a girls' outing." Because it wasn't only about the treats or the exposure to new experiences—things my own family couldn't afford. It was the quiet of her apartment, the way I had peace there. At home, I had four brothers and my mother's various boyfriends. I felt lost in the chaos—hardly even seen. At Mrs. Malcolm's, I could sit and read on the porch, without all the screaming and yelling, without anybody wanting or demanding anything from me. There were always fresh towels by the tub, and I spent hours in the bath, sometimes even reading in there!

Then we'd call it a night and I would sleep on the couch, which Mrs. Malcolm had carefully made up for me—sheets and blankets that I would fold up again just as carefully in the morning.

Something told me that I should never allow my mother to see how happy I was to be going to Mrs. Malcolm's. Maybe part of that was not wanting to hurt my mother's feelings, but mostly I was afraid that if I seemed too excited, my mother would put a stop to the visits. She could see that Mrs. Malcolm and I were becoming very close, and instinctively I knew that that was threatening to my mother. She already didn't like my 3 a.m. reading under the covers—when she caught me awake, she'd wallop me. But Nancy Drew, or whatever else I could get my hands on, took me away from where I was.

Mrs. Malcolm was white, and I'm conscious here of painting a picture of the white savior. I don't want to cast her in that role, or cast myself in the role of a Black girl who needed saving by a white woman. My mother was white, after all. It wasn't the white world Mrs. Malcolm gave me, but a *stable* world, an alternative to my chaotic life at home. It was a place of books and the time and space for reading them. A place where I felt listened to, but also where I had privacy and tranquility. Even now, after so many years working in the field of domestic violence, when I see women or children who don't have a bolt-hole of even temporary stability and calm, I think of what a gift that was for my ten-year-old self.

Eventually, Mrs. Malcolm asked my mother if I could live with her. She had been to the house to pick me up many times and had seen the disorder, the mayhem, the state of the house itself. She had seen my mother, who wasn't working then, sitting alone at the kitchen table, smoking, no doubt depressed. She said that if ever my mother would agree, she and her husband could adopt me. Not surprisingly, this didn't go down well with my mother. Her response was to bar me from seeing Mrs. Malcolm. My visits to her house stopped. The school year was over, so maybe it didn't seem so strange to me that I no longer visited Mrs. Malcolm. I understood that she and my mother had talked about *something*, but it wasn't until years later that I learned exactly what that something was.

The following year I went to middle school and soon lost touch with Mrs. Malcolm. But the people who've helped to shape us have a habit of coming back into our lives. Though Mrs. Malcolm and I would find and lose each other more than once over the coming decades, she's a part of my life now, and we share a unique bond.

When I think about Mrs. Malcolm asking my mother if I could live with her—the two women who were the most important people in my life mulling over who could raise me better—I feel for my mother. I was her only girl, her shining star.

She would say to other people, in front of me, "That child is smart." In a way I think Mrs. Malcolm's attentiveness toward me woke my mother up to my potential; she had always seen certain qualities in me—a feistiness, or "moxie," as she called it—but after Mrs. Malcolm, her expectations for me grew. Unfortunately, she never tried to give me the tools to meet those expectations or to realize my potential; maybe she had no idea how. She must have known that in an environment where I'd get the sort of attention she didn't have time to give me, where I'd be encouraged to read and be exposed to learning and culture, I'd thrive in a way I wasn't going to at our house in Eastside. But I don't blame my mother for saying no to Mrs. Malcolm's offer. I'm sure she didn't want to contemplate the possibility that someone else could do a better job of raising me. And she didn't want to let me go. Mom had so little agency in her life that refusing Mrs. Malcolm—*No, you are not going to take my child*—was a rare chance to exercise some control.

I didn't find out about all of this until I was in my thirties. My mother and I were talking one day about the difficult relationships she'd had with certain people in my life—among them, Cedric's mother and Mrs. Malcolm. "Well, you didn't know . . . ," my mother began, and then she told me what Mrs. Malcolm had offered to do. She asked me what I had said to Mrs. Malcolm about our home, or about her, that would have caused her to suggest such a thing. I hadn't told Mrs. Malcolm anything. She could see for herself. But my mother couldn't let go of that sense of grievance, of believing I had betrayed her and led Mrs. Malcolm to question her mothering, and I detected the slightest hint of satisfaction in the revelation.

My mother is someone who might have lived a very different life herself had she been given the chance. She was tough. As hurt as I was by her lack of warmth, and as stormy as our relationship was, I will always respect her for having been able to endure what she did, for not cracking. She had incredible resilience.

I spent a lot of time in my childhood dreaming of someone coming to save me. To learn so many years after the fact that someone had offered, and been refused, was disorienting and sad. It was a chance I had never even known I'd had. I don't know how I would have felt, leaving my mother's house, but if the decision had been up to me, I think I would have done it. And so I wonder still, as anyone would, what might have been.

CHAPTER 2

That Little Voice

Not long after I stopped visiting Mrs. Malcolm, I met my half brother Ric for the first time. I was twelve years old. Ric was twenty-one and had been drafted in February 1973, just a few months before the draft ended. He was on his way to basic training at Fort Ord, near Carmel, and he stopped in Riverside for a few days.

The reason I had never met Ric was that he had been estranged from my mother for many years. My mother's story had always been that when Ric and Will were about seven and five, her mother Wilma took them. However, Ric told me it wasn't like that at all. When I was a newborn, my mother put Ric and Will in the car, and drove them to her sister Pat's house in Quincy, California, where she left them. Ric and Will would live between Pat's home and Wilma's until they were old enough to be on their own. Ric remembers vividly the two-hour car ride and the drop-off in the middle of the night, the incredible sadness of it all. Neither of us is sure why our mother did that. Maybe it had something to do with my father having entered my mother's life. Maybe she felt her sister could offer the boys a more stable life. Maybe my mother simply felt overwhelmed with two young sons, a baby daughter, and the grief she must have been carrying from Robert's death. Whatever the reason, her decision spared Ric and Will from growing up with my violent stepfather, Alvin.

I was thrilled to be meeting Ric—my oldest brother, someone from the world beyond the one we lived in, where I often felt so trapped. We hit it off immediately. I remember during the days of his visit just wanting to be wherever he was. He is still the brother I have the most contact with.

Ric is a cowboy hat–wearing white guy and I'm a liberal Black feminist, but we have a strong and loving bond; I'm still his little sister. When I ask him now what he remembers of that first meeting, he says, "You were a doll. The boys were wild, but you were Mom's little girl."

By then we had moved to a much nicer place in the University neighborhood. Mom had gotten a house with the support of social services. In the two years between leaving Alvin and Ric's visit, she'd already been married and divorced again. She had also begun to work for the State of California, first as an administrative assistant and later dealing specifically with unemployment insurance. She was diligent and responsible, and took pride in doing a good job. My mother had her faults, but there was nothing lazy about her.

I was relieved to be out of the house in Eastside, but now I was in middle school, and life was suddenly harder in other ways. I distinctly remember early on in my first year at University Heights Middle School realizing that I was going to be bullied. I was skinny and homely and smart. I was an outsider who wore hand-me-downs from Goodwill, and I was mixed race. The Black kids wanted nothing to do with me because I was light-skinned. The white kids felt the same, but because I was Black. The taunting wasn't subtle. Kids sang "Half-Breed," Cher's song about the daughter of a Cherokee woman and a white man, and "Mellow Yellow," Donovan's hit from the mid-1960s that had nothing to do with race but that, for my classmates, applied well enough. I was always trying to find a place, or a state of mind, where I felt comfortable. And no one had stepped in to fill Mrs. Malcolm's place.

I was still a good student, and still loved to read. But because school was now a painful place to be, I began to skip classes. My idea of being "naughty" was finding a tree to sit under with a book. The school's vice principal would call my mother and say, "She's ditching class but I know where to find her. She'll be reading a book somewhere."

Middle school changed me, and my growing consciousness of race changed me, too. Adults and kids alike would ask my brothers and me, without thinking twice about how it might make us feel: "What *are* you?" I became awkward and introverted during those years, tormented into shyness, and even more uncomfortable about my looks. Now I didn't just feel unattractive; the way I looked, neither Black nor white, meant I was unacceptable. By way of comfort, my mother used to tell me looks didn't matter. She would say, "Oh, that's okay, honey, because you make up for it with how smart you are."

As I got into my early teens, I began to look for my Black heritage. Because I loved reading, it was natural that I would seek out books that might contain the answers to my questions, or ease this anxious sense of isolation. But I had no one to guide me, and so I grabbed anything that had a Black person on the cover. Unfortunately, one of the first books I stumbled on was *Mandingo*. It was set on a fictional slave-breeding plantation in Alabama, a world of violence and cruelty, where Black women were "bed wenches" as well as slaves. The book reinforced dehumanizing stereotypes, depicting hierarchies of power in which women were always at the lowest position. By the time I read it, *Mandingo* had sold millions of copies, suggesting that the world it portrayed was somehow attractive to readers, and that our society was capable of viewing such stories as entertainment. *If this was how people viewed Black women*, I wondered, *what did they see when they looked at me?*

Growing up in a mixed-race household, the issue of race was unavoidable. My mother was not good at keeping friends, either Black or white, but what social world she did have was mostly made up of Black acquaintances. This was especially true when I was younger, before she went to work and began to mix with people other than those she met through her boyfriends or husbands. As we got into adolescence, one by one my four brothers and I all began to establish our consciousness of race, and our relationship to being mixed race. ("What *are* you?" ringing in our ears.) One of my brothers was reluctant to fully acknowledge that he was Black. Another was militant about it. I recall him saying to my mother more than once, "You're nothing but a white woman, so you can't tell me shit."

I didn't know how I felt, except confused, and like I didn't quite belong anywhere.

Everything came together—the bullying, the growing sense of isolation and alienation, the loss of the one adult in my life who had made me feel worthwhile and safe—in the worst possible way. When I was fifteen, I decided that suicide would be the answer. I took a whole bunch of Tylenol. And then I panicked and told my mother what I had done. She called an ambulance and they took me to the hospital, pumped my stomach, and sent me home.

I didn't want to die. I knew that. What I had done wasn't even about wanting to harm myself. I just felt miserable, and didn't know how to change my life. I didn't feel like I had love from anyone. Even the glimmers of affection felt like someone trying to take advantage of me, especially when the interest came from boys or men. I was no longer a daughter or a sister or a studious young woman. I was an object, someone to be conquered. I'm not saying that is what every man who looked at me was thinking. I'm saying that was how I felt. Like someone to be preyed on.

That was where things stood when I first met Cedric.

It was my sixteenth birthday, the spring of 1976. Toward the end of middle school I had made a couple of friends, and one of them was a girl named Cheryl, who was also a neighbor. I happened to be at Cheryl's house on my birthday, and she was the one who introduced me to Cedric.

Cedric was nineteen. He had a car, and the next day he picked me up after school and we went to the mall. We clicked. Mostly because we were both outcasts, though for different reasons. Cedric was an only child, and by society's standards, he was not particularly attractive. He had a harelip, for which he'd had several surgeries. I had my own set of scars by then, emotional and psychological.

Soon, I would learn that Cedric had been bullied about his appearance, just as I had been about mine. He was being raised by his mother, and while she had a tendency to spoil him, his father was abusive. I saw the verbal abuse myself, and Cedric told me that when he was younger and visited his father, his father would beat him. Cedric had dealt with his troubles by becoming a bad boy—petty crime, and even stealing a car. My brothers knew him and didn't like him. They were a little wild themselves, but they didn't think Cedric was good enough for their sister.

To be honest, it was no great romance. I did feel he cared about me those first couple of months. But there was also a niggling feeling, a little red flag, that said something wasn't right. A little voice telling me, *Don't be fooled.* It wasn't that violence came to mind, necessarily; it was more a feeling of unease when I was around him. He put me on edge, and even early on he was verbally abusive, humiliating me in front of his friends, telling them what a dummy I was. He was just a very controlling person, and it was there in our relationship from day one. But I disregarded that warning voice, a fact I've thought about a lot in the years since. If I've learned anything by this point in my life, it's that as women we don't pay enough attention to our intuition. We're told we are being too emotional, that we're irrational; we're not using our brains. We think, *Aren't men supposed to be the predators? Aren't they supposed to dominate?*

No, they aren't. We should trust ourselves when we sense danger or feel uneasy. Whatever we might think about *why* a man is violent, let's pay attention to the voice that tells us something is off, even if we can't put our finger on what that is. If we sense danger, there is a good chance there is danger. And I sensed danger, even at sixteen.

Cedric and I were together for the next three months. But that June, he held a nurse at gunpoint in a parking garage and was arrested for armed robbery.

By that time, we had already broken up. And I was pregnant.

It was my mother who took me to the doctor when I missed my cycle. When we got the test back, I was devastated. Cedric was the first person I had ever been intimate with, and I can still remember feeling emotionally sick in those first days and weeks after I found out. My mother had often said, projecting her regrets onto me, "Don't be like me. Don't get pregnant." And now I had done just that. I felt like a failure.

I called Cedric to tell him. He said, "So what?" Then he said, "How do I know it's mine?" That was the last conversation I had with him before he went to prison.

When his mother, Albretta, found out, she wasn't one bit happy. Cedric and I were so young. But aside from that, Albretta was very class-conscious, and she had been appalled that Cedric was even dating me. My family was not as badly off as we'd been in Eastside, our worst period of poverty. We were still struggling—my mother had five kids to feed—but she was working. And we now had the newer house in the University section of Riverside. Cedric and his mother were a notch above on the social ladder, though. Albretta might be working two jobs (she was full-time at AT&T but also a notary and bookkeeper who prepared income tax returns on the side), but they were much closer to middle class than my family was. Albretta thought her son could do better than someone like me.

My own mother came unglued. Initially, she yelled and screamed, and then she more or less stopped speaking to me for about two months. She just found it too painful to talk about. The pregnancy strained our relationship to the breaking point. When she was finally able to speak to me, we did nothing but battle. In some ways, it was a classic mother-daughter struggle, but intensified by her disappointment in me and my own false impression that now that I was pregnant I knew all there was to know about the world. Desperate to get away from her, I rented a little house—it was hardly more than a shack—and my brother Ronnie and I moved into it. But it was a horrible place, the plumbing didn't even work, and I thought, *I can't raise a baby in this.* And so I went back home to my mother.

It wasn't just that my dreams were dashed now; in my mother's opinion, it was that hers were, too. Motherhood to her was transactional—she accepted and loved us according to how she felt about the things we did—and she was not a forgiving soul. But she had also genuinely wanted so much more for me, and now it looked as though I would have exactly the sort of life she had had, the life she'd hoped and believed I might avoid.

My son David was born in January 1977, while his father was in prison. I had dropped out of high school once I became pregnant, but I was trying to figure out with my social worker how I could get back to school, what I would need in the way of childcare, and so on. When David was a year old, I found childcare that was on the route to the "adult school." I would get on the bus in the morning, drop David off, and go study for my GED, which you can earn after passing a number of examinations. Government assistance helped me to pay for childcare and bus fare, and was what allowed me to earn my GED, which I did in April 1978. I was so proud. My high school class hadn't even finished their senior year yet.

What other people saw when they looked at me was something different, not a young woman trying to push back against the odds. They saw instead a walking stereotype: a teenaged mother with no money and a child whose father was in prison. There is a moment seared into my memory. David was just a couple of months old, and I was pushing him in the stroller one day near my mother's house in Riverside. A woman I knew vaguely from the neighborhood stopped to coo over David, and then she straightened up and said to me, "No surprise." She was smirking. She said something about how David was the first of many children I was sure to have. For good measure, she added, "You'll be able to collect welfare now."

People think they know you. They think they have the right to tell you who you are, or who you can or cannot be. That woman had looked at me and thought: *I know your type.* I was already well aware by then that the people in my life didn't think I would amount to much. But despite my doubts growing up, the self-consciousness about my looks, about poverty, about being biracial, I did have moxie. I might feel physically ill with fear, I might be saying to myself, *Who do you think you are trying to do this?* But when someone looked at me and assumed they could see who I was, I'd think, *You'll find out.* "No surprise," that woman had said. And I thought, *Actually, you're wrong. You* will *be surprised.*

CHAPTER 3

Below Myself

Cedric had broken up with me before he went to prison. But when it came time for him to go before the parole board in 1978, he got in touch. He said he wanted to see his son. David was almost two by then. I told him that he didn't have a son—*I* had a son. I had been reluctant to even visit Cedric in prison, but over the next few months, he convinced me that David shouldn't be without his father. And of course, a family looks good when you're up for parole. Albretta worked on me, too. She'd say, "He wants to see his child." She didn't want an out-of-wedlock grandchild, and to this day I believe she coerced Cedric into marrying me.

Not long after Cedric was released, his uncle got him a job as a janitor on the naval base in San Diego. We packed up David and our few belongings and left Riverside. We saw an ad in the San Diego paper that said something like, *Come get married by such-and-such a pastor next to a hotel poolside*. So in January 1979, that was what we did. There were just four in our wedding party—Cedric, me, two-year-old David, and a female friend of ours. I don't know whether it was true, but Cedric later claimed he'd been sleeping with her. After the ceremony, Cedric and I changed our clothes and called it good.

As dreadful as things would become, I loved him. For a time, anyway. He had his incredible moments. When he wanted to be sweet and affectionate, he could be. He was funny, too, and Lord, he could make me laugh. We both liked to dance, and though I don't think about him as much as I used to, when I do, it's often of us dancing. My fondest memories are of slow dancing with him. We had a synchronicity.

But he was also, quite frankly, an awful person. I can see that, too. Violent, controlling, and a constant womanizer.

The physical abuse began in San Diego, just weeks after the wedding. That was where Cedric first beat me up. The evening is still clear in my memory. We had argued about something and it eventually became physical. I was a skinny woman, but having grown up with four brothers, I was scrappy. I tried to hold my ground, but he punched me in the mouth, busting my lip open. I wound up with a black eye, too. The neighbors came and took me to their apartment, but I didn't call the police. In all the years we lived together, I never called the police on Cedric. I was afraid of what would happen if I did. Would he go to jail? Would he retaliate against me? Would I have to leave him or our home? What would happen to David? I had no idea what the consequences would be for any of us.

I had seen violence all through my childhood. So what did I feel when it came around again? My own husband. I was deeply hurt and disappointed, but there was a sense of resignation, too. Maybe the resignation came easier because I'd seen abuse growing up, but it was also what we—the women I knew, women in general—had been brought up to expect, from very early on. In Tarana Burke's memoir, *Unbound*, she speaks about the sorts of lessons young girls imbibe, particularly with regard to sexual violence. Tarana was raped when she was young. Years later, having worked with many young victims of sexual assault, she founded the "me too" movement in 2006. Tarana recalls being told as a girl to never let anyone touch her. "But I wasn't told why I had to protect my private parts, just that it was imperative that I did. Because of this, when I thought of my experience, I didn't hold my abusers accountable—I held myself to blame. In my mind, they didn't abuse me. I broke the rules. I was the one who did something wrong."

I hope it's different for little girls now, but when I was young, one of the first things girls learned about boys was that if they were being mean to you, that was a sure sign that they liked you. Any attention, the message seemed to be, was better than no attention at all. This may seem trivial, boys just being boys, but being taught to understand nastiness as a marker of affection is not an insignificant thing for a little girl to internalize.

Yes, I had heard the voice warning me when I met Cedric, but I was sixteen, hardly old enough to trust my instincts. And yes, I knew that the violence I'd witnessed growing up was wrong. But there was another sense in which verbal and physical abuse had been normalized, both within my own home and by our culture. And so, I resigned myself during our time in San Diego. I thought, *Well, I guess this is just the way things are.*

And for thirteen years, it would be.

———

People often think that victims or survivors of domestic abuse are weak or irrational, because we don't leave at the first sign of trouble. If you know nothing about domestic violence, such a perspective might seem obviously correct. But we need to stop thinking about the dynamics of domestic violence as rational—they aren't. Domestic violence differs from other kinds of violence, because it's perpetrated by someone you used to love, maybe still love, someone who may profess to love you and care about you, and might once have really done so. There are so many things it impacts that simply don't factor into other kinds of crime: whether your family will stay intact, for instance, or your ability to feed your kids and keep a roof over their heads. And it's insidious—abusers don't say when they meet you that they intend to start hurting you. At the same time, it isn't "heat of the moment" behavior; this isn't an "anger management" problem. It's about a person who needs to feel in control of another human being, and who chooses, systematically and repeatedly, to gain that power and control.

In the beginning, when everything is new and exciting in a relationship, we can all deny certain hints of trouble—your partner's tendency to want to dominate, for instance, or his habit of calling you a little too often—but as things progress, reality intrudes. You may not want what he wants at a given moment, you may look at him the "wrong" way; he senses that his hold over you isn't quite as firm as he wants it to be, and he sets about trying to re-establish control.

There is a statistic often quoted that the average abuse victim makes seven attempts to leave before finally exiting for good. I don't like that "statistic." If we start putting numbers on things, we aren't allowing for how varied and individual situations of abuse are. There are definite indications of increasing lethality, but there is no "average" abuse victim; nor is there an "average" trajectory for a relationship where abuse is taking place. When we talk about averages, we risk judging those who don't "measure up" to the "norm." We shouldn't commend someone who gets out immediately if that means reproaching the person who needs eight or nine or ten attempts before she can leave—or who is never able to leave. We simply don't know what the dynamics of a situation are, or the danger that leaving might put someone in.

After the first time Cedric beat me up, a woman I knew in San Diego said to me, "One hit and I'd be gone." Maybe. We don't know what we would do in a given situation until we're there. We think we do, but experience can prove us wrong, a fact I was reminded of when I read an article in the *New York Times* in December 2020 about the musician FKA twigs. She had just filed a civil suit against actor Shia LaBeouf, alleging that he had abused her physically, emotionally, and mentally over the course of their relationship. (Karolyn Pho, another ex-girlfriend of LaBeouf's, also accuses him of abuse in the suit.) FKA twigs had not gone to the police during that time—partly out of embarrassment over the alleged abuse, partly because she feared being responsible for harming his career (LaBeouf was trying to redeem himself in Hollywood at the time, following a couple of arrests), and partly because she didn't think she'd be taken seriously, a concern based on experience. She claimed that at a gas station one day, LaBeouf had thrown her against the car and tried to choke her. No bystander attempted to help.

Among FKA twigs's allegations are that LaBeouf criticized her constantly and would pick fights that lasted all night, depriving her of sleep; that he forced her to watch violent true-crime shows about women being raped or murdered; and that there were rules about how many times a day she had to kiss and touch him. She also said he kept a loaded gun by the bed.[†]

[†] In emails to the *New York Times* following the filing of the suit, LaBeouf insisted that "many of these allegations are not true," but said he owed the women "the opportunity to air their statements publicly and accept accountability for those things I have done." He also wrote that he had "no excuses for my alcoholism or aggression, only rationalizations. I have been abusive to myself and everyone around me for years. I have a history of hurting the people closest to me. I'm ashamed of that history and am sorry to those I hurt."

FKA twigs had more than enough money to support herself. At any time she could have bought herself a business-class ticket back to her four-story townhouse in London. But she said LaBeouf's treatment had eroded her sense of agency. "He brought me so low, below myself, that the idea of leaving him and having to work myself back up just seemed impossible."

That phrase "below myself" is telling—and so sad. You are "below yourself" because at that point there is no you. Everything has become about the abuser. Your entire life revolves around the questions of what's going to happen next with that person, and how you can carry yourself to reduce the risk of violence or the severity of it when it comes.

FKA twigs has alleged that in her case, the abuse crept up on her. It's very subtle, she said, the step-by-step process of getting somebody to a place where they lose themselves: "loads of tiny little things that get sewn together into a nightmare." When asked by Gayle King on CBS why she hadn't left LaBeouf sooner, FKA twigs said she wasn't going to answer that question anymore because the question should really be to the abuser: Why are you holding someone hostage? "People say, 'Oh it can't have been that bad or else she would've left' . . . no, it was *because* it was that bad that I couldn't leave."

When the woman in San Diego said to me, "One hit and I'd be gone," I really did question my own sanity. I didn't know anything then about the dynamics of abuse. What I know now is that leaving is usually a process, that it's never simple, and it's often dangerous. I know that when victims are leaving a relationship or pursuing a legal separation, they are at the greatest risk of being killed by their partners or former partners, particularly in the first three months.

The first time I tried to leave Cedric was shortly after that initial assault. Cedric had apologized to me, but the apology wasn't genuine and he was still on edge, still angry. I took David and we got on a bus back to Riverside. When we arrived, I called Mrs. Malcolm from the bus station and asked if she could pick us up. I had last seen her two years earlier, in 1977, when David was a baby and Cedric was still in prison. Mrs. Malcolm had two babies herself by then, and I can still see our three kids on the carpet between us, all equally innocent, but headed for very different lives. I had not gotten my GED yet, and Mrs. Malcolm was heartbroken that I hadn't graduated from high school. As I left her at the end of that visit, she said that she would try to help me however she could. But we lost touch, and I didn't see her again until she came to pick David and me up at the Riverside bus station in 1979.

I'm not sure what I was hoping for that day. I held Mrs. Malcolm on a pedestal, and felt she appreciated who I was—the version of myself she had encouraged me to believe in—and so I didn't want to tell her about Cedric assaulting me. We spent a couple of hours talking and then I got back on the bus and returned to San Diego. I wouldn't see Mrs. Malcolm again for many years, by which time I'd been to hell and back.

San Diego was hard. I was so young, and I didn't know anyone when we moved there. I was also working, sometimes two jobs—entry-level positions like a cleaner at the naval base, a parts driver, a clerk at 7-Eleven—while trying to take care of David. And I was very afraid. One night, Cedric threw me out of the apartment and locked the door. I was wearing only my underwear. I was banging on the door so he would let me back in, but I was in the hallway, and I didn't want our neighbors across the hall to hear me. It's not easy to think about this episode—to say it publicly—but this sort of humiliation is so common to abuse victims, and it's part of my story. I started drinking a lot during that time, and also began doing speed. Part of it was self-medicating, but I was also a woman in her twenties. I wanted to experiment and have fun, like other people my age were doing. For a while Cedric was buying speed for me. I'm five-foot-seven and I got down to ninety-five pounds. Whole days went by when I didn't eat, between the stress and the speed. The weight loss was so dramatic that Cedric eventually stopped buying speed.

———

In 1980, we moved to Colorado Springs. Cedric's father lived there and had gotten him a job at Digital Equipment Corporation, a huge computer company that had manufacturing and labs. Cedric went ahead to start his new job, and I stayed behind for a few weeks in San Diego with David, packing up. When we got to Colorado Springs, I realized almost immediately that Cedric was having an affair. (The affair would produce a daughter, Ida, who is still part of my life.) I confronted him and he became abusive. I took David and went to the women's shelter in Colorado Springs. They paid for a bus ticket so I could get home to my mother's in Riverside. I was gone for about two months, but Cedric convinced me to come back. I felt so guilty going back, thinking of how the shelter had paid for that bus ticket.

Once I was back, Cedric and I were okay for several months, but then something set him off—I can't even remember what it was—and he exploded. He was choking me on the sofa. When I got free, I grabbed David and we fled to my friend Lisa's house. I hardly knew anyone in Colorado Springs, and within an hour Cedric had found us. When we saw his car pull up, David and I ran down to the basement and hid. We could hear Cedric yelling at Lisa's mother at the front door, threatening to blow up the house.

When she finally got rid of him, she said, "I'm sorry, but you can't stay here." I understood why she needed to say that.

So I went home. There was no violence on my return. More a vibe of *Now I've got you back where you belong, let's just get on with the next thing.* Cedric was probably afraid I'd told Lisa and her mother too much about what was going on and that the cops might turn up on our doorstep.

People have often asked me if I thought Cedric experienced remorse after the violence or emotional abuse. I don't have a clear answer. On the one hand, I believe abusers get more diabolical as time goes on, that the whole business of breaking your nose and then buying you flowers (or cooking you breakfast or taking you to Acapulco, whatever the amends are) is part of the pattern of manipulation. On the other hand, I find it hard to believe that Cedric didn't feel some remorse. He wasn't a sociopath.

I doubt that Cedric thought, in the midst of an incident, of how he was harming me; in the moment, it was all about exerting or re-establishing control. The awareness of harm came afterward. But it was cyclical, a buildup that was crazy-making. One minute things would be fine, and the next I'd be walking on eggshells, wondering what was happening and why, and whether I was losing my mind.

There were days I dreamed of revenge. I can't tell you how many times I thought of hurting him. I never thought of using a gun. I was terrified of guns. Guns were what he used to control me. Instead, I would imagine waiting till he'd gone to sleep and then stabbing him. I thought about this more in the early years of our marriage, on the couple of occasions that he was sexually abusive. Afterward I would think: *I'm going to kill him.* As

I said, I was drinking a lot then, and I remember one night in particular, sitting on the stairs in our apartment in Colorado Springs, drinking and waiting for Cedric to get home. I had a knife, and I planned to kill him. Fortunately, I passed out before he got home. He found me on the stairs and dragged me up to bed. I don't know what happened to the knife, or if he ever saw it. But if he realized why I was sitting up waiting for him, he never said.

One day David looked at me and said, "Mommy, why are you always sick?" It wasn't long after that that I stopped doing drugs completely and cut way back on my drinking. I knew I had to do better by David, to be a more present and reliable mother, no matter what I was coping with in my marriage.

In 2019, journalist Rachel Louise Snyder published a study of domestic violence titled *No Visible Bruises: What We Don't Know About Domestic Violence Can Kill Us*. It's a good title for a book on this subject, because the image of the victim of abuse is still too often the woman trying to hide a black eye behind sunglasses. The physical violence is real and prevalent; domestic violence accounts for 15 percent of all violent crime in the U.S. But what I learned during the course of my marriage (and over the many years since, working in this field) is that the emotional and psychological abuse is the hardest to recover from. Bruises and split lips heal, but when someone keeps picking at your psyche, demeaning you, filling you with self-doubt, and taking away your sense of self, the damage that does is deeper and more long-lasting—and it makes you much easier to control. Which is the whole point. When you hurt someone badly enough, sometimes all it takes after that, to put her on notice, is a look.

But still you hold out hope that things will improve. With Cedric, the emotional abuse was always there, while his physical abuse was sporadic. Months would pass, sometimes a year, without physical violence. During those lulls, I would begin to feel hopeful. Then, when the physical violence finally did happen again, I would think, *Well, it's getting fewer and farther between, so maybe I can make this work*. Because I kept believing that somewhere, deep down, he was a good person.

Abuse in all its forms is so insidious that you can't *not* hope. The insidiousness, in fact, is a key ingredient of what's happening. I still go back to the fact that no one gets into a relationship because they want to be abused. They get into it because the other person seemed wonderful—maybe *was* wonderful, for a while—and it's hard to leave because, among other things, you want that person back, the one you remember from the beginning, who didn't abuse you. If you could be happy together once, then why not again?

Author, professor, and activist Beth Richie, who studies the experience of domestic and sexual assault among African American women, found that Black women were in relationships on average for about two years before violence started. That's more than enough time for a significant amount of emotional, psychological, and financial involvement to have developed, perhaps including coparenting and a web of extended family relationships.

It's also true that women have been enculturated to make excuses for their abusers, to believe that controlling behavior or jealousy is a sign of love, or that maybe he just doesn't know how to show love in the "normal" way. We're also taught at a young age that keeping the peace, keeping everyone happy, is our job. Other people's feelings are our responsibility.

———

Over the years, Cedric became far more inclined to terrorize me emotionally. It was that threat of what *could* happen that he used to maintain control. I would pick fights with him just to get it over with—a classic survival tactic of abuse victims. Anything was better than the tension and anxiety of waiting for it to happen. In the last house we shared together, on East Napa Drive in Aurora, there were nights I heard the garage door open and I'd be terrified, not knowing what mood Cedric would be in when he walked in the door. If I saw *that* face, I knew. He was going to be abusive. I was growing tired by that point in our marriage of not having control over anything. And sometimes it felt a little bit better knowing that while I couldn't change what he was going to do, I could at least control the *when* of it. I had control of *something*. Even the day he shot me, I was thinking as I pulled the car over, *Okay, let's just get this over with.* Of course, I didn't realize he had a gun and was planning to kill me; I thought he was just going to unleash some terrible tirade. But that's the point you reach. You are so worn down by it all, and the only thing you want is to get through the inevitable—the next fight, the next beating—so you can rest for a while.

By the time we left Colorado Springs in 1985 and moved to Aurora, just east of Denver, I had become so used to living in fear that in a strange way I had normalized it. I was petrified every single day, terrified that Cedric would kill me. Certain times were worse than others, of course. But I remember thinking that the longer we went without a fight or him hitting me, the more chance I had of dying the next time, as though I could feel what was building during the lull. And it wasn't just punching anymore. It was guns and empty brandy bottles; everything became a potential weapon, even when it wasn't being wielded. The overt violence, what I call the "hard abuse," happened less and less often, but even as it became less frequent, it became more volatile and lethal. The line he repeated till it made me sick was "I'm not going back to prison for you, but I'll kill you if you leave, so that means I gotta dust you, and I gotta dust myself."

We had gone to Aurora because Cedric got a job with the Colorado Department of Human Services, in the Youth Corrections Division. I soon had a job there, too. We often worked at the same place; it was another way for Cedric to keep an eye on me. In the beginning I was a driver, bringing kids to their appointments off the prison campus. Then I became a counselor, working with juvenile offenders. Anyone who became a counselor had to complete a fairly demanding written test, but otherwise we didn't receive much formal training, and to be honest, not many of us knew enough to really make a difference.

It was through my work at Youth Corrections that I met Pam, one of a group of women who would become very important in my being able to rebuild my life. My first encounter with Pam was at a team meeting where I was detailing something that had happened with one of the sex offenders. (We were assigned to work with certain types of offenders, and none of us liked to go into the sex offender pod, but occasionally we interacted with them.) This man would wind up in adult prison years later for trafficking a homeless minor, but at the time he was only sixteen or seventeen. He had been telling one of the staff supervisors who counseled sex offenders of his rape fantasies—about me. Some of this he had even written down. The supervisor thought it would be therapeutic for this young man if the three of us sat together and he confessed his fantasies to me. It's hard to put into words just how horrifyingly wrong this was, though I honestly don't think the supervisor meant it maliciously. We worked in a strange bubble then. The kids were our priority, and we thought first of what we needed to do for them so that they wouldn't keep offending. The supervisor was trying in his own way to hold the young man accountable—by making him face me—for what he had said and written; he genuinely thought it might help him. It just didn't occur to the supervisor to consider the effect it might have on *me*.

I think it only really sunk in once I'd left that room, and later at the team meeting I reported to the half dozen or so other counselors how violated I felt. I don't recall Pam being at that meeting, and our friendship would not really begin until soon after Cedric shot me, but she remembers that day clearly. She says it made such an impression on her that I was able to sit there and detail what had happened, to call it out for the offense that it was. She later told me she saw a strength in me that she admired. She didn't know, of course, what I was going home to every day.

Throughout this time, I said nothing to anyone about what Cedric was doing to me and, increasingly, to David. Cedric and I were building what looked from the outside like a nice middle-class life. *We were making it!* A young African American couple with a lovely home in Aurora. We played cards with friends on the deck. Our son was enrolled in the best public school system. Cedric never said explicitly to me, *Don't tell anyone what's going on*, but there was a pretense we were both keeping up. Eventually, I would stop participating in the lie, but during those years in the house on East Napa Drive, I colluded in the story. It wasn't the material things I was attached to—it was the fear of what awaited me if I walked away from our home. The memory from my childhood of the run-down house in Eastside was still with me. Is that what I'd be reverting to? What I'd be bringing David into? David wanted for very little when we were in Aurora—at least in terms of material security.

And so I told no one. I never called the police. I also had very little contact with domestic violence services over the years: I was terrified that if I had more to do with them, Cedric would find out and there would be hell to pay. But people can feel that something isn't right, they can sense the violence. Once Cedric's cousin, who had lived upstairs from us in San Diego, said, "I can't believe you're letting him do this to you."

I did try for a time to talk to my mother about the abuse. She knew enough to tell me I should leave, but mostly she didn't want to hear it, not really, and my anger with her general indifference has never fully subsided. During the later years of my marriage, my mother was attending Al-Anon because she was married to an addict. (Reese, her sixth husband, would die of a heroin overdose in 1997.) So she used to come at me with the Al-Anon script, suggesting I was codependent, making me feel as though *I* had done something wrong.

My mother-in-law was difficult in a different way. In the beginning she had scared me. She was a formidable woman who exuded an air of control at all times. Albretta was more educated than my mother. She had a degree in Business Administration from UC Riverside, where she'd majored in accounting. She was also a very serious Baptist. She had left her abusive first husband, Cedric's father, when Cedric was just four years old, and raised him on her own. She did not put up with bullshit. She used to say, sternly, if someone was out of line, "They need to come correct." She worked at AT&T for twenty-five years, part of that time as a manager, and ran up against racial discrimination from colleagues. Instead of just putting her head down and ignoring it, she took it to her supervisor and insisted she be transferred to a different department—not an easy demand to make in the 1970s. I wanted to get to know her and figure out how she became who she was, but I also wanted her to see and understand the truth about me. Apart from that period in middle school when I'd been bullied and had felt so unattractive, I had never considered myself weak. And during my marriage to Cedric I had wanted Albretta to see me for who I was—and to see what was keeping me from being my strongest self.

But Albretta didn't talk to me much during the years I was married to Cedric. He succeeded in manipulating that relationship as well. He would start in on me, and then, when I was very worked up, he'd call his mother and say, "Listen to her, how hysterical she is." Sometimes I called her, to try to get her to convince Cedric to stop abusing me. Instead she would say, "If you'd quit being hysterical, if you just stay calm, he won't act that way."

I was young and emotional, no doubt about that. But I was "hysterical" because Cedric was abusive. Albretta saw it differently—that it was up to me to manage Cedric, to manage the abuse. Albretta was blaming me, telling me the "right" way to do things. It wasn't about what Cedric was doing wrong. I look back on that and think, *How dare you?* She was enabling his abuse. But Cedric had achieved his aim; he had cut off the possibility that his mother and I could trust each other and become close, or become allies.

Eventually, Albretta and I would forge an honest and mutually respectful relationship. It would require her to accept the truth about her son, while I would need to forgive her for having not wanted to know, and even for having blamed me. But all that happened years after Cedric died.

CHAPTER 4

Leaving

On March 3, 2021, a thirty-three-year-old marketing executive named Sarah Everard disappeared in South London. She had been walking home from a friend's house. Her body was found a week later in a woodland in Kent, about fifty miles away. It was in a builder's bag and had to be identified from dental records. Sarah had been kidnapped, raped, and murdered.

Sarah's death might not have attracted international attention were it not for two things. The first was that she was raped and killed by someone entrusted with public safety, a police officer named Wayne Couzens, who would later receive a life sentence for the crime. (Another officer, who was assigned to the case, was removed for sharing a joke meme about the murder in a WhatsApp group.) The second was that women in London reported that, following Sarah's disappearance, police were going door-to-door advising them to stay home, for their own safety—the same thing women were told forty years earlier when serial killer Peter Sutcliffe, the "Yorkshire Ripper," was on the loose. In a sick twist, Sutcliffe gave this advice to his own sister, a harrowing example of how violent perpetrators manage to compartmentalize their lives, presenting one face to their victims, another to their unsuspecting friends and family.

The advice in 2021 sparked outrage again. Many women turned the logic on its head, in order to reveal how reducing violence against women is still, fundamentally, seen as the responsibility of women. Instead of encouraging restrictions on women's freedom of movement, they asked, why not impose a nighttime curfew on men? Perhaps if men were losing their freedoms, more might be done to improve street safety. If a curfew was too extreme, wrote Jenny Jones, a Green Party member in the House of Lords, then it could be stipulated that men are "only allowed to walk along well lit busy roads in the evening, even if this adds another 10 minutes to their journey."

No government in the world would take such suggestions seriously, and these women surely knew that. They were making the point that, as British journalist Helen Lewis wrote, a radical reframing is long overdue, one that allows us to view "street harassment, sexual assault, and rape as problems for men to solve rather than an inevitable hazard for women to avoid." Lewis and the other women who wrote about Sarah's murder were clear that they were not tarring all men with one brush; we are talking about a minority here. But until some kind of reframing occurs, Lewis wrote, "the conversation will be stuck on whether women are taking the right precautions to protect themselves."

There is a horrible irony, of course, in women being advised to stay home for their own safety, given that most incidents of sexual assault and physical violence within families happen in the home. The continued lack of understanding around this was made depressingly clear by the governor of Texas. While defending the rollback of abortion rights (even in the case of rape), Greg Abbott said that law enforcement would "eliminate all rapists from the streets of Texas by aggressively going out and arresting them and prosecuting them and getting them off the streets." The belief that women are only raped by strangers who jump out of alleyways is alive and well, despite the fact that eight out of ten rapes are committed by someone known to the victim—and very often happen in the victim's own home.

This is a book about domestic violence, but domestic violence, and the rape and murder of Sarah Everard, are part of the same family of crimes, which also includes stalking, sexual assault, and intimate partner homicide. And one of the traits domestic violence shares with these other crimes is that all over the world, people too often continue trying to explain it or prevent it not by addressing the perpetrator's behavior, but by looking at how the victim might adjust or adapt to the threat in order to minimize or avoid it.

You can lock down your neighborhood. You can put women under curfew. But there will always be other neighborhoods, and there will always be women. Similarly with domestic violence. You can tell a woman to leave, but what about the abuser's next relationship? Is it then up to that woman to leave? And the one after that? And so on and so on. To focus on victim behavior fails to address the root problem and its causes. We will continue to have domestic violence until we start making abusers and not victims responsible for the violence, until we shift the conversation from "Why don't you just leave?" to "How can we help you, and how can we reduce male violence?"

Many people think leaving an abuser is as simple as walking out the door. But because that act is very likely to put you in even greater danger than you're already in, the decision about how and when to do it can be harrowingly complicated. So you read the landscape, you think about your timing, you wonder who else will be put in danger, who you need to protect even as you try to save your own life. (One recent study of intimate partner homicides found that 20 percent of homicide victims were not the abuse victims themselves, but family members, friends, neighbors, people who intervened, law enforcement responders, or bystanders.) You think about the practical things, too. You wonder where you can stay and for how long, whether you might wind up homeless, and what that would mean for your children; you fear losing custody of your children, either to social services or to the abusing parent. You ask yourself how long the money you've been saving will last and whether your abuser will take full control of your shared bank account or assets. Maybe you come from a religious or cultural background that is especially conservative, and so you think about the shame of breaking up a home, and whether people will support you, or judge you, or ostracize you. Whatever your background, you probably think about the shame of friends and family finding out why you left, what's been going on behind closed doors.

All of this you contemplate from within a state of psychological, emotional, and physical depletion, as someone who has been menaced into believing that she knows nothing, deserves nothing, is nothing. Judith Herman, whose book *Trauma and Recovery* is a key text in trauma treatment, writes of the "insidious, progressive" PTSD that develops in people subject to prolonged abuse: "The victim of chronic trauma may feel herself to be changed irrevocably, or she may lose the sense that she has any self at all." Our ingrained habit of pathologizing the victim (surely she wouldn't remain in a situation of chronic abuse unless there was something wrong with her to begin with?) needs to be reversed to reflect the reality: Chronic abuse *causes* real psychological harm, eroding the sense of agency that would enable a victim to leave.

And yet, victims do it. They leave. And this, too, continues to amaze me: they risk everything in order to escape, knowing what their abuser is capable of. There comes a point where a switch is flipped and you say to yourself: *It's worth the risk of dying.* That switch may need to be flipped more than once, and for different reasons. I told myself that I left because David was in danger, and that was true, but it was just as true that I was desperate to regain myself. I was exhausted from living a lie and being controlled by someone else. It came down to the question of why I was even alive. If I'm supposed to be alive, I thought, then surely my life isn't meant to be like this.

———

A few things came together that enabled me to leave Cedric. The main catalyst was the effect he was having on David. This is not unusual—for a lot of women, the decision to leave is made when the man begins to threaten the child or children. (One difference between being a POW and a victim of domestic violence is that in the latter case, you also have to protect your children.) During the years we lived together, Cedric held a gun to me twice. The second time was when David was fourteen years old. As David had grown up, he had become more of a target for Cedric's abuse—it was mostly name-calling, which was horrific enough, but not long before the incident with the gun he'd broken David's eardrum, something I didn't learn about until several days after it happened.

One day I got a call at work to say that David was really struggling at school. My first question was "Did you call his father?" When they said, "Yes," I panicked. I knew Cedric would be enraged. I hurried home. By the time I got there, Cedric had cornered David in the house and was threatening him. I jumped on Cedric's back and he threw me against the wall (for three weeks after I couldn't walk without a searing pain in my back), and David ran up the stairs. Cedric pulled a gun on me and we both went upstairs after David. At one point, as we stood in David's bedroom, Cedric aimed the gun at me, looked at our son, and said, "If you bring one more F into this house, I'll kill your mother."

I was so traumatized and terrified by then I could hardly think (I was going to sleep at night wondering if Cedric was going to kill us all), and I remember saying to myself, *I can keep putting up with this, or I can kill myself.* But I also knew that both of those options would be disastrous for David, and a couple of days later I was sitting on the patio, and I thought, *I can't kill myself. I love my son too much. What would happen to him if I did that?* I knew I had to get us both out of there.

I had already reached my limit on keeping up the charade. Yes, I'd come from nothing, as Cedric liked to remind me, and now I was part of a middle-class family with a hot tub, a rose garden, and two cars in the garage. (Never mind that Cedric would disconnect the wires in my car to keep me from going anywhere without his permission.) We were a three-minute walk from David's great school. But I had already told Cedric that I wasn't going to pretend anymore that what was happening was okay. That didn't mean I'd gone out and told everyone, but something in me had shifted, and I think Cedric knew that that part of the show was over. I wasn't going to keep colluding in the sham. I had also reached the point where my fear of what I knew—the abuse and violence David and I were facing at home—finally exceeded my fear of what was "out there," the world outside my home, the world of the unknown. Finally, I had come to believe that whatever happened to David and me, however we had to struggle, it couldn't be worse than what we were already living through.

Eventually, I did tell someone, a colleague named Regi, who was working in gang intervention when Cedric and I were both still with Youth Corrections. Regi was a confident, no-nonsense woman who also had an air of fun about her. She had known Cedric before she knew me, but I began to run into her at events. In 1991, Regi was doing an internship at Lookout Mountain Youth Services Center, a locked youth corrections center west of Denver. We chatted a few times when we crossed paths on the campus. One day, Regi was on break and I went outside to smoke a cigarette, when I saw David walking onto the campus. David was in his school baseball uniform. Regi remembers better than I do that my whole demeanor changed when I saw David. I looked suddenly very concerned, even afraid. She thought there was something triggering for me about having David turn up there, and she was right. I had been growing more and more concerned for David's safety.

The next time I saw Regi, it all spilled out. We were both on break again, still on the campus, and I remember saying, "That SOB is hurting me." Up to that moment, I had told my mother and Albretta about what was happening, but they weren't conversations in which I went into detail and they certainly didn't take place in a context of trust or support. With Regi it was different. There was something about her that enabled me to believe that if I told her the truth she would help me to understand I wasn't crazy. That we could even become friends. (My instinct was correct. Regi and I have been close ever since. She and Pam are the two women I call my godsisters.) For the first time, I spoke honestly and in detail about Cedric's abuse. It was also the first time I felt listened to—*heard*. Regi was stunned. She told me later that she'd thought, *What the hell? I don't even know this woman.* I think a lot of people sensed that there was something not right with Cedric and me, and maybe Regi knew we weren't the happiest couple, but she'd had no idea how serious the situation was until that day. The charade had been successful. Even years later, I would run into people who had known Cedric and me and they would ask about him and be shocked to hear the truth about us and about how he'd died.

Regi's reaction was: "You have to get away from him immediately. You need a plan, *now*."

That conversation was another catalyst in my leaving Cedric. It wasn't anything Regi said—I knew by then that I had to get out—as much as it was hearing myself say out loud, in my own words, what was happening.

Why did I hesitate for so long to confide in someone? If I were mugged, or the victim of a hit-and-run, would I have hesitated to tell anyone? Would I have thought twice about calling the police? Domestic violence is so often kept hidden, out of fear of the abuser, or the psychological effects of gaslighting, or the deep sense of shame and humiliation that comes with being abused by someone with whom you're intimate. But there is also the fear that other people won't understand or will be upset by what you tell them—in other words, victims often just don't know how to share something like this.

Telling Regi, allowing her to know me and know the truth about my life, was a big step. I didn't realize it at the time, but what happened that day was something I would repeat over the years to come and that would become a really significant part of my moving forward and recovering from abuse: the act of telling my story. It's different for every victim, and I would never say that, because we need to normalize the conversation about domestic violence, every victim should stand up and tell their story. I respect a victim's right to privacy and silence. But for me, speaking out has been crucial. Over the next couple of years, as I began to confide in more of my friends (and later to speak publicly as a survivor), I became aware not only of how telling my story empowered me but also of how I was helping to educate people at a deep, personal level. I saw that the two parts of that experience of story-telling—the convergence of empowerment and education—were inseparable and interdependent. Seeing people's reaction, realizing that they understood things in a new light, only strengthened my resolve to keep speaking out.

———

Leaving Cedric, getting my own apartment, didn't free me from him. Cedric harassed me, he stalked me, he taunted me; he sat outside my apartment building until there was a spot worn in the grass. Sometimes he slept there, when he'd been drinking and passed out. I saw little point in calling the police. I knew they couldn't make him stop. And I still felt that I knew best how to handle him. Like a lot of victims, I thought: *I know him, I know how to keep a lid on it, and eventually he'll stop.* Cedric was not in his right mind those days—which is not to excuse him, but simply to state a fact. He was doing various illicit drugs, drinking even more than he had been, and now I had left him. He'd lost control not only of his own life, but now of David and me, too. I think he must have imagined that the only thing he could regain any control over was me. And so he kidnapped me.

It was the end of March, and I'd been gone for about four months when he showed up in the parking garage of the apartment complex and abducted me at gunpoint. He had already been to the apartment and had told David that he was going to go down and wait for me, so that we could talk. But David had noticed that Cedric had a gun, and immediately called the police once Cedric left the apartment.

Cedric made me drive to his house and park a couple of blocks away. We got out and walked the rest of the way. Once we were inside, he had me call David to find out what he had done. (We had seen the cop car flying past.) I spoke briefly to David and tried to reassure him I was okay. He told me that he had called the police, but I was careful to show no reaction, so that Cedric wouldn't suspect anything. I just said, "All right, good, I'm okay, see you a little bit later." He also told me that his stepsister Ida, who was ten, was at the apartment. When I hung up, the phone rang. Cedric picked it up—it was the police. I thought about screaming, but I was afraid of what Cedric would do. He gave me the phone and made me tell them everything was fine, while he pointed the gun at me.

I was certain he was going to kill me. Before we left the house, I said, "If you're going to kill me, please make it quick."

He said he wasn't going to kill me, he was just going to make me watch him kill himself. "You need to know how much I love you," he said.

He led me back to the car and told me to drive to a liquor store at 6th and Sable, where I walked in with a gun at my back and bought a bottle of gin and a bottle of brandy, which Cedric wanted. I think the store clerk sensed there was something off about us. Then we went across the street to a Traveler's Inn and I signed for a room, still with Cedric holding the hidden gun at my back. I was afraid if I moved or tried to signal to anyone, he would shoot me.

When we got into the motel room, the first thing Cedric did was turn on the Final Four basketball game to check the score—in the middle of a kidnapping. I asked if I could talk to David again, and Cedric agreed. I can't remember whether the police were still with David at that point, but in any case they wouldn't have been set up to trace a call, and this was long before you could track people's locations through cell phones. David said he was safe and wanted to know where I was, but I knew if I told him Cedric would be enraged. David and I talked in code, as though we were having a normal conversation, just reassuring each other that we were all right. I said, "Make sure the hamburger is thawing on the counter," and he told me it was. He kept saying, "Mom, just do what he says," and I would agree, and say, "That's fine."

The poor kid, my fifteen-year-old son, was amazing.

After I hung up with David, Cedric handed me his gun and said, "If you don't kill me, I'm never going to let you go."

I spent the next four hours at Cedric's mercy, thinking this is where they're going to find my body. I fully expected that he was going to rape me and kill me, and then kill himself. He said more than once, "There's one thing I want you to know. I'm never going back to prison over you."

However many times Cedric begged me to kill him, I knew that even though my life was in danger, I wasn't capable of doing it. Which meant I had to figure out how to survive—and how to keep him from ending his own life. That wasn't something I wanted to witness, and Cedric was still David's father. I didn't want David traumatized any more than he already was.

Cedric was drinking throughout that afternoon, and was forcing me to drink, too. I felt if I appeared to be drinking with him, it would show that I had calmed down, but when I filled my glass, I added mostly water. The last thing I wanted was to get drunk. I was trying to keep my head straight. I had figured out at some point that the only way we were both going to make it out of there alive was if I told Cedric what he wanted to hear—that I would come back home. So I lied. I knew I was never going back, but I said, "I just need time to get out of my lease. Then I'll come home." That's the reason he didn't kill us both that day, because I managed to convince him that we would be together again. It's incredible to imagine now, but I don't think Cedric could really have comprehended that he was no longer in control of me. If I said I was coming home, I must mean it. Why would I lie to him? That would only have been possible if he'd actually lost control.

In the end, Cedric just exhausted himself, physically and emotionally. The level of tension over those few hours in the motel room was horrific. He got very drunk, and then very sleepy, and finally couldn't sustain the threat any longer. He softened enough that he stopped talking about killing me and killing himself. After what seemed like forever, we left the motel room.

I don't even remember driving away. But he told me to go back to my apartment and drop him off nearby. His car must have been parked somewhere in the neighborhood. I ran inside to check on David and Ida, but the apartment was empty. I was terrified Cedric was going to come back, and I'd be trapped with him again, so I left and drove to a nearby Conoco station and called the police from the pay phone there. By then it was 10 p.m. Cedric had held me for more than five hours.

While I was on the phone with dispatch, an officer arrived at the gas station. I was crying and shaking. "I'm so scared," I said. "I can't find the kids, and I need to know if they're okay."

The officer assured me that they were fine—David had gone to a friend's house and Ida was at home with her mother. Then he said that Cedric was already in custody. It turned out that a SWAT team had been called to Cedric's house, and an officer who'd been tasked with directing traffic away from the house had spotted Cedric walking down the street and arrested him. The Aurora police charged Cedric with carrying a concealed weapon and handed him over to the Denver police for the kidnapping charge.

I went with the officer and gave my statement. I never saw the full "Offense Report" until the fall of 2021, when I requested it from the Aurora Police Department. It arrived in my inbox like a small bomb. Reading the fifteen pages was a reminder of what trauma does to the brain. There was so much I'd forgotten or blocked out—including the act of actually writing out my statement. But there it all was, the kidnapping recounted in my own handwriting, so many details that brought the texture of that day back and made it all fresh in my mind.

A few things jumped out at me from the report. The way I was referred to throughout as V-Glenn (V is for victim), while Cedric was S-Glenn (S is for suspect), our relationship now reduced to one of victim to suspect. I was also struck by the fact that on page one of the report, under General Offense Information, was the notation, "Family violence: No." I understand that Aurora wasn't handling Cedric's arrest for kidnapping, as it was outside their jurisdiction, but surely if he was picked up on a weapons charge related to the gun he had just used to hold his estranged wife against her will, shouldn't some indication of the presence of domestic violence have been prominently noted on the report?

But maybe the strangest aspect of the report was how my statement contradicted my memory of who had been driving that day. For years, I'd had a very clear picture of driving to Cedric's house in my car, while he was in the passenger seat, then switching to his car to drive to the motel, and Cedric dropping me off at my apartment at the end of the ordeal. The first part is correct—we did travel in my car to his house, while he held me at gunpoint. But we never switched cars. We went into his house, where he got the bullets. Then I drove to the motel, still at gunpoint, and later I drove us back to my apartment, where I dropped Cedric off. It made sense that it had happened that way. It would have been hard for him to drive and keep the gun on me.

Why had I been so certain all these years that we'd switched cars? Trauma wreaks havoc with our ability to remember things correctly, but I also think that sometimes we misremember things in a certain way because the made-up version better reflects how we felt in the moment. I had zero control of what was happening. Cedric had a gun. I was at his mercy. Maybe being driven in his car somehow captured that feeling of helplessness better than the memory of being the one behind the wheel, which we usually associate with being in control. Or maybe it was a way of trying to explain to myself how it could have happened, or even to forgive myself: He *must have* taken me in his car. I didn't drive myself to a kidnapping!

I hoped, as I read the report, that today things would be handled differently. That the kidnapping would have been a point of intervention that could have prevented Cedric's subsequent attempt to murder me. That maybe he wouldn't have been released the very next day (he was let out on $10,000 bail) and without anyone even informing me. I think, too, about all the people along the way the afternoon of the kidnapping who might have intervened: the maintenance man at my apartment garage, the liquor store cashier, the hotel clerk, the people Cedric and I passed walking those couple of blocks from my car to his house, the cops who flew past us on the road. I remembered that old feeling of being trapped in abuse and violence, of being isolated and unseen. The anxious thought: *Does anybody see me? How can I get someone to see what's happening?*

That night was the first time in thirteen years of abuse that I had ever called the police to report Cedric's violent behavior. Their reaction wasn't reassuring: For an hour I experienced what amounted to an interrogation. They kept returning to two things: that I'd been drinking, and that I was still married to Cedric—which meant that, in their minds, what had happened was a domestic squabble, a marital spat more than a crime. I had the distinct sense that at least one of the officers didn't believe that Cedric had actually kidnapped me.

The Denver Police charged Cedric with second-degree felony kidnapping, and a court date was soon set for June 23, 1992. David and I went to SafeHouse in Denver, the shelter we'd been to briefly right after we moved into the apartment, and then we stayed with a friend for several days before going back to the apartment. Cedric did have an automatic emergency protection order placed against him following his arrest, and on April 15, about two weeks after the kidnapping, he was served with a final protection order. But it's not as though an order comes with round-the-clock surveillance.

To make certain I understood that I still wasn't safe, Cedric called me right after the sheriff had delivered the order. "A protection order won't stop a bullet," he said.

Unbelievably, about ten days after that, with Cedric still actively threatening my life, his lawyer coerced me into signing an affidavit. He was going to use it in his attempt to get Cedric's case "continued," meaning that the court would postpone any findings, and the case could be dismissed once Cedric had met certain conditions. The affidavit the lawyer had drawn up stated that my "primary concern" was that Cedric receive counseling, and that I believed that the "most appropriate" disposition of Cedric's case was a deferred judgment and a lessening of his charge to a misdemeanor. "That way, he would receive the treatment I believe he needs and at the same time not end up with a criminal record as a result of this incident." The affidavit also stated that I believed it was "important for Cedric and the community for him to keep his job with the Division of Youth Services."

The language of this document is shocking. It's all about what is best for Cedric—with a nod to the well-being of the larger community, which would somehow, it seems, be served by having a man who had committed a violent felony continue in his role as a youth counselor. No mention whatsoever of the victim of his crime or her well-being.

Why did I sign? For starters, I was in a vulnerable, confused, traumatized state. I also had no one advising me legally—at that point I hadn't even met my victim advocate. I wanted Cedric to be held accountable, but, like most victims, what I wanted more than anything was for the harassment and violence to end. I actually thought that maybe if he went to counseling, he *would* stop. Finally, I was afraid of what Cedric might do if I didn't sign—he wasn't in prison, after all, and no protection order was going to keep me safe if he decided to hurt me for not going along with his lawyer. So I signed.

During that time, I watched my back more than ever, and kept as close an eye as possible on David. I knew there was little point in moving to another building in another part of the city. ("Even if you're in Alaska, I will find you.") The State had put Cedric on paid leave immediately after his arrest, so at least I didn't have to see him at work. But not knowing where he was could be just as nerve-racking as knowing, and after finally getting officially fired on June 1, he severely escalated his threatening behavior.

I think back on the days and weeks following the kidnapping and ask: What should have been done differently to protect David and me? It wasn't just that the legal system placed Cedric's right to not be incarcerated above my right to be safe from harm—a situation that would nearly cost me my life about three months later. It was the fact that no one from within the criminal or legal systems ever used the words "domestic violence" to describe what was happening to me. It was that the police didn't do the work (and maybe didn't know how) that would have allowed them to properly assess the danger I was in; having been kidnapped at gunpoint apparently wasn't enough. What I needed—and what any victim in that situation deserves—was for someone to take a full history, one that would reveal patterns of abuse. Law enforcement needed to investigate rather than interrogate: to ask the pertinent questions with a nonjudgmental eye, and to try to see the situation from the victim's point of view rather than from the perspective of the abuser's rights.

We live in a system where we try to protect people from being wrongly accused, which is a good thing. However, if someone comes forward and says she's in danger, we have to take what she's saying seriously. We have to understand the dynamics of domestic violence—including the fact that if a victim has not yet left an abuser, or has only just left, that doesn't mean the abuse hasn't "been that bad," and it certainly doesn't mean that the danger is past. Leaving isn't the end of the story—rather, it's often the beginning of its worst chapter.

I should have met my victim advocate much sooner than I did. I only saw her for the first time when I went to the court hearing, after I'd signed the affidavit Cedric's lawyer had drawn up. I still remember Cedric getting very close to me as I was walking up the courthouse steps and whispering, "You're not going to live to see the next court date." He actually stuck close to me inside the courtroom until his lawyer arrived, and then it seemed everyone who had anything to do with the case—except me—was having a conversation. I felt absolutely alone. Only then did my victim advocate appear and introduce herself to me. All of that was absurd—no victim should be subjected to her abuser's taunts or threats at a courthouse. And every victim should have the support of an advocate, first and foremost, from the moment she comes into contact with law enforcement.

When I left Cedric, Colorado was one of only two states in the U.S. that did not fund their domestic violence programs. (That has since changed.) David and I were largely on our own. I reached out to numerous people for counseling for both David and me, but it took some time to find someone I could afford. Victims of domestic violence, and their children, need immediate access to free counseling. For children, especially, there should be no statute of limitations on availability of these services. Children who have witnessed violence and trauma sometimes aren't able to address it for years—I know this from my own son—and when they are ready, they should not be told that it's too late, or that they have to pay an arm and a leg if they want help.

Obviously, if Cedric had been denied bail after the kidnapping and remanded into police custody, he would not have been able to attempt to murder me almost three months later. But he was let out. I don't know what kind of conversation the police had with him the night of his arrest, but once he'd been released, there was nothing in his behavior in the weeks after the kidnapping that makes me believe the police left him with the impression that he was going to be held accountable for what he'd done.

Two days after the kidnapping, the *Rocky Mountain News* reported that Cedric had released me "unharmed." The word may have come off the police blotter or it may have been the journalist's choice. I imagine—I hope—that today a journalist might at least say, "physically unharmed." I had been taken at gunpoint by someone very unstable who I knew was capable of violence; I had been kept for hours against my will; I had had my life threatened repeatedly. I was not *un*harmed. (Nor was David, who hadn't been present at the hotel but who knew what was happening, knew his own father, and believed that he was never going to see me alive again.) But because I hadn't been beaten, bruised, or shot, I was deemed unharmed. Language can diminish the perceived severity of what victims experience, especially with regard to emotional or psychological abuse. It has been these latter "invisible" forms of harm that have been the hardest for me to heal from, but society tends to take physical wounds more seriously. Well, soon enough, I would have more of those, too, and the harm would be horrifically, plainly visible.

CHAPTER 5

Woman, 32, shot in head . . .

June 17, 1992

The things you remember: How beautiful the evening was as the sun was going down. Seeing his car in the rearview mirror. His arm out the window. My hand on the gearshift. A buzzing in my ears. Blood everywhere, and thinking, *Oh my god, my white shirt*. That my arm, flopping as I lay on the ground, might have saved my life. That later, when I went back to the car wash, there was a bloodstain the size of a dinner plate on the tarmac.

That evening wasn't the first time I'd spotted Cedric in my rearview mirror. I used to take East Evans Avenue to and from work, and several times I had checked the mirror and noticed him behind me. Once, when I had David in the car, Cedric had forced me to pull into a barbershop parking lot. He said he needed to take David for a haircut. I managed to talk him down and drove away, David still with me.

So, while this kind of stalking was nothing new, June 17 would be different. Cedric's court date for the kidnapping was in just six days. As I was about to learn, in a twisted piece of logic, Cedric had decided that in order to avoid going back to prison for the kidnapping, he would prevent me from testifying against him—by killing me.

Cedric called me that day to say he had stolen some things from my car, including the registration and insurance. His name was still on the car along with mine, and he still had a set of keys. Sometimes he actually stole the car itself; it was another form of control, another way of reminding me that I wasn't free of him. He would find the car wherever I'd parked it—at work or near the apartment—and drive it away and not tell me where he'd left it. David and I had made a game of it: *Let's go find the car!* I called the police more than once on those occasions. I'd say, "My car is missing and I believe that my husband has stolen it." They would ask if his name was also on the vehicle's title. When I said yes, they would tell me that there was nothing they could do.

This time, Cedric had cleaned out the glove compartment. He'd even removed the bumper sticker I'd put on the back. It was an escalation of that particular "game." Maybe I should have seen this latest harassment as a sign that the danger was growing, though *should* is not a word I like to use about myself or other women in that situation.

Recall that since mid-April, Cedric had been under a protection order because of the kidnapping. In spite of that, I didn't feel remotely safe. Recently, after leaving work one evening, I had found pictures of David and me on the seat of the car. Cedric had torn them in half and left them there.

When he called on June 17 to tell me he was going to return what he'd taken from the glove compartment, I told him not to bother, that I was going out to meet friends and didn't have time to play games today. It was the strongest I had ever been with him. I was still frightened, but I was also extremely pissed off. *Here you are, still messing with me.* He had abused me for years, he had stalked and harassed me after I left him. He had taken my car, taken my belongings. He had kidnapped me at gunpoint.

"Leave me the fuck alone," I said.

When I hung up, I felt both scared and relieved. I had infuriated him. I knew that, and knew there would be consequences. I thought there was a chance I'd just signed my own death warrant. But as I'd sat there on the phone, listening to him tell me what he had taken, a change had come over me. There was a freedom I felt in that moment, even knowing the danger I was in. I had been so petrified of Cedric that the fear had immobilized me, physically and emotionally. But I had just broken his grip on me. I could feel it. So could he, and he was enraged.

Around eight-thirty, just as the sun was beginning to set, I got into my car and headed out. I remember very clearly that as I turned right onto Dayton Way, just outside my apartment complex, I had the feeling that something was wrong and wanted to turn back. (Later I would think that if I'd gone back to the apartment, maybe Cedric wouldn't have shot me—but

I doubt that; he'd have figured out a way to break into the apartment, or would have found me somewhere else the next day.) That's when I saw his car in my rearview mirror. He had obviously been waiting for me to pull out. I thought, *Okay, Ruth, don't panic.*

I figured I had better keep going, so I took a left onto East Iliff Avenue, a main thoroughfare. By now Cedric was honking and flashing his lights. Within minutes, he was right up on my bumper. I could see his arm out the window, waving for me to pull over. I didn't want to get off the main drag, and I knew I wasn't going to outrun him—I was in a tiny little Hyundai and he was in his big Buick. I didn't see any other option but to pull off to the side, get whatever it was over with, and get away from him. About two miles from my apartment, I turned into the parking lot of the White Glove Car Wash, in a strip mall on East Iliff. At least it was out in the open on a well-trafficked road. It was still light out, so people could see us.

Cedric pulled up in front, backed his bumper right up against the front of my car, then got out and walked toward me. As I sat there in the driver's seat, I remember thinking: *He's going to beat the shit out of me.* I had already resigned myself to that. My only hope was that he'd make it fast.

He walked up to my window, looking like the devil incarnate, even more frightening than he'd looked the day of the kidnapping. Then he just lost it. He cursed at me, said I didn't deserve to live. He said if I thought David and I were safe I was crazy, because he could get us anytime he wanted. "David can't even take out the trash without me knowing," he said. He called me a bitch and a slut and said he didn't even know how many men I was fucking. He said I'd left him because he was Black. As mean as he'd been over the years, some of these things he had never said before.

I was in shock. He was yelling so loudly I could hardly understand what he was saying, and he was so enraged he was actually spitting on me. I remember wiping my cheek, and wanting to say, *Don't spit!* but I thought, *Just say nothing.*

I kept the car running and my right hand on the gearshift while he spewed venom.

"You know what, bitch?" he said. "You're not going to live to see June 23 and David isn't either."

Finally, he turned around and walked away. *Thank God*, I thought, *that's it for today.* But as I looked down to put the car in reverse, I realized he was back at my window, this time with a gun. He raised it to my eye level and pulled the trigger twice.

A gunshot is the most awful sound. The smell is even worse, especially close-up. I remember those two blasts, each one distinctly. The first went under my scalp, the second skimmed my forehead. When a bullet hits you, you feel a stinging sensation, distinctly metallic, like being burned or getting an electric shock. I thought, *This can't be happening*, and *Must be my time to go*. I wasn't in pain—it wasn't until later, when the shock wore off, that I really felt the pain—but there was blood everywhere.

As Cedric was walking away I had a moment of the starkest clarity. *He's going to get David now*. I knew it. In his eyes, our son had betrayed him, too. *I have to reach David*, I thought. I opened the car door to get help, but fell out onto the pavement. As I was lying there, I could hear Cedric pulling away, and I told myself to look dead until I couldn't hear his car anymore. But he realized that I was still alive and did a U-turn and came back. I could see the car coming toward me.

I thought he was going to run me over. I wasn't capable then of getting myself out of the way, and I just kept thinking: *Pretend you're dead*. But the body does strange things when it's in shock, and my arm started twitching and shaking and I couldn't do anything to stop it.

Cedric pulled up close to where I was lying.

"You're not dead yet, bitch," he said.

Without getting out of the car, he shot me again, this time in the arm. I think in his confused rage he thought that was the way to kill me—my arm was the only part of me still moving, so he aimed at that. And then he drove away and left me for dead.

There's no way I'm going to survive this. I thought he'd hit me in the side, and I was aware of my knee hurting—I had fallen onto it when I'd toppled out of the car. At that moment, my knee hurt more than the bullet wounds did. In my shock-addled brain, I puzzled over my stinging knee. I briefly blacked out. But when I came to, I immediately remembered David.

Somehow, I crawled back to my car. Blood seeped into my contact lenses, but I could see that there was a Vickers gas station straight ahead, about two hundred yards away. I managed to climb into the driver's seat and head toward it. *I can't let him get to David*.

I pulled up in front of the gas station. There was a man outside pumping gas. When I stumbled out of the car, I said, "I've been shot." The man helped get me inside the shop, where the cashier, a very young woman, freaked out. I fell on the floor right in front of her booth. I remember looking up from the ground and there were crates and crates of Mountain Dew and thinking, *What's with all this Mountain Dew?* (In fact it wasn't Mountain Dew, as the pictures taken for evidence will show. It was Mello Yello, an irony I can't but roll my eyes at now—"Mellow Yellow" was the song kids taunted me with in middle school.) There were one or two other customers inside, and everyone hunkered down on the floor—they were worried the shooter was following me—and the cashier closed the station.

The man who'd helped me inside was trying to staunch the bleeding from my head, while making sure the cashier called the cops. I began reciting my address over and over, asking them to please get the police to David because Cedric was going to kill him.

By the time the ambulance showed up, the cops had already radioed in about a big pool of blood next to the car wash. The paramedics couldn't believe how coherent I was, given that I'd been shot in the head. I said, "I won't let you touch me till I see my son." Of course, they didn't follow that order.

Cedric went straight to the home he was sharing with his girlfriend, and the two of them took off. The getaway must have been panicked, because when the SWAT team arrived, there was a half-cooked meal in the kitchen. It was a three-level condo, so it took SWAT some time to figure out if Cedric was still in there. In the process, they tore the place apart.

Meanwhile, I was at the hospital. They treated my wounds, "debriding" my arm—a process of tissue removal to ensure all the bacteria on the bullet didn't cause an infection. They also gave me a CAT scan. They were certain I couldn't have survived the shooting without permanent brain damage. The bullets had taken chunks out of my head. I had a severe concussion, a debilitating headache, a busted eardrum, and some bleeding in my ear from the gunshot blasts (not from the bullet itself). I had a twisted ankle, an injured knee, and a ruined white blouse—which I was disproportionally pissed off about.

Ultimately, there was no brain damage. The doctors were amazed. Two centimeters over, they said, and I would have been dead. What might have saved me was the fact that I was looking down at the gearshift when Cedric came back to shoot me—so the bullets hit the top of my head, instead of penetrating my forehead or temple.

It felt like it took the police forever to convey to the hospital that David was safe, and that they were bringing him to me. When he finally did get there, he was so angry with me: "I told you he was going to do this!" he said. He also said, "I can't believe it . . . two centimeters and you wouldn't be with me."

As time went on, I would come to understand just how angry David was with himself, for not having been able to protect me. To this day, if we go too long without speaking, he gets anxious. He wants to be able to see me and know that I'm okay, and not lying hurt somewhere. I reassure him that I'm alive and I'm here. But the damage of that day, and the years leading up to it, have impacted us deeply, and we both continue to reckon with them.

It was only after I saw David in the ER that everything hit me. I began sobbing. That night in my hospital room, I saw the story of the shooting on the late evening news—there was my car, and a picture of Cedric's face—and I lost it. The nurse was holding me, calling out, "Cut off the TV!"

I was in the hospital for three nights, under guard by the police. They had admitted me using an alias ("Susan Smith"), and kept me in an extra night because they didn't know where Cedric was, or where I could go that would be safe. When they discharged me, they gave me a cowboy hat to wear as a disguise. My life had never felt as out of control as it did during those days. And yet, that was the beginning of the long road to my taking back control.

There is a "before" and an "after" in my life. Though I would never wish that shooting on my worst enemy, I am who and what I am today because of it. It wasn't only that it required me to discover my reserves of strength and resiliency. It was that once I began to emerge from the trauma, I was motivated to work toward ensuring that others *never* undergo the violent abuse that I did.

The headline in the *Denver Post* on June 19 read: *Woman, 32, shot in head, drives 200 yards to gas station for help*. In the years to come, as I began working as an advocate, I would think back on that headline. By then I understood how diminishing it was to not mention domestic violence. And what was with the passive voice? *Woman shot in head?* As though it were a thing that had just happened out of nowhere, for which no particular person was responsible. No, somebody shot that woman. What about this for a headline? *Husband attempts to murder wife, who drives 200 yards for help.*

———

Regi had heard about the shooting from Pam, and her first thought was to feel responsible. She had been adamant when we spoke about the abuse that I needed to leave Cedric immediately. Even now, she remembers how frantically she tried to convince me to go stay with a friend of hers. Six months had passed between leaving Cedric and the shooting, but when it happened, Regi felt she shouldn't have pushed me so hard.

I understand—all of it. The not knowing what to do, the wanting to protect a friend and feeling helpless to do so, the blaming yourself when things go horribly wrong. Domestic violence has its own dynamics. Unless you've been through it or work in the field, there is a lot that you may not understand. There were things even I didn't see clearly until I had the perspective of time and distance and education. Regi blamed herself because she felt she'd been naïve, that she hadn't grasped the potential consequences and should have encouraged me to proceed with greater caution. But I had done everything right when I left. I had carefully, quietly laid the groundwork so that David and I could escape. I had given us the maximum lead time before Cedric would discover that we were gone. I had moved into an apartment building that had a security door. I had gotten a temporary restraining order as soon as Cedric found out where we were living.

The shooting, of course, wasn't Regi's fault. That's on Cedric. It's also on a system that failed to protect me from someone who had already been arrested for kidnapping me, and who should have been nowhere near me.

There was a sad realization from those days, one concerning my mother. She never came to visit me in the hospital. At first, I didn't say anything to her about that. It was Pam who prodded me months later to bring it up with her. When I confronted my mother, she said she was just so scared of Cedric. That much I understood—when I left him, he threatened a lot of people, including my mother. As soon as he realized I was gone, he called her and anyone else he thought I might have run to and warned them that they'd better not be helping me. But I also knew that *nothing* would have kept me from my child if he were lying in a hospital. I understood something else then, too, about my mother: She simply didn't know how to nurture. She didn't know how to be a mom.

Soon after the shooting, and for only the second time in my life, I made contact with my birth father. I told him what had happened. It was that same feeling I'd had when I was twelve—*Can you save me?*—but he hardly reacted. I could tell he was drunk; by then I'd realized that he was an alcoholic. That was the last time I ever talked to him. I wouldn't even learn of his death until two years after it happened. My half brother Ric, a genealogy buff and the unofficial keeper of our complicated family tree, called me in 2005 to tell me he'd just learned my father had died in 2003. I had long since resigned myself to the fact that I would never truly know my father. But that didn't make his death easier. Maybe, when it comes to our parents, some shred of hope always persists.

It was my friends who came through for me after the shooting, the family of women I was beginning to assemble. Regi's mission, once it became clear that I was going to be okay, was to get me a new white blouse, to replace the one that had been ruined in the shooting. Weeks later, when a few of us gathered at a bar and restaurant, she presented me with it. It was way too big for me. She laughs at that now: "I think I bought it so huge because I had an image of you as a superhero."

———

David and I went to a motel outside Denver after I got out of the hospital. Catholic Charities paid for us to stay there for a couple of weeks. Karen, my victim advocate who worked for the Arapahoe County Sheriff, negotiated with the manager of our apartment complex to move us to a different apartment off the ground floor and into another building in the complex. Karen was wonderful in so many ways. She supported me emotionally and practically, keeping me informed but also understanding *how* to communicate with me while I was so traumatized. She was firm with others and compassionate with me. I don't know how many times she went and picked David up from school because I was afraid to leave the house. She even made me laugh. When there was confusion about which office was actually responsible for the case—because the car wash is located on a patch of land where Arapahoe County, Denver County, and the city of Denver meet—Karen said, "You don't do anything the easy way!" I was grateful for that little bit of humor.

For the next four months, I was on high alert. In the beginning I was off work, recovering from the shooting, so I had a lot of time to think and worry. David and I lived in a constant state of fear. Project Safeguard found a lawyer to help me with legal issues and paperwork. As far as support groups, I didn't avail myself of those. Partly because I'm very strong-willed, and if it's not an immediate crisis, I used to think I'd work it out myself. But the main reason I didn't use a lot of the resources? I was terrified to drive downtown.

I was terrified to go anywhere. I knew Cedric was out there watching my every move, just waiting for one more chance. This time he'd make sure I was dead. An Arapahoe County Wanted flyer, which I would only see after Cedric had died, said that he had been seen by acquaintances three times in July in the Montebello neighborhood of Denver, only a twenty-minute drive from my apartment. According to the flyer, the police thought Cedric might be staying in the area because he was waiting for a $12,000 "retirement" check to be deposited by the state into his credit union account. (Fortunately, DHS had ignored the affidavit I'd signed under pressure from his lawyer requesting that he be allowed to keep his job, and had fired him.) The police never told me that Cedric had been seen in Denver, but that flyer explains why the detective was so adamant that David and I stay hidden. They knew Cedric was around, they just didn't know where. In the past, when I'd been at the shelter, the staff had been angry and upset that I had insisted on calling Cedric; they didn't understand that I needed to know exactly where he was. Knowing was always better than not knowing, and in the days before cell phones, if he picked up the phone, I knew he was home and I was safe.

I believed at the time—and still do to this day—that Albretta was helping Cedric when he was on the run. She denied it, and she still blamed me for what had happened, but I wrote him a note and sent it to her anyway, asking her to pass it on to her son. It read, *Please do what's right and turn yourself in.* I still have a letter I received from Albretta that summer. Her phones had been tapped and the FBI had come to the house several times. She wrote that she knew I was surviving, blessed with health and strength and a well-paid job, and that the situation could have been much worse. She was dealing with a lot at the time, I get that. But it wasn't the most supportive letter I've ever received.

For the most part, I had physically recovered within a few weeks of the shooting. The emotional and psychological damage was longer lasting, of course, but my other wounds had healed. I started working again for Youth Corrections, but only from home. Someone would bring me whatever files I needed, and I would do what I could without leaving the house. But after about three months, I returned to my actual workplace. They put me on the graveyard shift. Just a few nights after I was back, I answered the phone around 2 or 3 a.m., assuming it was the control tower. Instead, I heard sobbing. The caller wouldn't identify himself, but I realized it was Cedric. I said, "I know it's you. Please turn yourself in so we can be done with this." The sobbing intensified then, but he still wouldn't say a word, and he soon hung up.

Cedric had a tight network from our work and social lives, and someone must have told him that I was working graveyard, which is how he knew where and when to find me. I told Karen, my victim advocate, about it, and she reported it to the police.

I was still petrified and was doing whatever I could think of to stay safe. Sometimes I asked coworkers to pick me up so that Cedric wouldn't spot my car on the road and follow me again. Everyone knew about the shooting, both the kids I was dealing with and the other staff members, all of whom had worked with Cedric. It was awful. Most of my coworkers had no idea how to communicate with me, whether they should acknowledge what I'd been through or politely avoid any discussion of it. I felt incredibly isolated, on top of the trauma. Eventually I asked to move out of that unit, and they transferred me to an administrative position.

Pam was such a bright spot in those first dark months. Our friendship was actually forged during the worst days of my life. Pam and I are different in so many ways. She is logical, careful, and balances her checkbook; I am spontaneous, impulsive, and not always sure what's in my account. Pam is white, I am Black. Pam is a morning person, I come to life sometime after noon. But we share a lot. Neither of us knew our fathers; our mothers were both emotionally unavailable. We had children when we were too young and became trapped in dysfunctional marriages. When no one at work knew what to say to me, Pam seemed to understand, intuitively, how to connect with me. While I was out of work recovering from the shooting, Pam had inherited my office. She noticed that, like her, I liked to use colored pens. One day, after I'd come back to work, I lost my pen, and Pam loaned me hers. After that we started exchanging colored pens. It was a simple form of kindness and communication that gently laid the foundation for a friendship. Pam would help to make my return to the world possible, bearable, even enjoyable. Thirty years later, our friendship is still one of the most important in my life.

And then, on October 11, almost four months after the shooting, my victim advocate showed up at my apartment. Karen sat David and me down and told us that Cedric was dead. He had shot himself in the head in a motel room near Columbus, Ohio, where he had been staying. (Ohio was where Cedric was from, and where Albretta lived.) Information wasn't as instantaneous back then, and more details trickled in over the next several days. I learned the police had found him through the woman he was with. She'd been arrested at a truck stop in a stolen car, and she had led them to the motel where she and Cedric were staying. The Franklin County Sheriff's SWAT team arrived at the motel, and a deputy got Cedric on the phone. The deputy was trying to convince Cedric to give himself up when he heard the gunshot. Cedric lived for twelve hours in the hospital before he died.

Hearing the news of Cedric's suicide from Karen felt like a gust of wind blowing past. It was almost as if Cedric were saying, *It's okay now*. I wasn't surprised he had done it. I knew he was adamant he was never going back to prison, so I'd thought there was very little chance they would take him alive. I felt an indescribable sense of relief. And then I felt guilty. Then sad. *How could I be relieved?* Cedric was the father of my child, he was someone I'd once loved. There was a huge mix of emotions in those first few hours. I walked around outside the apartment complex, sobbing.

By the time I got back inside, Cedric's face was all over the news. David saw it, too. He had very little reaction—actually, he had little reaction to anything at that time. His father had taught him that men don't show emotion.

I have been asked if Cedric's suicide made me feel cheated out of justice—not getting to see him tried, convicted, held accountable for the things he'd done. I understand why victims feel that way, but it's never been foremost in my mind. I did feel it was the coward's way out, leaving without facing up to his actions. But I've known so many victims who don't get any kind of justice, even when an abuser is apprehended, and many victims who continue to live in fear. Cedric's abuse, his terrorizing of David and me, was over. I'm sorry the story had to end with his death, but I'd be lying if I said I wasn't relieved.

———

I talked to Karen about the people who had helped me at the gas station after the shooting. I hadn't gotten an opportunity to thank them. So after Cedric died, and I knew I was safe, I went back. The young woman was there. She was shocked to see me—though not quite as shocked as she'd been the first time. She apologized to me for something she had said that day—she'd been worried, with all that blood, about HIV. It was 1992, and HIV/AIDS was still very scary for people. I reassured her and told her it was okay. She didn't know the man who'd been there, or how to find him. I still don't know his name, the man who helped save my life. Regardless, I feel a deep connection with those people. I understand just how traumatic that day must have been for them, too.

I was still a mess. I was on Zoloft and something else for anxiety, plus two kinds of painkillers. The skull fracture was taking longer to heal than I had expected and causing me severe headaches. But saying thank you was therapeutic for me. I sent cards to the detective and the hospital staff and even called the ambulance station. The guy I spoke to said, "Hey, it's my job." The man at the gas station is the only one I haven't been able to say thank you to. I wish him well, as I do all of the people who were a part of my survival that day.

When I started working on this book, I decided to go back to the car wash. It had been years since I was there. It's only a few miles from where I live now, but not a place I have reason to pass. The minute I turned down Dayton, I became almost frightened. An ominous feeling hit me. But I kept driving. It was a beautiful day in late May, very like the day of the shooting. I pulled the car up along the curb outside the car wash. I could see the gas station ahead of me, now a Circle K. I went through it all again in my mind. Details came back to me, not just about the shooting.

I thought about episodes from my marriage. I thought about the kidnapping, too, the feeling of terror, driving while Cedric pointed a gun at me, the thought, still so clear: *Does anybody see me? How can I get someone to see what's happening?* I thought about those questions, how that desire to be truly seen had run through my life.

As a kid, lost in the tumult of so many brothers, in the darkness that pervades an abusive household.

In school, casting about for some understanding of who I was as a shy, studious mixed-race girl.

As a sixteen-year-old single mother, stopped on the street corner by that snide neighbor who cooed over David in his stroller and thought she could foresee my future.

And as a woman, abused in her own home, who had been able, finally, to say out loud: *Look at me. Look at what is happening to me.*

PART II

After

CHAPTER 6
Picking Up the Pieces

Here are a few statistics from around the time my husband tried to kill me:

- At least 21,000 domestic crimes against women were reported to police in the U.S. each week.

- More than 90 women were murdered each week, 9 out of 10 of them by men.

- The total number of aggravated assaults, murders, and rapes against women committed in American homes, both reported and unreported, was estimated to be upward of 3 million annually.

- There were three times as many animal shelters as battered women's shelters.

Numbers. They are important, but they have a way of making our eyes glaze over; especially when they're very large, they can leave us feeling powerless to bring about change. In 1992, in order to come to a "more vivid, more human" understanding of sexual assault, domestic violence, and intimate partner homicide, the Senate's Committee on the Judiciary published a report titled *Violence Against Women: A Week in the Life of America*. The aim was to create a snapshot of violence against women that spoke louder than statistics. The (all-male) Committee on the Judiciary was chaired by then Senator Joe Biden, who had already introduced the

Violence Against Women Act (VAWA) in 1991 and begun holding hearings on domestic violence, rape, and the existing legal landscape.

The report on a week in the life of women in America surveyed a cross-section of cities and towns around the country, gathering stories of individual women who suffered violence during the first week of September 1991. Much of the document is taken up with thumbnail descriptions of violent crimes. It is not an easy read.

The writers of the report seem shocked themselves by what they were conveying, stories they knew were only the tip of the iceberg: Their approximated total domestic crimes, they wrote, was "*an extremely conservative estimate.*" (Italics theirs.) Only seventeen states even collected information on domestic crime. Many states excluded categories such as rape and kidnapping, or didn't classify certain rapes and murders as domestic crimes even if they occurred between spouses or family members.

The bulk of the report was essentially a sampling. The writers noted, "If we were to have included every reported incident, our timeline would be *2,000 pages* long—just for a single week. And if we were to add all the unreported crimes, our timeline would have to be extended by over *7,000 pages.*" (Again, italics theirs.)

The mosaic that takes shape is shocking. There are numerous stories of women setting out to engage in ordinary activities—catching a bus, getting an estimate for landscaping services, taking a taxi, playing tennis, sitting at home—only to wind up beaten, raped, or dead. There is a woman whose arm is broken by her boyfriend with a hammer. Another who is pushed out of a moving car by her husband. Yet another assaulted by her husband with an axe (he also rapes her). A woman in Baltimore is beaten, choked, and raped at knifepoint by a former friend. A woman in Texas, eight months pregnant, is denied food by the man she lives with, who won't let her leave the house. One women is beaten with a metal pipe, another with the butt of a gun, another with a broomstick. A woman is dragged by the hair through her house—after her husband tried to run her over in his car.

Over and over again, as the report put it, women are assaulted. In every possible venue; at 7 a.m. and at eleven at night; rich women, poor women, homeless and working women. Many of the domestic crimes recorded took place even after legal protection from abusers had been sought and obtained.

A Week in the Life of America is a remarkable document. The harrowing picture it paints certainly contributed to the passage of VAWA two years later, the first comprehensive legislation on domestic violence. There is something about seeing story after story on the page, stripped down to its worst details, *over and over again*, that sends shivers down my spine.

Each entry begins with a time and location stamp:

3:00 p.m., a city in Oregon
Time unknown, a town in Texas
6:05 p.m., a city in New Mexico
Morning, Kansas
2:00 p.m., suburban Connecticut
Afternoon, a city in southern California
8:15 a.m., northern West Virginia
Night, a small town in Tennessee

These time stamps read like scene headings in a screenplay. But they come at you so relentlessly you get the queasy sense of looking through a camera that is swiveling wildly, trying to catch each moment as it happens, unable to keep up. *Here. No, over here. Look here now. Now look over there.* And you realize: *It's everywhere.* You are surrounded by it, whether you see it or not, whether you know it's happening or you don't.

Some of what is reported is so horrific I don't want to reproduce it here. But I will include the final entry for the week, a woman whose name we will never know, but whom the system failed to protect:

Time unknown, a city in Texas.—A woman calls a shelter because she and her two children are fleeing her abusive husband. The shelters in the area are full and she decides to go to her sister's apartment. She begins proceedings for a protective order and agrees to keep in touch with the shelter. Later, she and her husband are found dead. She has been stabbed repeatedly and her throat has been slit. Her husband has hung himself.

———

A Week in the Life of America was published just a few months after Cedric shot me. Years later, I will share a stage with Joe Biden in Washington,

D.C. He will be the vice president by then, and I will be heading a major advocacy organization, the National Coalition Against Domestic Violence. We will be part of a gathering to commemorate the twenty-year anniversary of the passage of VAWA. But in 1992, as I reeled from the trauma of the shooting and Cedric's suicide, all that was light-years away, in the realm of the unimaginable.

My memory of those first couple of years after the shooting is murky. Things are jumbled or just not there at all. Cedric's funeral is a blur, punctuated by snapshot memories, images and things that were said that have stayed with me for three decades. In late October 1992, I drove to Springfield, Ohio, with David and Ida. What I recall about the moment of my arrival at Albretta's house is how she looked me up and down to see—I was sure of this—whether I'd really been shot. Her attitude toward me that day was one of tolerance. Clearly someone had told her I should be there, so she was going to put up with it, but she didn't like it. She would have preferred if just David and Ida had come.

I remember walking into the funeral home and seeing Cedric laid out, his head covered with a cloth, and saying to Albretta's husband, Mannie, "Why do they have a towel on his head?"

Anyone in her right mind would have known immediately why his head was covered, but I was a wreck emotionally, and still on pain meds.

Mannie said, "They can't show his head."

That was the moment when it officially sunk in. Cedric was dead. I cried throughout the entire service at the church.

Mannie insisted David, Ida, and I travel with him and Albretta in the limo back from the church. There was a heated discussion about what to do with all the flowers. Albretta was well known in the Springfield community; she did a lot of volunteer work at nursing homes and hospitals, and serving food to the homeless. Many people had sent flowers. Now she was fretting about where they should all go; she wanted to make sure they got to a certain nursing home. Mannie was getting frustrated. Finally he said, "Do we really give a fuck about flowers right now?!" But that was Albretta's way of getting through the day: focusing on the fate of the flowers.

Ida got through the day in her own manner. She was connecting socially, which was her way, showing empathy as well as sorrow. David kept to himself. He cried briefly at the service but otherwise he was very unemotional, kind of checked out. I remember looking at him at one point, sitting next to me in the church, and it suddenly hitting me, just how angry he must be. David would move on with life after that, or seem to. And it would be a couple of years before I realized just how much trauma he was carrying, and how much trouble he was in.

———

Back home again, I began to pick up the pieces.

My friends remember details of that period that I can't summon. They saw me from the outside, saw the brave face I was putting on. Regi recalls the "amazing, I'm-going-to-survive Ruth." There were plenty of tears, she says, but it was the stoic and shielded me she saw more than the raw, scared me. She refers to that period as "a very different chapter in our relationship," meaning she doesn't define me or our friendship by it. She says she wants to believe that even if none of the awful stuff had ever happened, we would still have become friends. I feel the same.

Pam says, in her typical straightforward style, "You were a mess." Pam was still working with violent juvenile offenders at the Department of Corrections, covering the 6 a.m. to 2 p.m. shift. I was so depressed I had trouble getting out of bed and kept coming in late to work; they were getting irritated with me. So Pam began to call me in the mornings to make sure I got up and into the office. It didn't matter that I might have had her on the phone only hours before, one of my middle-of-the-night calls in need of support. She still got herself out of bed, she still got me out of bed.

It was Pam who would eventually yell at me for sending flowers to Cedric's grave. Yes, I did that for a few years. I was stunned, traumatized. I was also in a very complicated sort of grief. I had been so relieved when they told me Cedric was dead. He couldn't hurt me anymore; David and I were out of danger. And then almost immediately I'd felt guilty for feeling relieved. There *was* a time I had loved him. He *was* David's father. His life had ended violently and horribly. No matter how I might condemn his behaviors, I felt incredibly sad that he had never been able to figure out another way to live than hurting people, and that he'd been tortured enough to take his life. The usual conventions of mourning didn't seem to apply in any neat or predictable way. But I felt it was important for me, for David, for Cedric's mother, for all of us to understand that Cedric was cared about. He wasn't just a set of behaviors, he was a human being. So I marked his passing with a ritual. He was buried in Ohio, and on his birthday I would send flowers and a note: *From your son and Ruth.* After the first couple of years, I just signed them from David. David was struggling with both hating his father and feeling love for him. I had to help him see that he could love him, while not liking the things he had done.

One day, Pam said, "What the hell are you sending flowers to this man's grave for? He tried to kill you!"

I stopped the flowers. We laugh about it now. We roll our eyes. But the impulse was one of compassion, and even all these years later I don't dismiss or negate it.

Regi and Pam, my godsisters, were great that way. They were unfailingly compassionate but not afraid to call me out if they saw me doing something they didn't think was in my best interest. They entered my life at its most dramatic and difficult moment, and they stayed. It wasn't just that I was trying to recover from the violence; I was also having to relearn how to build friendships, how to trust people again. Regi said once, "Some people stay with you for a season, others for a lifetime." They will both be with me for this lifetime. They weren't scared away by anything I was going through, and I was dealing with a lot, not just psychologically but practically. I was still trying to figure out then what I had done wrong, what I could have done differently to prevent what had happened, as though the violence were my responsibility. And I was managing the mess Cedric had left behind. Because he'd committed suicide, I wasn't able to collect life insurance. Because we weren't divorced, I was responsible for his unpaid bills. I had a son I needed to care for, who was traumatized himself. I was in survival mode.

David and I got each other through. I was so young when I had him, in some ways we grew up together. David had always been clear as a child that he stood with me, not his father. We had been bonded by the trauma of Cedric's violence and abuse. Now we were united in surviving. Any time I felt like it was never going to get better, I thought of him. David is the kindest person I know, and I don't know how he has such a good heart after all he witnessed and experienced.

But we each had to find our own way out of what happened. David went to counseling after the shooting. For almost a year, he wouldn't talk about his father. The counselor said, "He's just not ready to touch that stuff." When I tried to get him to talk to me about what he was feeling, he would clam up. It wasn't only the anger—what I'd seen so clearly in the chapel that day—it was also his guilt over not protecting me, not being able to stop the bad things from happening. It was feeling responsible for things that should never, ever be put on a child. When Cedric pointed a gun at me and said to David, "If you bring one more F into this house, I'll kill your mother," he was telling our son it was down to him whether I lived or died. David was just fourteen years old.

I could see by his late teens that something had changed in David's personality and his response to life. He had a new set of "friends." I was only starting to learn about the effects of trauma then, and I thought (and hoped) that the change in David might just be adolescence, a teenager being secretive or difficult. I wasn't immediately able to acknowledge the toll it had all taken, and I didn't see the early signs of his drug use, something he still struggles with today. Looking back now, I know that his response during that time to all that happened, ending in his father's suicide, was an attempt at avoidance: *If I change my friends, if I make my life look different, I won't have to relive anything I've lived through.* Drugs blocked the feelings not only about his father's death, but about his own sense of guilt. He tells me that himself now—that they were part of his avoidance. I know I'm not the only mother who has wished she could wave a magic wand. I wish I could impact David the way I've impacted others over the years. I say what I believe are the right things to him, and when I feel like it's not making a difference, I want to reach for the magic wand. Of course there isn't one. But as a mom I never give up hope. I keep loving unconditionally while holding him accountable and setting boundaries. I may have stopped accepting his behavior because he hasn't chosen to deal with the hurt, but I will never stop loving him or trying to guide him or wanting things to get better.

———

Traumatic events, particularly those where we can neither resist what is happening nor escape it, overwhelm our normal systems of adaptation and self-defense. They produce changes in our systems involving physiological arousal, emotion, cognition, and memory—functions that are normally integrated but which trauma can sever, so someone may be hypervigilant in the absence of danger, or feel no emotion at all when recalling traumatic events. Our ordinary responses to danger live on after the event(s), but in altered form. Judith Herman writes that this sundering, in which trauma "tears apart a complex system of self-protection that normally functions in an integrated fashion," is a critical element of PTSD. She distinguishes between the post-traumatic stress that follows a single traumatic episode and that which follows trauma that is repetitive and persistent over time. Victims of domestic violence tend to be in the second group, chronically traumatized and suffering from a more complex form of PTSD.

In those first few years after Cedric's death, things hit me without warning. One day I was driving down the highway and went rigid with fear: I smelled gunpowder and my body just froze. I had to pull over and call a friend to come get me. The strange thing was, it was a new car, not the one I'd been driving when Cedric shot me.

Other times, I sensed danger where there was none. When Pam decided to leave her husband, I freaked out. She had told him she was leaving him, and had moved into their spare bedroom, but she was working on a big academic paper and didn't want to move out until she had finished that. This was beyond my comprehension, that you could say that to your husband, negotiate that arrangement, and not wind up dead. So I would call her two or three times a day to make sure she was okay. Pam's husband, I thought, could be controlling, but he had never been violent with her or threatened to harm her. Nevertheless, I was convinced that her life was in danger. Finally, she said, "Ruth, enough! He's not going to kill me!"

———

Some months after the shooting, I began therapy, first with a woman named Barb, who would come to refer to herself as my Jewish angel, my Jewish mother. We would meet at her home, in the room where she saw clients. Even before I walked in the door I would be crying. Barb was very put together—the big sprayed hair and the matching business skirts and blazers. I loved her. She was the one who allowed me to recognize that everything I was feeling was legitimate—including guilt—but she also helped me to understand that I didn't *have* to feel all those things. I could let some of them go. What had happened hadn't been my fault. It would take me some time to really internalize this truth, but I did. Now I don't even like the term "abusive relationship." The word "relationship" implies mutuality, shared responsibility. It may seem like splitting hairs, but there is an important difference between calling out abuse within a relationship and saying that someone is *in an abusive relationship*. The latter suggests something inherent and reciprocal, as though we're talking about two people with a common purpose. But if what we're really talking about is a situation where one person is the aggressor, the one who is harming, and the other is the victim of that harm, we should not assign blame to both parties. Abuse within an intimate relationship shouldn't be confused with codependence. Hamish Sinclair, who works in violence prevention, has noted that violence is not a "relationship problem." It's a problem of one person's "commitment to violence."

At a certain point, Barb said I needed to do something that would give me a feeling of control over the memory of what had happened. She sent me to a woman she knew who specialized in PTSD and practiced regression therapy.

My sessions with Diane did not involve hypnosis, but there was a hypnotic quality to the process. With Diane, I revisited traumatic events in the safe environment of her consultation room. I would close my eyes and she would take me back, help me recall the details of a certain day—including the days of the kidnapping and the shooting—and how I felt as those things were happening. (Oddly, I don't remember my emotional reactions from those sessions with Diane so much as I remember my physical ones: breaking out in a sweat, my heart racing.) I also imagined other scenarios that might have unfolded. The purpose of that wasn't to explore the possibility that I could have changed the outcome—quite the opposite. As victims, we so often fall into the trap of believing that if we had only done X or hadn't done Y—if I'd dropped the kids off earlier, dressed differently, not spilled the coffee that morning—he wouldn't have beat or abused me that day. Whether it's everyday verbal abuse or an attempted murder, we are always asking ourselves what *we* did "wrong." The phrase "Maybe if I'd just . . ." is one we need to free ourselves from. Working with Diane, I began to understand, and to really believe in my bones, that even if I had left the house a half hour later, or pulled over somewhere else, Cedric was hellbent on killing me, and there was likely nothing, short of him being in prison and unable to get to me, that would have kept him from trying to do it. Maybe it would have happened the 19th of June rather than the 17th, but it would have happened.

Victims make mistakes, just like every human being does. But that does not make a victim responsible for an abuser's behavior. Diane and Barb helped me to understand that, and to really believe it. With both women, I worked toward accepting what had happened, that I was never going to erase it from my history. It had gone into the shaping of me, so how was I going to respond to that?

David and I had moved into Cedric's condo. An odd choice, but I was desperate for a house, a stable home, where I could raise David. It was a practical rather than an emotional decision. Cedric's retirement fund had helped me catch up on the bills he'd left, and the home owner's insurance covered a deep cleaning and repairs. The SWAT team had done a lot of damage when they went there the night of the shooting looking for Cedric. After that, the house had been off-limits while he was on the run.

We stayed in that house for a couple of years. Sometime in there, my mother came to live with me for a few months. (As I said, it was a crazy, mixed-up time.) My mother hadn't been there for me when I was shot—not at the hospital and not in the months afterward. When she finally did show up in my life, in my house, it was less about coming to help me than about hoping to be with someone who cared about her. She thought I was going to take care of her, that we were going to spend our evenings sitting in rocking chairs together. But I had a job, and was raising a teenager, and trying to keep my own head above water. When my mother realized I didn't have time to care for her as well, she left.

Eventually, David and I moved out, too. This time the decision *was* emotional. There were days the place felt haunted with memories or presences, and I knew I couldn't be there any longer. Every time I drove down the street, I'd think of how we'd driven down that same street the day Cedric kidnapped me. In a bizarre twist, I sold the condo to Pam, one of my godsisters, who went on to live there for more than twenty years. We had a running joke in the beginning. There was a microwave on the counter that had a habit of flashing *HI* (for the "high" setting) for no reason, and we used to say it was Cedric, living in the microwave. At some point, Pam saged the house to chase Cedric's spirit out. But we still laugh about the microwave.

It might seem strange to be able to laugh about a thing like that, but if you're with someone you trust, someone you know you're safe with and who understands exactly how serious your situation is, laughter can be part of healing. It's an element of your humanity, it's your birthright. And it is definitely one of the things that got me through. I try to laugh a lot.

There were so many days back then when, in order to keep going, I had to believe in a future I couldn't yet see, whose particulars were in no way clear to me. But what I learned is that just as we can't foresee the challenges and crises that the future holds, neither can we imagine the gifts that will come our way: the kindness and friendship, the stretches of peace, the inner strengthening that will allow us to navigate the challenges. Maybe I always knew this, intuitively. In my worst times, even going back to when I was a girl, there has been a voice that said: *It won't always be like this.* That voice kept me moving forward. Gradually, I would learn how to trust myself again. In a way, I had no choice. It was a new life, and every decision was on me.

I put one foot in front of the other.

CHAPTER 7

The World Would Cease to Function

In the spring of 1993, I was glancing over a newsletter published by the Colorado Domestic Violence Coalition (now Violence Free Colorado) when I saw my name. The woman in charge of the Coalition's information and public education campaigns was named Connie—someone I would come to know and love—and Connie had decided that one way to combat domestic violence was to tabulate statewide fatalities that were related to it. Her spring 1993 newsletter listed all such deaths from 1992, including suicides, homicides, and infanticides. She regularly scoured Colorado's two dailies, the *Rocky Mountain News* and the *Denver Post*, and had seen the news of Cedric's standoff in Ohio with the police. The articles on his suicide also referred to his attempted murder of me and to the kidnapping. So there I was, reading Connie's newsletter, when suddenly I'm staring at my own story.

Shortly after that, in May, I contacted the Coalition. I was still having a very hard time—not even a year had passed since the shooting. Despite the therapy, friendships, and freedom from violence, I had sunk into a dark depression. I was struggling with what my place on earth was. *What was the point of it all?* I had survived. But what was I supposed to do with myself now? I called the Coalition and asked if I could volunteer there. I said, "I don't know what to do," and they said, "How about stuffing envelopes?" So initially they got me doing administrative work. It turned out that performing mostly mindless tasks in a safe and supportive environment, with people who understood what I was dealing with, was exactly what I needed.

Throughout my life I've felt buoyed, nurtured, ferried along, by a series of women. Some passed through, helping me in the moment, but others came into my life and stayed. Connie and Pat, the two women at the Coalition who sheltered me emotionally and are themselves survivors of domestic violence, are among the lifers. (I have a warning I give to new acquaintances I click with: *Be careful, once I meet you and like you, I won't let you go!*) They have watched me emerge from my shock and uncertainty, and they have nudged me gently along.

Connie had come to the Coalition by chance, as I had. She'd been working in sales but had a degree in journalism from Northwestern (as well as a PhD, with a thesis on female novelists of the eighteenth century), and had heard that they needed a volunteer editor for the Coalition newsletter. So in she went. The more she saw of the office, the more help she realized they needed—particularly with their public relations and outreach: Connie was a survivor of domestic abuse, and yet, she realized, she had never heard of the Coalition until recently. So she drew up a job description and said, "This is what I think you need, and I can do it." They hired her.

Connie is brilliant, a wonderful writer, and a lifelong advocate for victims of domestic violence. She is more traditional than I am, but just as strongly feminist, and not afraid of challenges. She has run reading groups in women's prisons and, after leaving the Coalition, worked with the Colorado Bar Association on a new program called Domestic Violence: Make It Your Business. The program's aim was to make businesses aware that they probably had at least one employee who was either a domestic violence victim or a perpetrator, and that this kind of violence often spills over into the work setting—for instance, when an abuser shows up at a victim's workplace. (I can think of my own case, going out to the car after my shift and finding the pictures of David and me, torn in half and left on the seat of my car, and knowing there was a good chance Cedric had been armed when he paid that visit.) Domestic violence was something businesses should view not as a private matter but as a risk to their organizations and employees. Connie trained businesses in risk assessment, prevention, and response. There are many such programs now all around the country, and Connie was in at the ground level.

Pat was also a survivor. She had been in a relationship for a year with an extremely violent man. Pat had had no experience of abuse before that, but she met this guy when she was a single mother and at what she calls a "crazy place" in her life. A couple of years after she had left him, she felt the need to give back to other survivors. (Pat's abuser later went to prison for severely beating a woman he was with after Pat.) She began to volunteer in various capacities—working in a shelter, as a volunteer coordinator, running a twenty-four-hour helpline. When she moved to Denver, she became the office manager at the Coalition.

Pat remembers me walking through the door that first day, dressed to the nines in heels and a fancy jacket, and announcing that I was the new volunteer, which makes me sound more self-assured than I remember being. Both Connie and Pat recall that I was rail thin. (Connie says I was so skinny that when I turned sideways she could hardly see me.) The shooting had happened only a mile from Pat's house, and when I said, "You might have heard about my story . . . ," she said, "Yeah, I certainly did."

Connie, Pat, and I became close friends when I joined them on the Survivors Task Force, a group they had created because they believed that survivors needed their own committee within the Coalition. There were a dozen or so of us on the Task Force, and we were a diverse group in terms of class, age, and race. Not all were volunteers at the Coalition. One woman was a district attorney, another a hairdresser. We also had different experiences of abuse, and viewing domestic violence through the eyes of other women taught me more than what I already knew from firsthand experience about the many forms it can take and its effects, both the insidious ones and the more obvious. I learned that sometimes survivors believe they haven't been abused badly enough to qualify as victims of domestic violence, and that we shouldn't assume we can gauge damage by looking only at the most obvious signs. It's more than black eyes and bruises. It's all the violations of your autonomy and your sense of safety that aren't necessarily physical. Cedric pulled a gun on me only (*only*) twice when we were living together, but the mere presence of that gun in our house had an intimidating and coercive effect on me. That's an impact you can't easily see or measure.

The Task Force got together one night each month. It was both a support group and the public face of survivors, and it helped to change the whole tenor of the discussion within and outside of the Coalition. Up to that point, service providers often treated survivors as though they had to be hidden away for their own protection. Sometimes this is absolutely true, as I knew all too well. But there were many survivors who were perfectly glad to go out in public and say: "This is what happened to me, and it's not all right." This commitment to speaking out was in contrast to how survivors had often been viewed, as fragile and damaged. *Yes*, some women were saying, *we've been abused and that trauma is ongoing, but not only can you survive abuse; you can heal and thrive within a supportive community*.

One of my early tasks at the Coalition was staffing a photo exhibit Connie had organized for Domestic Violence Awareness Month that October. It featured the work of Donna Ferrato, a series called *Living with the Enemy*. Donna was a photojournalist doing important and groundbreaking work—both as a photographer and an advocate—on behalf of victims of domestic violence. She had stumbled into the subject. While on assignment to cover the swingers scene in the early 1980s, she saw up close a man viciously beating his wife. She photographed it—she said that otherwise there would be no evidence and no one would believe that it had happened. Then she tried to intervene. Witnessing that beating changed the direction of Donna's work, and for the next ten years, she went around the country documenting domestic violence and the fallout from it, a problem she realized was widespread and yet hidden from public view. She rode in police cars and spent time in courtrooms, hospitals, and women's shelters. She attended women's self-defense classes, and even stayed in violent homes—both rich and poor. She also spent time in women's prisons, and was outraged to find women incarcerated whose only crime was trying to save their own or their children's lives from violent partners.

Donna wasn't a stranger to sexual violence—she had been raped as a college student. When her photos of domestic violence began appearing, her father revealed to her that his father had regularly beaten his mother, something Donna hadn't known about. The domestic violence that she had been exposing in other homes had been a part of her family, too, just as hidden.

Our exhibition was put together on a shoestring. Connie gave $500 of her own money and got nine other people to chip in the same. The space was offered to us for free, and artist friends of Connie's donated their time and materials, designing and printing posters. The mayor of Denver came to the opening night.

The fact that Donna's photos were being shown around the country, and had already been collected into a book, *Living with the Enemy*, was a sign that change was in the air. For the first few years she had been documenting domestic violence, no magazine was interested in running her stark, intimate photos. But when she won the prestigious Eugene Smith Award in 1985, editors took notice. In July 1994, a few weeks after Nicole Brown and her friend Ron Goldman were viciously murdered—and O.J. Simpson, Nicole's ex-husband, had been charged with the crimes—one of Donna's photos was used on the cover of *TIME* magazine. It was a close-up of a woman with two black eyes. The headline read, *When Violence Hits Home: The Simpson case awakens America to the epidemic of domestic abuse.*

The year 1994 was a watershed for domestic violence awareness and legislation, for reasons both good and bad. The good was Congress passing the Violence Against Women Act (VAWA). Although federal funds had been designated for programs serving battered women and their children in 1984 under the Family Violence Prevention Services Act, the scope of VAWA was much broader and more comprehensive. It brought together for the first time representatives from the legal system, social services, and nonprofits to create and support a range of services for victims of domestic violence, sexual assault, dating violence, and stalking. Shelters, rape crisis centers, and legal aid for victims would be funded under VAWA, as would advocacy organizations and training on sexual and domestic violence for police and judicial officials. VAWA would also support prosecution for federal crimes involving such violence.

At the time of VAWA's passage, there was no national domestic violence hotline in the U.S. (There had been a toll-free number set up in 1987 by the National Coalition Against Domestic Violence [NCADV], but it had been forced to shut down five years later due to insufficient funding.) Now there would be money guaranteed for these incredibly important services.

The other big news that year about domestic violence—the terrible news—was the murder of Nicole and Ron. The two had been stabbed to death at Nicole's house in Los Angeles on June 12; Nicole had been nearly decapitated. Ron was tragically in the wrong place at the wrong time—among the 20 percent of victims of homicides related to domestic violence who are family members, friends, police, or people who try to intervene. At the time of the murders, law enforcement knew that Simpson had a history of battering, harassing, and stalking Nicole; he had pleaded no contest to spousal abuse in 1989. In a 911 tape from 1993 that would become public at the trial, a terrified Nicole says, "Could you get someone over here now? . . . He's back. . . . He's O.J. Simpson, I think you know his record. . . . He broke the back door down to get in. . . . I don't want to stay on the line. He's going to beat the shit out of me. . . . The kids are up there sleeping and I don't want anything to happen. . . ."

Nicole's words will sound horribly familiar to victims of domestic violence: the repetition of abuse, his refusal to leave her alone, the police knowing all about it while she remains at risk, her fear of a beating, her fear for her children.

The murders and the trial that followed would bring together several ugly strains in American life: violence against women, racism and police brutality, victim-blaming, misogyny, and the way we turn a blind eye to the worst behavior of our sports heroes. (Simpson would be acquitted in criminal court—a verdict one juror would later say was payback for the LAPD's beating of an unarmed Rodney King in 1991—though in a civil suit Simpson was subsequently found liable for Nicole and Ron's deaths.) The crimes placed domestic violence on the front pages of the nation's newspapers. If a rich white woman could be battered, who was safe? If a handsome all-American hero could be a batterer—maybe even a murderer—then domestic abusers were not just people on the margins of society but were in our midst, successful professionals with perfectly charming public faces.

In one sense, that *TIME* magazine headline was correct. The murders had awakened America to domestic abuse. But the awakening was largely temporary, as it tends to be with every sensational case that hits the headlines. In the end what we were left with was a missed opportunity to teach the public about the dynamics of domestic violence. Nicole had endured all the classic tactics of abusers. What happened to her should have been a case study in our education. But as the trial got underway, it became more about Simpson than about his victims, and about the divide in America between those of us who believed he was guilty and those who didn't. The racial narrative, and the narrative of police misconduct and bumbling, overshadowed the crime itself: The man who many believe murdered Nicole and Ron went free. America might have been awakened, but we didn't learn enough in the moment.

Like 95 million other people, on June 17 I watched Simpson lead the police on a two-hour, low-speed car chase in Southern California. The chase took place two years to the day since Cedric shot me. Simpson was to have turned himself in at the police station that morning, as he'd been declared a "person of interest" in the murder investigation. But instead of going to the station, he had disappeared for several hours—until he turned up on the freeway in the now famous white Bronco.

The following day, Connie and Pat approached me and said that Channel 9 News in Denver was looking for a domestic violence victim who would speak about her experience of abuse, someone who could put a face on our movement. I was still pretty shaky then, and my initial response was "No way."

But I kept thinking about Nicole. Her experience felt like a mirror of my own. I was wishing there was something I could do about these crimes, about the fact that men got away with them. I was wondering why I was still so fearful about showing my face, given that Cedric was long dead. Connie and Pat convinced me, and the next thing I knew, I was sitting in front of a camera crew talking about the worst thing that had ever happened to me.

I still have a VHS recording of that interview. For decades it was packed away in a box in the garage, gathering dust. I got it out recently because I wanted to remember more about that year of my life. I bought a VCR player on eBay, and the day it arrived, I slid the cartridge in.

What I saw moved me—how young I was, how new to the whole experience of going public with something so painful and private. I was identified only by my first name, and I was filmed in silhouette. Those were things I had requested, maybe for David's sake as much as my own. What also struck me was how calm I seemed. I said that what happened to Nicole was causing me to replay everything I had gone through two years ago. I explained that the violence I'd experienced was because of Cedric's need to control me, and I pointed out that domestic violence was far more common than people might think. I could hear a shift in my tone as I was talking, as though even over the course of the interview I was actually gaining in courage or confidence. I recalled that as I spoke I had begun to feel angry. I remembered distinctly thinking, *Wait a minute, I can't believe we even have to be talking about this.*

That was the first time I spoke publicly about my abuse and Cedric's attempt to murder me. It broke the ice—or maybe the dam.

A couple of months later, I got involved, through the Task Force, in Denver's version of the Clothesline Project. The Clothesline Project had started in 1990 in Cape Cod. The women behind it had questioned why we record and commemorate men killed in battle, while women were dying unrecognized, unmemorialized, from another kind of violence right here at home. (The figure 58,000 dead is well known in this country—it's the number of Americans killed during the Vietnam War. But during those same sixteen years, there were 51,000 women murdered in the U.S. by their husbands or boyfriends. More recently, 3,200 members of the military were killed between 2000 and 2006, while 10,600 people, the vast majority of them women, died by domestic homicide.) The message of the Project was that domestic violence was far more prevalent than we wanted to believe, and those who suffered it should be recognized and remembered.

The Clothesline Project invited women affected by violence to decorate a T-shirt expressing their thoughts or feelings about what they had endured. The shirts, which functioned as a form of public testimony about the problem of violence against women, represented the end of silence: the "dirty laundry" victims were airing. (Gratitude is due to the women behind the first such public event, a speak-out on rape in 1971 organized by the New York Radical Feminists.) The Clothesline concept quickly went global. Six thousand shirts would be displayed at the 1995 NOW Rally for Women's Lives. The project brought survivorship out of the closet.

Here in Denver, all kinds of women were coming forward. It was a version of what would happen later, on a much larger scale, with #metoo. When someone starts the ball rolling, it's hard to stop its momentum. In 1994, our Task Force invited every person affected by domestic violence, either a survivor or family members, to create a T-shirt with whatever message they wanted to convey, honoring the victim. On September 30, we put these T-shirts on a clothesline and marched the clothesline around the grounds of the state capitol. Then about two hundred of us assembled on the capitol steps. Governor Roy Romer joined us to help hang the clothesline on rebar we had set up around the capitol building. Someone beat a drum every fifteen seconds as a reminder of the frequency of abuse against women in the U.S. I was one of the speakers that day. I stood at the podium, my voice trembling. As I told my story I was actually in tears. But when I was done, I felt strangely composed, and I joined the small group of media people who wanted to ask me more questions.

———

In our little corner of the world, victims and survivors were contributing to a larger movement to get out from under the shame we felt about what had been done to us. More immediately, the Task Force, and particularly the Clothesline Project, changed the whole tenor of how the Coalition approached its work. It had been somewhat inward-looking, focused on protecting victims and survivors by keeping them out of sight. I was part of a group of women who rejected that ethos, who said, "I'm not ashamed, and I'm not hiding." I may have felt self-conscious about my background or my level of education. But that didn't stop me from telling the truth about my family circumstances growing up, about what I'd gone through as a young woman, or about the effect of domestic abuse on my son. I shared it all. Hiding the truth, pretending things were fine, hadn't served me well. I was done with that. And unlike many victims I knew, I no longer had to be afraid. My abuser was dead.

The time I spent volunteering at the Coalition was life-changing. Connie and Pat gave me a platform where I felt safe. That was their gift to me. In return I brought my energy, my heart, and my ability to keep seeing the positive in people and situations. After those first nervous public appearances, I began to do a lot more public speaking. I became active on the Coalition's Speakers Bureau. I also became the Task Force's representative to the Coalition board. I had known domestic violence intimately, but now I was beginning my education in other facets of it—advocacy, the provision of services, cultural forces that enable violence against women and perpetuate myths about its victims. I was coming to understand just how widespread the problem of domestic violence was, and how often it wasn't taken seriously—deemed a private matter rather than a crime for which perpetrators should be held accountable. It was becoming ever clearer to me that what I had experienced—being continually stalked and harassed by someone who was actually under a restraining order—was something many victims experienced, a clear systemic failure to protect those who've been abused and are still in danger.

I think back on those years and see two realities coexisting: I was still in shock, but I was also regaining my voice. In fact, I was gaining a new one. When I had shown up at the Coalition in 1993, I was skinny, scared, and lost. It was painful working with other survivors, hearing their stories, but I hung in there because I wanted to heal, and I seemed to know, intuitively, that here was a path for me to do that.

Pat says even from the start, there was something about me that was never quite settled. I wanted to keep doing more, going forward, even on the darkest days. Connie remembers I seemed like a young woman on the brink of something. I was stepping over a threshold. I may not have known what was next, but I was moving ahead, and in a way that was careful rather than reactive. I assessed before I leaped. I've always had drive, what my mother called "moxie," and what I jokingly call "the R factor." Something that told me on those dark days: *One day this won't be me.* I bounce back instead of giving up, and I wanted to figure out what my life could be, to prove the doubters wrong. I know that inside, there was a huge amount of tumult and fear, but to Connie and Pat I looked like someone determined, as Connie says, to keep sailing her boat.

Connie told me recently that someone had asked her if she thought I was an outlier, in the sense of having been able to rebuild my life after that degree of violence. She had answered that if you look at the stats, the number of women affected every year by intimate violence, and you dig into the stories, you realize that these women are all around us—working, rearing children, contributing to their communities, taking care of aging parents, going out with friends on a Friday night. They keep on going. "Keeping going," she said, "might be the most essential thing about Ruth, but she's not unusual in doing it." She said that I was absolutely typical, in fact, representative of what women all over the world do.

"Think of it," she added. "If every woman affected by domestic violence took to her bed and put the blinds down, the world would cease to function."

CHAPTER 8
Educated

Abusers want control. They don't like you to be or say or think a single thing that doesn't somehow include them. Because like all tyrants, they are insecure—dangerously so.

Education, on the other hand, represents freedom. At its best, it enables you to think critically about all sorts of subjects, including your own life. It exposes you to people and ideas outside the confines of your home or your small circle. And, in the mid-1990s (before student debt became crippling), it was a solid path to greater economic independence.

Obviously, education isn't something abusers encourage for their victims. Cedric had always told me I couldn't go back to school. "You don't need to," he'd say. "You'll work where I work." Going back to school would have been a declaration of my autonomy, which he couldn't bear.

When I had been volunteering at the Coalition for a couple of years, I saw an ad in the *Denver Post*: *Are you a woman who wants to get your education on the weekends?* It was a special program designed for working women at the University of Denver's Weekend College. The fact that it was women-only made it easier. I knew I'd be nervous attempting to go to college. Every major decision I made during those years caused a psychic disturbance in me. *Who do you think you are?* I'd hear myself saying. *You can't do this.* I'd be sick to my stomach with fear. I would hear Cedric's voice, telling me I wasn't good enough.

Sure enough, my first day on campus I was sitting in an empty classroom overwhelmed with panic. A counselor walked in and spoke to me.

Her name was Amy. She sat beside me and calmed me down. "You can absolutely do this," she said.

Amy was another one of those angels who showed up at just the right moment. Maybe it wasn't a coincidence that she went on to work at SafeHouse and other important nonprofits whose missions are to protect the vulnerable.

Years later I bumped into her and reminded her of that day. "Yeah," she said, and laughed. "I didn't know what a beast I was unleashing!"

I was among the odd ones out at college that first year—one of just a handful of women of color. But the experience I had at that school was the one I'd always longed for growing up. I got involved in everything. I became an overachiever. I marked up all my textbooks and went at my homework ferociously, just as I had when I was a kid in Mrs. Malcolm's class. Corny as it sounds, there was nothing more thrilling to me than pulling into the school parking lot.

I had been drawn into the academic orbit by Pam. The paper Pam was writing as she was splitting up from her husband—the paper she had wanted to finish before she left their house, the situation that had given rise to such panic in me—had evolved into a master's thesis. Seeing Pam immersed in her academic work reminded me of my old love of reading and learning, and helped rekindle my desire to go back to school. Pam was getting a degree in Criminal Justice at the University of Colorado, and her topic was domestic violence. Her thesis included lengthy interviews with both perpetrators and victims. She focused on three women who had been abused. One of them was me.

I went in-depth with Pam about my experiences, in a way I hadn't done with anyone till then, apart from my therapists. (Many of the details in this book of the abuse during my marriage, and of the kidnapping and the shooting, I've taken from the interviews I did with Pam for her thesis, when all those things were still fresh in my mind. It's been painful, but invaluable, revisiting that source.) One of the interviews Pam did with me was on July 5, 1994, just over two years after the shooting. David and his friends were setting off firecrackers in the street, and every time one popped I jumped out of my chair. Any loud noise sent me right over the edge—and still does. As I spoke to Pam, I was repeatedly jolted, my heart racing and my hands shaking.

Nevertheless, in the pages of Pam's thesis, I sometimes manage to sound pretty together and surprisingly optimistic—not quite how I remember myself at that time.

"I feel for once in my life that I'm important," I told Pam. "I'm not as scared of things. I've gotten more assertive. . . . This period that I have been by myself has really helped me grow and understand that I don't need to have someone always controlling me, telling me what to do or how to do it or when to do it or why to do it. . . . If you don't want to do it, you don't do it. . . . It feels wonderful. It's funny, it's like a rebirth. . . . I became much more involved in everything. My friends, my work, doing things I never thought I should or could do. . . . I feel like living again. . . . A lot of times it's even scary. I like it. If I fall on my face, I fall on my face, which I do on a regular basis. I can still do that good."

There were two sides to me, and the contradiction is understandable. I was feeling the excitement of new possibilities, that sense of rebirth, and there *were* times I felt strong and competent. But I was still in a bad way. When I closed my eyes at night, I went over it all, again and again, the choices I'd made, the flashbacks to the shooting, the various traumatic episodes leading up to it. I could go for days sunk in a state of disarray. Hours and hours I spent curled up in a ball, crying. Or praying for peace of mind. The unending questions. *Should I buy a home? Should I go back to school? How can I help David?* Every decision felt like it weighed two hundred pounds. And I still wasn't well physically. I wasn't eating right, sometimes I ate hardly at all, and I had frequent headaches.

But the disconnect between what I remember as I look back today, and what I said to Pam in 1994, might also be because everything in life is relative. Compared to where I'd been for the previous several years—living in a state of terror, not in control of my own day-to-day existence—where I was that July, sitting in my backyard with Pam, no longer afraid of being hunted down, felt pretty good. From the perspective of today, though, when I've healed that much more, and am so much surer of who I am, I look back on that young woman assessing her life and her prospects, and I see her shaky, flinching at loud noises, and uncertain of her future. I see her putting on a brave face, determined to sound determined.

Things were scary, but I was okay with that. Because it was good scary. It was about risks I wanted to take to grow and change, and not allowing a fear of failure to limit what I was willing to try. I hear myself saying, *Let's see what's next, let's see what's over here.*

I started school the year after that interview, going for my bachelor's in Communications, with a certificate in Women's Studies and Writing. Once I was going to classes, along with my full-time job, the volunteer work became too much—but I didn't stop the speaking and advocacy I had begun.

When I think of the "firsts" in the new life I was building—my first time speaking about domestic violence on television, my first job that had nothing to do with Cedric, my first trip to Europe—I still think of school as the most important, the "first" of which I'm the most proud. I had always been proud of myself for getting my GED, but I had also felt, all my adult life, like an imposter. Someone only pretending to be smart, capable, lovable. There was nothing legitimate about me, I thought. I don't mean that an academic degree or any external stamp legitimizes anyone. I mean that education just happened to be one of the things that allowed me to move forward. It was something I wanted to do and that I had been denied for so long. When you're being abused and living in fear, your imagination constricts. You are preoccupied by the question of surviving, of how to limit the damage to yourself or your children, of how to de-escalate danger.

Now, though the past still haunted me, and though I was still working through some very complicated and painful feelings, I was free to think of other things. I found that I was more than capable of being a good student, setting goals, participating in school events, enjoying myself. School was something that I had loved as a child, so the act of going back to study was also the act of reclaiming and reconnecting with a part of myself that I had lost during the years of my marriage. School was tied to who I felt I was, deep down, the self most people had been incapable of seeing underneath the impoverished child, the mixed-race misfit, the teenaged mother, the abuse victim.

This question of being seen is one that has been with me throughout my life, both in terms of feeling as though my most authentic self is obscured from view by assumptions or prejudice or stigma, and in terms of going public with my story. The willingness to be seen, the insistence on it, can be a powerfully political act when it occurs in the context of testimonials about violence or injustice. I wanted to be seen so that I felt some sense of harmony between my inner world and my outer life, but I also wanted to show people that there is no shame in being a victim of abuse. Neither is that abuse the sum total of who you are. As Roxane Gay wrote in *Hunger*, her memoir of being gang-raped and the traumatic fallout from that, she didn't want anyone "to think I am nothing more than the worst thing that has ever happened to me."

Letting go of that feeling that I was an imposter didn't happen overnight. But setting foot on campus in the fall of 1995 was the first step. I began to come out of my shell. Part of that was writing for *The Weekender*, the college's newspaper. I wrote about the things and people that mattered to me. I wrote about being shot and left for dead by my husband. (I was told that the school administration was very resistant to publishing it, but in the end, the newspaper ran it.) I wrote about testimony I gave to the Colorado State Senate in support of a bill on domestic violence intervention programs (the bill was defeated). And, in a nice sort of symmetry, I wrote about Pam. While Pam was typing up her thesis, I was publishing an article about my friendship with her titled "The Sources of Resiliency." I talked about how we had entered each other's life at a critical time, how she'd befriended me during my first rocky days back at work: "We were both dealing with major pain, and we were not sure how to go forward without taking too many steps backwards." But I also said that we both felt an exciting phase of our lives had just begun and there were many adventures we looked forward to sharing.

Judith Herman speaks of people emerging from the traumatic past and creating a new future, including victims of domestic abuse, as being like refugees entering a new country, a sort of psychological immigration when you have to mourn all that's been lost or destroyed and discover a sustaining faith that will allow you to take on the task of developing a new self. The survivor forges this new self, this new life, as though in a radically different culture. "Emerging from an environment of total control, they feel simultaneously the wonder and uncertainty of freedom. They speak of losing and regaining the world."

This is what I was telling Pam, in my own way, the day she interviewed me in my backyard and I described my state of mind as both wonderful and scary: "It's funny, it's like a rebirth."

After so many years of feeling constrained and defined by Cedric, by his abuse, by my own fears and doubts, I was entering a new country. School wasn't just a practical undertaking—it was a symbol of the freedom I now had to make, and remake, myself. It provided crucial tools that became a part of my healing. It taught me how to place my own life experiences in a larger social and cultural context, and it allowed me to get more distance and perspective on the things that had happened to me. I gained in self-confidence. I was expanding my comfort zone, slowly inching back toward the life that Mrs. Malcolm, and even my mother, had once foreseen for me. And I was learning, bit by bit, how I could use the trauma of my past to help others.

CHAPTER 9
Finding My Communities

In her searing and beautiful memoir *Memorial Drive*, former poet laureate Natasha Trethewey tells the story of her mother's life and death. Gwen was murdered by her ex-husband (Natasha's former stepfather) when she was forty and Natasha was nineteen. Gwen had been divorced from this man for nearly two years at the time of the murder; he had already tried to kill her once by injecting her with battery acid, but was convicted only of criminal trespass and spent nine months in prison. After which, as Natasha says, he came back to finish the job.

Does it bear repeating? Leaving is no guarantee of safety.

Memorial Drive was hard for me to read. There are many parallels between Gwen's story and mine. Gwen had taken her children and fled to a shelter after years of abuse. Her husband had explicitly threatened her life. (Gwen wrote in her diary that he "told me quite calmly that since I had decided to leave him he would kill me.") He forced her into her car at gunpoint and held her against her will, as Cedric had done to me. He later shot her at close range—when he was not supposed to be anywhere near her. (There was an arrest warrant out for him because of threats he'd made, but the policeman assigned to watching the house had left his post in the middle of the night.) Like Cedric, he was tracked down at a motel, where police found him with the gun he'd used to kill Gwen. He said he'd been intending to turn it on himself. Unlike Cedric, he didn't follow through on that intent. He went to prison for several years and was released in 2019.

Victims of domestic violence can be invisible for many reasons. We may not want to see them because we'd rather believe it isn't happening. Or we don't see them because we think they are weak or fatally flawed and therefore undeserving of our full attention. Natasha has talked about how she wanted to tell her mother's story—the story of a beautiful, loving, educated woman (she had a master's in Social Work)—in order to give Gwen back the place in her life that she felt was being erased. Gwen was Black. Natasha's father, who was white, was a poet, and Natasha found that people drew a line from her father to her, as though he alone explained who she had grown up to be. There was something "racialized and patriarchal in this assumption that I'm who I am because of my father. . . . People didn't understand that the thing that hurt me into poetry, that the thing that I had tried to contend with my whole adult life was the loss of my mother."

Natasha was a guest at the NCADV conference in 2020, by which time I was heading the organization. She spoke eloquently about what sharing her mother's story has meant to her. As horrific as the murder of her mother was, she said she has come to think of the trauma—the "existential wound"—less as a burden and more as a source of illumination, a place where the light enters. It is only through these wounds, she said, that we can come closer to the kind of knowledge that allows us to do things in the service of the common good.

In the immediate aftermath of the shooting, I certainly was in no condition to think of my trauma as an opportunity to do something for the common good. I was too busy just surviving. My very self had been eroded by abuse, violence, constant fear. I had a lot of healing and rebuilding to do. I had to reimagine my whole life, and I had no idea what the path would look like or what it would require of me.

But gradually, I began to recall that I was, and always had been, much more than the abuse I had suffered. As my friend Connie said, victims and survivors are not *just* the awful things that have happened to us. We also work, exercise, study, take care of our families, have fun with our friends. We find and make meaning in many other aspects of our lives. I go back to Roxane Gay: I am more than the worst thing that has ever happened to me.

One of my own avenues for making meaning out of my life has been telling my story. Since that first day at work when I opened up to Regi about the truth of my marriage, I've learned a lot about trauma, about remembering and narrating it. I know that memories of traumatic events can feel "set apart" or cut off from our ordinary stream of thoughts, feelings, and memories; that traumatic moments can suddenly break into my consciousness—smelling gunpowder as I was driving down the road—because our brains encode and retrieve those memories differently. I know also that the story we tell ourselves about our lives influences our level of well-being, and framing our life story solely or primarily around traumatic experiences tends to leave us with a feeling of ongoing distress.

I didn't want my life to revolve around or be defined by its worst moments. And yet in order to get to the place where it wouldn't be, I had to look squarely at those moments. Paradoxically, it has been by giving those traumatic events their due—I was abused, kidnapped, and shot; such things change you irrevocably—that I have been able to relegate them to their proper place within my *whole* life story. To integrate them into the weave of my life—as a mother, a grandmother, an advocate, a boss, a friend, a sister, and a woman who dances in the grocery store when the spirit moves her.

I seemed to intuitively understand what I needed to do if I was going to move on in life, not ruled by what had happened to me, but not attempting to flee, repress, or deny it either. Sometimes we know what we need. Just as an inner voice had told me to be wary of Cedric when I first met him, that same voice later told me I needed to speak out if I was going to heal. By then I was starting to listen to my instincts.

What I was doing, without realizing it, was practicing what might now come under the heading of narrative exposure therapy, or NET. NET is a PTSD treatment for people who have suffered complex and multiple traumas, and it has been used particularly to treat refugees, former child soldiers, victims of organized violence in war zones, and victims of domestic violence. NET helps people establish a coherent chronological life narrative in which they can reorganize and contextualize their traumatic experiences—integrating them into their lives as a whole and fostering a sense of personal identity (just what I had lost through the years of abuse). Because NET has been used so much with victims of war, it is also often linked with explicit human rights advocacy. One is not only narrating one's own life story, one is "testifying." It turned out that the thing that helped me heal was, after all, in the service of the common good.

I began to make myself increasingly visible as a victim and survivor in order to enable my own healing but also to connect with others and—I hoped—inspire them to rebuild their own lives after trauma and abuse. Violence can toughen the hell out of you, because becoming cold and tough feels safer. I certainly felt cautious in those early years, but I never lost the sense of openheartedness I'd always had. Despite the trauma—and partly, I think, because of it—I found myself able to reach out to others, to be honest about what I was feeling, and to be open to what they had experienced and what they were feeling.

Strangely, this "coming out" coincided with a new reason to feel self-conscious. The effects of trauma aren't just psychological or emotional, of course—sometimes they're written on the body. In my early twenties, I had noticed a couple of white spots on my hands and arms. I didn't worry too much about them, but two or three years after the shooting, these discolored patches had suddenly started to spread all over my limbs and face. I was subsequently diagnosed with vitiligo.

Vitiligo is a condition where the body's immune system destroys the skin cells that produce melanin, the chemical that gives skin its pigment. Michael Jackson is probably the most famous sufferer of vitiligo. There is some percentage of vitiligo that runs in families, but it isn't necessarily inherited. As far as I know, none of my siblings have it and neither of my parents did. It can be triggered by autoimmune diseases and stressful life events, both of which were part of my history. By then, I had already been diagnosed with Epstein-Barr and chronic fatigue syndrome. When I went to the doctor for the vitiligo, one skin specialist told me, "Your skin is an organ, and when it's had to be hypervigilant, on high alert, it can do strange things once it's been released from that vigilance."

Vitiligo sometimes spreads very quickly, and I can tell you it's a startling experience to watch your own appearance change. There were a couple of months when I didn't feel comfortable looking in the mirror. Vitiligo isn't physically painful, but it hurt psychologically to see my skin, my face especially, changing color. It was like some essential part of me was being taken away, something so much mine that I'd never even thought of it as a thing I could lose. From one year to the next I just looked totally different.

One doctor suggested I get ultraviolet therapy, which was intensive and cost a lot of money. I knew I didn't want to lighten my skin any more than the vitiligo already had. I had loved my skin tone—a smooth olive brown. I thought about what to do and concluded, *If this is the worst that's happening to me, I'll be all right.* It might have been a coincidence, but as soon as I accepted the presence of the vitiligo, it pretty much settled down and stopped spreading. Now I'm careful in the sun, as I burn so easily. I wear very high SPF and even driving gloves. You figure things out, right? Life goes on. It was another hurdle, a temporary setback, then the realization that I could deal with it without imploding.

All the while, I was building communities for myself. After years of silence, of the shame and isolation that come with domestic abuse, of the mask of middle-class propriety (*Nothing wrong here!*), I had begun to reconnect with people through narrating what I had endured, what I had lost, and how I had reclaimed myself and my life. And it wasn't just that I was integrating the trauma into my own life as a whole, it was that I was coming to understand how what had happened to me was part of a far larger story that was unfolding every minute of every day, all over the world: the story of domestic abuse and of violence against women.

Sometimes I think of my community narrowly, the community of victims and survivors. But there are other communities I am also a part of—my city, my country, my fellow human beings—and the connections I've made with those have been sometimes surprising.

One day in the early 2000s I spoke to a group from the local Kiwanis chapter. For whatever reason, I hadn't thought about the demographic when I was invited to speak, and I walked into a conference room and saw a sea of older white men and thought, *Oh my God, whose idea was this?*

It was probably the most impactful presentation I've ever given. We victims of domestic violence often don't talk about our experiences because we think no one wants to hear about it all. Occasionally that's true, but what I've found time and time again is that it's more likely the case that people *will* listen. I had my own assumptions as I looked out over the Kiwanis crowd—namely, that a bunch of old white guys weren't going to take kindly to a Black woman coming to lecture them about violence against women. I say "lecture," but actually it never feels like that; it feels more like an invitation to communicate, because people invariably wind up telling me their own stories, or the stories of loved ones. And sure enough, after I was done speaking that day, some of the men approached me. They wanted to hug me and shake my hand and tell me how sorry they were for what had happened. They also shared stories of their mothers, daughters, and sisters who had experienced domestic violence. It was very emotional, for the men and for me, and it reminded me not to assume that I know which people will be open to hearing me and which won't.

As with everything in our lives, going public with a story of domestic violence or other trauma is a personal decision. But at some point, sharing our secrets with someone we trust can be empowering. Telling your story means, first, finding your comfort zone. That may be one true friend, a therapist, a whole support group, or the national stage. When I stand behind a podium, or with a mic in my hand, I'm in charge of my story. Early on, that sense of being in charge began to spill over into other aspects of my life. By speaking honestly about the worst things that have happened to me, I have been able to fully inhabit the rest of my life.

At the same time, connecting on an intimate level with a new partner has remained very difficult. Being in a relationship with an abuser eroded my capacity for trust. Even Cedric's seemingly kind gestures were manipulative and coercive. When I left the marriage, I had to relearn how to read people, especially men, and it wasn't easy. Everyone seemed suspect, in overt or subtle ways. I would ask myself: *Does this person really care about me, or does he just want something? Is his iffy behavior a one-off, because after all nobody's perfect, or is it a sign of what would be a habitual need to control me?*

I clearly remember a date I had in the mid-1990s with a guy I'll call "Craig." He took me to a Denver Broncos football game, and brought along a cooler, in which he'd packed some turkey burgers. I really don't like turkey burgers, and I said, "I think I'm going to get a bratwurst."

Craig got very angry. He said, "I can't believe I made this and you aren't going to eat it!"

I thought: *He didn't ask me what I liked, and now he's angry that I don't happen to like what he's giving me?* How dare I make a choice about what I want to eat!

Insisting on my right to eat bratwurst may seem trivial, but it was one of those moments when I felt I was taking charge of my life. I had a knot in my stomach going to the concession stand, but my tolerance for any kind of controlling behavior from others was pretty much zero, and there was no way I was going to eat something I really didn't like just to keep this guy from getting angry with me. There was something a little too familiar about what was playing out. I never saw Craig again.

There have been a couple of long-term relationships, and one of those men wanted to marry me. I found every reason not to. But really, I think, it was because I couldn't trust enough. That may be the most difficult part for me of the legacy of abuse and violence: learning how to trust again.

———

While I was volunteering at the Colorado Coalition, I had begun to educate myself about policy and legislation. But it was picking up what I could on the fly—whenever I had to talk to police or Colorado legislators, my friends and colleagues in the field would brief me beforehand. It was really only when I undertook my master's degree that I started to learn in a more systematic way about how and why laws too often let victims down or leave them unprotected. The Center on Domestic Violence had been founded at the University of Colorado in 2000, and offered an academic program that was focused on building and strengthening organizations and leaders committed to ending violence against women. (The program now concentrates on "gender-based violence.") It was the only program of its kind in the whole country, and it just happened to be right here in Denver.

I had gotten my bachelor's in 2001, a degree in Communications with a focus on Women's Studies, along with a Writing Certificate. My half brother Ric, who had recently come back into my life, attended my graduation. I hadn't seen him in years and it felt wonderful. My mother was also there, at the age of sixty-four. I remember that day as the first time I could really feel her affection for me.

Now I was back in school again, this time for a master's degree in Public Administration, with a concentration on Domestic Violence. I obviously knew a lot about the dynamics of domestic violence from firsthand experience, but now I had a program that would enable me to understand and advocate on issues from a solid knowledge base. I learned about how to provide services and run a nonprofit, about training other advocates, about ensuring that when we talk about the problem of domestic violence we also talk about the root causes—patriarchy, racism, misogyny, classism—and all of the related social ills that are linked to those root causes and that exacerbate the problem: income inequality, inadequate housing, poverty, discrimination, the systemic devaluing of women and children, prioritizing of the rights of abusers.

I was seeing, more and more, the big picture, which was deepening my commitment to supporting change on a larger scale, and leaving me better equipped to do that. It wasn't just the texts and the course work that provided my education, it was also the other women in the program. Between my classmates and the teachers, there were several who were executive directors of domestic violence programs, or working as advocates. One of those was Jacque Morse, who now heads SARA House in Fort Morgan and is still a dear friend. Jacque in particular educates me about service provision from a rural perspective.

Getting my master's was one of the hallmarks of my personal survivorship—exactly what I needed at that time to keep building my own sense of empowerment. I had been living under the shadow of imposter syndrome. I think it was really only when I graduated with my master's degree in 2003 that I was able to shed that. I remember standing in the sweltering June sun and being hit with the thought: *I can do this. I am the one doing it! I am the things I was afraid I was only pretending to be.*

Around the same time, I began to gather regularly for dinner with a small circle of friends. Our group grew, evolving organically to include about a dozen women. Some of them had started out as friends of mine; others were colleagues or former bosses who became friends. All of us were committed in one way or another to issues of social justice, whether it was domestic violence, gang violence, better legal advocacy for children, or improving the fairness of legal and judicial systems. We began to meet one Friday each month, taking turns hosting, a tradition that continues to this day. We have heated discussions, as well as a lot of laughs and sometimes a lot of wine. At some point, one of us referred to the group as the "Usual Suspects," and the name stuck.

Gradually, I was accumulating good people in my life. These friends would turn out to be my rocks as I moved through the ups and downs of the next several years. They gave me everything I could ask for—high-spirited nights out, access to their guest rooms, permission to dominate the conversation with my woes or my opinions, but they also did me the favor, when it was needed, of calling me out. Telling me, "All right, Ruth, you've wallowed enough, and now you're going to stand up again and you're going to be okay." They gave me a safe haven, each one of them individually, but also collectively, and there was something incredibly nourishing about being part of this community, this healthy family. I had never had a community quite like this—not as a little girl in the household I grew up in, not in school, never as a young woman in the workplace or during the years of my marriage. I hope I've given back to each of them some of what they've needed.

In the early 2000s, around the time the Usual Suspects was forming, another good person came into my life—or back into my life.

I hadn't spoken to Mrs. Malcolm since my visit to her around 1980, after the first time Cedric assaulted me. We had talked at her house and then she had dropped David and me off at the bus station in Riverside. After that, we lost touch. Then one day I get an email from my brother Brady's wife saying that a Mrs. Malcolm had called the auto body shop that Brady owned. She was trying to reach me.

Within minutes, I had Mrs. Malcolm on the phone. I found out that she had tracked me down through ancestry.com. She didn't know my married name, but when she found my brothers, and saw me listed there with them, she said she just broke down crying. She told me that her two children had grown up knowing about me, the girl named Ruth whom their mother had loved as though I were her own daughter.

She knew nothing about the shooting, nothing about the twists and turns of my life. It all came pouring out. I filled her in on what I had gone through. We cried, partly out of sadness, but also from the joy of reconnecting. Being a teacher—which she still was—she was thrilled to hear that I had gone back to school and was now working on my master's. That phone call was the beginning of the second act of our friendship, which has continued to this day.

To lose someone good from your life and then gain them back again brings with it not just the happiness of friendship renewed; it also reminds you in a strange and sudden way of who you were when you counted that person among your blessings. I had known Mrs. Malcolm when I was a bright young child—not a child with an easy or carefree life, not a child with a happy home, but a child nonetheless, full of tentative hopes and with no idea of what lay ahead. Hearing Mrs. Malcolm's voice that day, I felt as though I were meeting her on the other side of a breach, a span that contained all that had happened to me since that year she had taken me under her wing. There had been so much pain in the interim, and there was still a lot of pain, but I was also, undoubtedly, on the other side of something. I couldn't have been happier to meet Mrs. Malcolm there.

CHAPTER 10

Time for Advocacy

I had been working at DHS since 1985, and my roles had evolved from my first job driving kids to their appointments off the prison campus and later serving as a youth counselor. By the mid-1990s, I had moved out of the Division of Youth Corrections and into the admin side of DHS, which is how I met Roz Bedell. She was an expert in industrial and organizational psychology—how people behave in the workplace and how you can solve problems that arise. When Roz was named director of training and staff development in the HR Department, I became her staff assistant, working on training new hires and development for existing employees. It was a big department, and I covered staff from the state hospital, Youth Corrections, nursing homes for veterans, and other institutions. It was also more diverse than many other state agencies because of the communities we served. Eventually, we had an executive director who was a Black woman. We did a lot of diversity training, the sort of thing that is fairly standard now but that back then we were still developing a language for. Those were also the dinosaur days of tech, and I found I had a knack for certain techie things. I set up the internal communications program and video conferencing network.

I worked for Roz while I was getting my bachelor's. By the time I began my master's program, I had moved from the staff development group over to the communications team in the DHS Public Information Office. I managed the intranet, along with our marketing, newsletters, and other communications. I also served as backup for our public information officer. All of these roles gave me more visibility within DHS.

In 2003, Roz left Human Resources, and we saw each other only rarely. Roz is one of those friends I knew immediately I wasn't going to let go, so I invited her to join the Usual Suspects. When Roz eventually formed her own consulting company, her first client was NCADV.

Those years at DHS working under Roz, which coincided with my going back to school, were critical for my confidence. It wasn't just about continuing to gain, or regain, my voice, it was about speaking with self-possession, how I inflected my language. I wasn't combative or aggressive, but I was learning how to be heard. A part of that growth was the trust that Roz placed in me. She never balked at my growing confidence; in fact she celebrated it. She was a role model of strong female leadership.

But I had outgrown my role as an administrative assistant. Even the communications work wasn't fulfilling me. I was almost finished with my master's degree, and I was itchy for a new challenge. I didn't actually want to be anybody's assistant. *Now that I have my feet under me,* I thought, *how do I keep growing, and how do I make a difference in the field of domestic violence?* I knew I couldn't work directly in service provision. It would just be too painful. I was sure I would be triggered by other survivors, and as a result wouldn't be capable of providing them with the support they needed. It never crossed my mind that I would do something removed from the world of domestic violence; it was very clear to me that that was where my passion lay.

Around that time, the director of what was then called the Domestic Abuse Assistance Program at DHS, a former nun named Mary Ann, had let it be known that she was planning to retire. This program had a staff of only two, but it managed the distribution of funds for domestic violence service organizations throughout Colorado. I knew Mary Ann, and I went and talked to her. "Maybe I'll apply," I said. "What do you think?" She was absolutely supportive and encouraging.

"Go for it," she said.

I mulled it over, but it was pretty clear this was the right step. I had gained a lot of confidence through school. Through work and my own advocacy and speaking, I had met plenty of women who were strong leaders. Now here was an opportunity to learn more about domestic violence and service provision, to put into practice the theory I'd been studying at school, and to make an impact as a public employee. It would also move me into a leadership position: I would be in charge of figuring out how DHS could best serve the domestic violence programs we funded.

One day I woke up and it all made sense. I was more than ready. With a lot of support from Regi, Pam, and the Usual Suspects, I decided to apply. It would be an epic step for me, making domestic violence the center of my professional life. And while I wouldn't be serving victims directly, I would be living and breathing the issues. I knew that one of the challenges would be making sure the work didn't consume me.

I took over as director of the Domestic Abuse Assistance Program in the summer of 2004. My office was the size of a small closet. But when I walked in that first day, I thought: *This is right. This is where I belong.*

———

The initial year or so on the job was all about getting a handle on processes and procedures, the bureaucratic chain of command, and better informing state agencies what the programs we supported were all about and the critical services they provided. Our own program needed to be dragged into the twenty-first century. Mary Ann had done a wonderful job, but the administrative systems being used were outmoded. Everything was still on paper. In fact my whole office was stacked from floor to ceiling with boxes of paper files that I needed to sift through. One of the first things I had to do was hire a program coordinator, and I ended up choosing a woman named Brooke Ely-Milen, who had been a classmate of mine in the master's program. Brooke was extremely thorough and had very strong opinions. She would keep me on my toes during the nine years she worked for me. When I left as director in 2014, Brooke took over the directorship until she became ill. In 2021, Brooke died at the age of forty-seven from a rare form of cancer. Her death stunned the domestic violence community in Colorado. Brooke and I had our conflicts, but we shared a passion and learned from each other, and her death was a huge loss.

I also made sure, early on, that we renamed the program. When you're trying to make a change in an organization, there's a lot to be said for a rebranding. It wasn't just cosmetic. We needed to align ourselves with all the programs we were funding or liaising with, and we needed to have "violence" in our name, as they all did. We wanted the Colorado legislature to recognize us as *the* domestic violence program, and we couldn't do that unless we called our work what it was. We dropped Domestic Abuse Assistance Program and rebranded ourselves the Domestic Violence Program.

Even in the midst of this bureaucratic work, I could feel that something fundamental had changed—the change was both inside me and in the way I interacted with others. Ever since the shooting, and maybe before that, I had been walking around with a red "V" on my chest. It was there in the police report for the kidnapping, right? There was "S-Glenn," Cedric the suspect, and there was "V-Glenn." Me. The victim.

But taking over as the director of the Domestic Violence Program marked a turning point. I moved out of the victimization space and stepped into the survivor space. It might seem strange that in taking on full-time work in the field, which would remind me every day that I had been the victim of violence, I felt myself shedding the red "V." Part of it was that I was also stepping into a position of authority. I was an authority *because* of my victimization, but also because I'd worked to understand the issues and dynamics around what had happened to me. I could inform others now, but as an authority. My whole life I had never felt like other people had confidence in me. I had given so many presentations with all the old tapes playing in my head—that I wasn't good enough, or that I was going to get triggered and wouldn't be able to handle it. How many times had I apologized beforehand, warning people that I might start crying? (I still get triggered on occasion, and I still cry, but I'm not ashamed of it and I know how to manage it.) It was a good feeling, letting go of the "V" as my identity. I thought, *Okay, now I'm here. How can I honor what happened to me and also be a force for change as a government employee?*

What I was experiencing, what I wanted to "make" out of what had happened to me, is not unusual. A lot of survivors work through their trauma and make some kind of peace with it at a strictly personal level, and I support them 100 percent in that. But others feel the need to connect our recovery from the horrors of the past to political or social action. I couldn't change the past, and I would never see Cedric held accountable in any legal sense. But I had come to realize that what had happened to me wasn't just about me. It wasn't just my bad luck. It was linked to much larger problems, about our laws and our justice system, about our acceptance of violence (especially gun violence, and especially violence against women and children), about the socialization of men toward violence, and our failure, culturally and legally, to place responsibility for domestic violence where it belongs. I didn't want anyone to suffer what I had suffered, and what countless women I knew had suffered. I was well enough now in myself to want to contribute to systemic change. I wanted to help, in whatever way I could, to create a safer and more just society, one that protected victims and held perpetrators accountable.

Many times during those first years on the job, I would be attending meetings with the directors of other government agencies, and I would feel an unmistakable resistance to my new self-assurance. I noticed that as I became more comfortable expressing my opinions unapologetically, some people celebrated it and others resented or resisted it. I was a Black woman, and often the only person of color in those meetings. When I spoke forcefully, I was seen as an *angry* Black woman. No one says to you, *Stop being an angry Black woman*, but it isn't hard to read the atmosphere. I can guarantee there isn't a Black woman in this country who hasn't, at some point, felt that message coming at her when she's making her views known to a room full of white people.

The reception I got from professionals in my field was different. One of the groups that reached out to me was the Colorado Organization for Victim Assistance (COVA), which supported crime victims in healing and rebuilding their lives. COVA was, and still is, led by Nancy Lewis. When Nancy came to COVA in 1994, it was tiny, with a $300,000 budget and 1.5 employees. As a membership agency of organizations that came into contact with crime victims, COVA was very focused on training. Nancy started the COVA Academy in 1999 as a formal structure for training people working in the victim support space.

I don't remember when we first met—there just came a point when Nancy was in my life. Nancy tells me now that one of the things that stood out about me was that I presented as a professional first and a victim second, which is ironic, because what Nancy did for me, from the moment I met her, was help me to understand at a deeper level that I had been victimized. She legitimized the many things I felt about that. She remembers early on feeling like I had something to teach her. She was among the leaders in Colorado's victim services who had encouraged me to go for the DHS job, saying, "Ruth, you can do this." She invited me to speak at the Academy, which I ended up doing more than once. There were lots of newbies at those sessions, and they wanted to save the world, an impulse I admire. But I was honest with them: You aren't going to solve domestic violence; you're there to serve in the moment.

At the Academy sessions, advocates could ask any question they wanted, and one question I was asked was why I had gone to Cedric's funeral. I said there was a part of me that still loved him. I owned that. I wasn't beating myself up for it anymore. I never relinquished the belief that he was a human being who was worthy of love. But I had also come to understand that feeling love for someone doesn't mean you need to stay with him if he is hurting you.

———

One afternoon, a few years into my job as director of the Domestic Violence Program at DHS, I answered a phone call in my office from a woman who was clearly very upset.

"This is Ruth," I said, all business. "How can I help you?"

"Are you the head of the DVP?" she asked.

"Yes, I am. What can I do for you?"

I already knew I was talking to a victim or survivor—you just know. But I was surprised she had reached me through the office line. I wasn't a direct service provider, not like someone working a hotline. But victims would find me. I had a public profile, and victims can be very resourceful and adaptive when things get desperate.

The woman told me her name—I'll call her Carol—and said she was in rural Colorado. I could tell from her voice that she was older, maybe sixty-five or seventy. She mentioned that she lived on a small ranch.

She said, "My husband will be home in an hour or two. He beats me up, and I can't take it anymore."

I was struck by the fact that she used that phrase—*he beats me up*. It's something you seldom hear from victims. They don't like to say it out loud, especially not at first. They might say instead, "He's not being very nice to me." There are reasons for this. The abuse could be terrifying, he could be exercising the most heinous and chilling forms of control, but maybe he never laid a hand on her. There is also the fear of being judged. It's humiliating to admit that someone who is supposed to love you, someone you may be dependent on financially, is beating you up—even if you're talking to a woman who heads a domestic violence program.

I asked Carol if she'd contacted her local agency, and she said she had but they wouldn't help her.

"What?" I said. "What do you mean?"

She said, "They won't let me take my mother's desk."

"I see," I said. "Tell me about this desk."

Carol said that the rolltop desk had been passed down through her family for generations. "I know that if I leave here, he'll destroy it."

I asked if there was anyone who might be able to come and take it, and Carol said no. She had thought of dragging it into the shed, but she knew her husband would find it there.

I asked her to call Catholic Charities in Denver. Sometimes they were able to help with things like furniture. I said, "Please call me back and let me know."

"I have to do something fast," she said. "He'll be home in an hour."

"Let me know," I repeated, and we hung up. I didn't get her number, which I regretted, because I never heard from her again.

My conversation with Carol wasn't long, but it affected me then, and has stayed with me since. It upset me, not knowing what happened to her, and whether she found safety. At the time of Carol's phone call, I was in a strange state. I'd begun to feel transactional in my job, functional. I was a funding administrator, a very narrow administrative lane that I wanted to get out of. I wanted to *advocate*. I'd been feeling myself losing compassion, and Carol was a wake-up call. She was a reminder of what our work was really about, what our agency should be, and the complicated issues women face when they think about leaving home or separating themselves from an abuser.

To someone who has never been in Carol's situation, her concern with the desk might seem irrational. To me, it made perfect sense. The desk was something precious to her family, it was part of her own history, and leaving it behind would be very painful. But it wasn't just about her husband having yet another way to hurt her. It was about control. Abusers want control over everything a victim holds dear. If they cannot destroy the attachment—whether it's to objects, family, friends, or activities—then they have to control it. (The minute I left Cedric he saw David and me as a unit—we'd both betrayed him, we'd both ruined his life. The day he kidnapped me, he went first to see David; he was making the point that he still had access to the person who meant more to me than anyone else in the world.) Talking to Carol, I understood all over again how an abuser will always zero in on what matters most to you. Carol was very emotionally tied to what that desk represented—it might have been the last thing she owned that felt truly hers and that linked her to the life that had existed before she was with her husband—and my role was not to convince Carol to abandon the desk, but to help her find a way of bringing it with her.

Over the years, I have come to understand that our systems—judicial, social services, law enforcement, and so on—aren't set up to support victims of domestic violence. It isn't that they're "siding" with the abuser; I don't believe that. I persist in believing that most people are coming from a place of good. But the responders and service providers don't have all the tools and resources they need to properly support victims.

It starts with the woman leaving home. Is there any other crime where the changes necessary for prevention of additional harm are in the hands of the victim? If a neighbor burgled your home, no one would suggest you move out and become homeless while the burglar remained comfortably housed. In the early days of VAWA, getting a woman into a shelter was often the beginning and the end of the support available. Shelter options have expanded since, and we have begun to think about ways of providing housing for victims that offer greater stability than traditional short-term shelters.

This is where transitional housing comes in—or would come in if our services were adequately resourced. Shelters are intended for crisis situations, and they are an essential part of the support network. But many victims don't want to leave their homes and go to a shelter when they know it's only a short-term respite. They would likely be far more open to shelters if they knew that there was something waiting on the far side other than the choice between going back home and being left to make their own way, to find their own housing, and so on. Transitional housing is the logical and compassionate stepping-stone to independent living. As soon as a victim arrives at a shelter, a rapid assessment of her needs should take place—including her housing situation. We should then be able to offer her housing, either in the area where she lives or elsewhere, if that is what she wants. The logistics of leaving a home and setting up a new life can be daunting for anyone, even in the absence of trauma and abuse. When there is trauma, and probably violence, those changes can feel overwhelmingly scary. We should be able to say to victims that once they take the first step, we have the resources to help them transition to a new life.

My conversation with Carol reminded me that we needed to advocate from the perspective of victims and survivors rather than from the perspective of the bureaucracy. I decided it was time to make changes. My small staff and I developed and provided training to other departments and social service agencies on victimization issues and perpetrator tactics. We also had to educate our colleagues and supervisors about how we should be measuring the performance of domestic violence service providers. As a funder, we needed to make sure that they were providing the services they said they were—and the state required programs to measure performance, and count services, in very specific ways. But gathering data on victims of domestic violence or service provision for those victims differs from how data can be gathered on other programs. For example, a child who encounters the child welfare system for the first time will be given a case number, and that child will be followed throughout their various interactions with the system, from agency to agency. (Children do fall through the cracks, of course, but there is a system in place to trace them, which also allows for accountability among those overseeing their cases.)

The same isn't true of domestic violence victims. They are often in extremely fluid situations, and their use of services is also fluid. If a victim comes to your shelter, she may only stay for an hour while you're finding a place for her in another shelter, which may be in a different state. We simply don't track victims of domestic violence like we do children or other users of social services. There are confidentiality and safety issues that make this kind of tracking inadvisable, and even impossible. When I was asked at a meeting, "How many victims were made safe last year?" I had to explain why we would probably never be able to arrive at a precise answer to that question. It's a little like trying to gather statistics on people in 12-step programs. They come and go, they don't give their full names or addresses, they move around from one meeting to another. If they appear once and never again, you don't always know what has happened to them. They may have relocated, they may have died, or they may simply not need the service anymore.

I was definitely in favor of hard data, but I argued that we should be counting services—we can ensure a shelter is meeting state health and safety standards, that it has appropriate staffing levels, and so on—rather than focusing on individuals served. In other words, collecting data in the aggregate, and not adding another layer of administrative work to organizations already overburdened and operating on a shoestring.

For the first couple of years running the program at DHS, I sometimes held back, trying to get along with everyone. Eventually, I thought, *No, I'm not going to do that.* I knew what my experience had taught me, and I knew the things that needed to be said. There were times I was wrong—isn't everyone, sometimes?—and days I got myself into hot water. There were meetings I walked out of furious, because I didn't think people were listening, or because I wasn't sure I was serving as the advocate I aspired to be.

All the while, I had to make sure that the work didn't swallow me up. Occasionally during my tenure at DHS I fell into significant depression because of the work I was doing. But what I was learning, again and again, was that I could come out of those dark periods by relying on the people who loved me and fully inhabiting the other parts of my life. *Okay*, I would think, *I can make an impact, but then I can go home to my friends and my son and (soon enough!) my grandchildren. There is a life outside of my work, and on evenings and weekends, I need to live that life, and enjoy all that it has to offer.*

———

One day in 2010, while I was still at DHS, I got a call from Lynn Rosenthal. I had never met Lynn, but I knew who she was. She was a well-known activist and a force to be reckoned with. She had started at the grassroots level, as director of a rape crisis center and women's shelter in Florida, before going on to serve as executive director of both Florida's and New Mexico's Coalitions Against Domestic Violence. She had also been the director and president of the National Network to End Domestic Violence. At the time she contacted me, Lynn had just been appointed by President Obama and Vice President Biden as the first-ever White House adviser on violence against women. Lynn wanted to know more about my story. In October, which was Domestic Violence Awareness Month, the White House was going to be holding an event to mark the unveiling of new federal programs to reduce domestic and sexual violence against women and children, and Lynn was doing some background work for the event.

Lynn and I clicked immediately. The questions she asked me—particularly about financial and housing issues—really delved into parts of my survival story that I hadn't thought as much about and made clear she understood the multiple impacts of domestic violence. The way she asked those questions, in a very thoughtful and caring way, made me trust her.

The next day Lynn called me back and asked if I'd be part of the event—if I'd come to the White House.

I was sitting in my office and had to play it cool. "Yes!" I said as calmly as I could.

When I hung up that day, I felt both thrilled and panicked. I called everyone in my group of friends—they mostly wanted to know whether I'd get to meet President Obama. Two years before, with my Usual Suspects friends Susan and Regi, I had attended Obama's speech in Denver, when he'd accepted the Democratic Party's nomination. Now they were as excited as I was to think that I would be in the same room with him.

Roz took me shopping for something to wear. She said I needed a brightly colored outfit so I'd stand out. I bought a royal-blue jacket (and sure enough, it's visible on C-SPAN). The White House wasn't paying for the trip, so I asked the NCADV—the organization I would one day lead—to fund it. I had spoken many times at their request, and I thought they would consider it a worthwhile investment to send me to Washington, D.C. They said they couldn't do it. Nancy Lewis from COVA stepped up and got me a plane ticket and hotel room. I will be forever grateful—not just for the financial support but for her recognition of the importance of the event and the honor of being invited.

I arrived in D.C. on October 27. I was standing outside of National Airport when President Obama's speechwriter called on my cell. He wanted to know if it would be okay if the President used my name when he spoke.

I bit my lip and tried—again—to stay calm. "Of course," I said.

Other than Lynn, whom I knew only by phone, I didn't know anyone in Washington in those days. I got a taxi to my hotel and started getting ready for the event. I was delighted with my bright blue jacket, but I felt very alone. I remember also feeling self-conscious about my vitiligo, which was noticeable on my face at the time. I had made my peace with the ways that this condition had changed my appearance, but I still wasn't entirely comfortable around other people, especially strangers, and especially on a day like this. But what could I do? I got dressed, and off I went.

My hotel was close to the White House, and I walked to the event on my own. It would have been a remarkable feeling stepping inside that building no matter who was president, but the fact that it was Obama just blew me away. I felt proud of him, like he was a brother from another mother. What he had achieved by becoming our first Black president was extraordinary, but there were aspects of his experience that I could identify with, and like so many people of color in this country, I felt a kinship with him. We were both biracial, with white mothers. Both of our fathers had been absent when we were growing up. As a biracial person, I had known since childhood the feeling of not fitting in to either the Black world or the white one, of not being fully accepted anywhere. Sometimes the snub was subtle and sometimes it wasn't; when I first began volunteering in the 1990s, I tried to join the women of color working group at the Colorado Domestic Violence Coalition, only to be told I wasn't Black enough. Some of the other Black women in the group were even more offended by the comment than I was, but it made me uncomfortable enough that I didn't go back. And I knew the feeling, as an adult, of having to be extraordinary in order for white people to accept me; I, too, have been congratulated for being "articulate." I also absolutely believed that Obama recognized the importance of addressing domestic violence, and of course I already knew that Vice President Biden did. I had been one of the millions who had campaigned to get Obama elected, and now here he was—and here I was!

From the door of the East Room a uniformed usher led me to my assigned seat in the second row. Lynn was flitting all over the room and I couldn't speak with her. I felt shy and a little awestruck—Lynn, Valerie Jarrett, Vice President Biden, President Obama, four people I had such enormous respect for, all in the same room with me.

Lynn was the emcee for the day, and she kicked things off by talking about how the commitment to address domestic violence has to come from the top. She paid homage to Vice President Biden for his twenty years of dedication to the issues confronting victims, dating back to the pre-VAWA dark ages when, as the vice president had said, domestic violence was "the dirty little secret" that nobody wanted to talk about. She said that, to this day, wherever Vice President Biden traveled in the country, women would come up to him and whisper in his ear, "Thank you for helping us."

Valerie Jarrett took the stage next. She was the chair of the White House Council on Women and Girls, which Obama had created to ensure that federal agencies considered the needs of women and girls in all their policies, programs, and pieces of legislation. Valerie introduced Joe Torre, the legendary MLB player and manager who had started the Safe at Home Foundation. Joe grew up witnessing his father's severe physical and verbal abuse of his mother. When Joe's father learned that his mother was pregnant with him, he threw her down the stairs. Joe has been a strong voice speaking out about the damage domestic violence does to children—whether they are the targets or the witnesses or both—and about what we need to do to provide safe havens for our children.

When Vice President Biden took the stage, he spoke about VAWA as "the single most significant thing I have ever been a part of in my life." Biden didn't grow up with any experience of violence, but his father had passed on a strong message against the abuse of power, and he had an instinctive empathy for victims of violence. He described being allowed to listen in on some of the 22,000 calls that come in to the National Domestic Violence Hotline every month. He understood what it took for women to reach out like that, the risk such calls represented to their own lives. "I love these guys who talk about courage," he said. "*That* [calling] takes real courage."

He also emphasized how the legal system has to do more to help victims stay safe once they get away from their abusers. He mentioned the case of Dorothy Cotter, a woman who had been murdered by her estranged husband in 2002. William Cotter had a long history of abusing Dorothy. All the warning signs of escalation to murder were there. Even while subject to a restraining order, William had held Dorothy hostage in her own home and threatened to kill her—all in the presence of one of their daughters. Following that incident, and with a warrant out for his arrest for assault and violation of the protection order, William had turned himself in. Astonishingly, he was released on $500 bail. Five days later, he showed up at Dorothy's house and shot her at close range with a sawed-off shotgun. The daughter who'd witnessed the earlier incident was home that day, too.

Victims need effective legal representation, the vice president said, if they're going to be able to escape domestic violence. And yet less than one in five low-income victims ever see a lawyer. The Department of Justice was launching a new effort to help victims find lawyers to represent them pro bono, and he called on lawyers to join the fight against domestic violence.

Being a lawyer, he said, isn't just a profession, a transactional business, but a calling to fight for justice and help those who need it the most.

At the same time, the vice president clearly understood that violence against women wasn't just a legislative or criminal justice problem, it was a problem of "attitudes that remain deeply embedded in our culture" about what constitutes appropriate treatment of women, cultural assumptions that we needed to reverse. He cited studies he'd seen on both children and young adults—one that found that 25 percent of sixth-graders felt it was acceptable for boys to hit their girlfriends, and a quarter of the older boys who had girlfriends reported having punched or slapped them.

Finally, President Obama took the stage. We've come a long way, he said, since domestic violence was regarded as a lesser offense, a private matter, and he lauded the progress made by those in government who were working to support survivors and end domestic violence. But much of that progress, he emphasized, has been down to the willingness of victims to speak out. "If there's one group I want to thank, am grateful for, it's people who are willing to tell their stories." He then mentioned Joe Torre, Lori Stone, and me. Lori had suffered years of abuse from her husband, who also destroyed her credit, leaving her to spend her limited savings on legal representation to retain custody of her children. Lori and I had in common that we had both emerged from violent abuse in our marriages, returned to school to earn our degrees, and became advocates in the field. Lori was a founding member of the Michigan Coalition to End Domestic & Sexual Violence, and has worked hard to educate policy-makers and steer legislation.

President Obama referred to my story then—how I had been viciously attacked by Cedric *after* I had left him—as a reminder of how that period is critical and often extremely dangerous, and that we need to do much more to help and protect victims, particularly during this time.

"We need to ensure," he said, "that no one has to choose between a violent home and no home at all."

When the President had finished speaking, he came off the stage and started greeting people seated near the front. We were all standing by then, and of course everyone wanted to shake his hand and have a word, and I was afraid I wouldn't get to do either. So as he made his way in my direction, I decided to be a little brave. When he'd finished speaking to the person in front of me in the first row, I reached out and grabbed his hand. I said, "It's so nice to meet you, Mr. President," and I thanked him for his speech. There was a moment when he was still on autopilot, in the meet-and-greet mode you need to have mastered by the time you're the President, flashing his million-dollar smile. I edged forward and whispered in his ear, "I'm Ruth Glenn," and his expression changed. "Oh," he said as he realized he'd just been talking about my life. The big smile faded and in its place a look that was compassionate and gentle and touched with sorrow. And then President Obama leaned in closer and hugged me.

"Thank you," he said.

PART III

Advocacy

CHAPTER 11
Shelter

In late 2013, I left my job as the director of the Domestic Violence Program at Colorado's Department of Human Services. I had honed my own expertise on domestic violence policy and legislation, and learned how to shuttle between local, state, and national organizations to get things done. I was now a go-to person on domestic violence issues, and I felt confident of my role and my voice.

When I resigned, I had no idea what I would do next. And I had no clue that I was about to be blindsided by a painful personal crisis involving my son.

David had been through the mill as a child and a teenager. He had deep scars from the abuse he had witnessed, which he felt powerless to prevent. He was scarred from the loss of his father, and from his guilt over not having been able to protect me, particularly from that last act of violence. He had been kidnapped himself by Cedric once, held for twelve hours against his will at Cedric's house, not long before Cedric kidnapped me. He had been threatened by Cedric, and he had been told he was responsible for my survival: "One more F, and I'll kill your mother."

When I resigned from my job and was living in a house on 29th Street in Denver, David tried to take his own life. He was thirty-six and had been struggling with drug abuse for years. He was a binge user. Before that (and since), he has had periods of being sober, the longest being about a year. But much depends on what's happening for him emotionally. At one point, David had his own business; for almost two years he was laying carpets. But when the business folded, he collapsed.

He was living with me on 29th Street, and things weren't easy between us. I had begun to confront him about his drug use. Then, one day, I opened the door to the front porch and found him lying there unconscious. I don't know what propelled me to open that door, because I never went in or out that way, but thank God I did.

David had had suicidal ideation over the years, but this was his only serious attempt. This time he hadn't said anything about how he was feeling. He had just overdosed on pills. I called 911, and they rushed him to the hospital. He was there for three days. It was during that time that I finally fully admitted to myself the extent of his torment. At that point, I needed to come to terms not only with his addiction, but with my own long-standing denial. For too long, I had just wanted it all to stop. I thought if I just closed my eyes, it would go away.

David and I also needed some independence from each other. We had been bound for so long by trauma. Living in the same house didn't seem to be helping David figure out his life, nor was it improving my well-being. A couple of months later, I told David I was leaving that house. I put my things in storage and moved out.

My friend Susan, a member of the Usual Suspects, took me in. Susan is not just intelligent, she's wise. For much of her life, she lived according to the expectations set for her by society about how women should move in the world. (It was okay to get educated, as long as you didn't plan to use it.) It was only in middle age, when her marriage ended, that she began to understand that the path she'd taken had been determined by those outside expectations rather than by her own possibilities. Her sons were teenagers by then, and the divorce pushed her into using her education to take care of herself and her boys. There is something about that discovery of other possibilities later in life that means Susan really revels in the present, as though making up for lost time. She has the curiosity and liveliness of a much younger person.

I had met Susan in the early 2000s through Regi. It was inevitable our paths would cross, as Susan's work involved domestic violence. She was the program director at the Denver Metro Chamber Leadership Program. The organization arranged continuing education for lawyers. Susan had a big say in which areas would be focused on, and she included domestic violence education. She was on a committee that was looking, along with the

DA and others, at how police and courtroom protocols could be reformed to better serve victims and their children.

The first thing a lot of people know about me, even before they've met me, is that I was shot by my husband. Susan met me first as an advocate. Only later, as our friendship grew, did she come to know the details of my story. From the beginning there was a spark between us. We seemed to recognize quickly that we could be outlandish together. Susan has a wonderful and irreverent sense of humor, and humor has been vital to our friendship. So we had laughter and we had mutual respect. Not a bad foundation.

Immediately after David's suicide attempt, Susan came to the hospital and sat with me. As I talked about what was happening in my life, all the turmoil I was in, she began trying to figure out how she could help. She had raised her three sons on her own and had the house to herself now. Her mother had died recently and left her some money. I needed shelter, a quiet space, a safe haven from all that was going on, and Susan offered to take me into her home. Once I had managed to get out of my lease, I arrived on her doorstep.

Neither of us was sure how our cohabiting would go. As it turned out, it was pretty amazing. Susan still tells me she felt lucky to be able to help. I felt at sea and lucky to have such a landing pad. She gave me a lot of space, and we established an easy rhythm, talking or not talking, watching Broncos games together, leaving the TV on all night—a quirk we shared, needing the low noise to fall asleep.

I cleaned her house furiously. That was my therapy. Susan isn't the most organized person—at least not to the untrained eye—and I cleaned her pantry, throwing away the out-of-date food, and organized her closets. I bought a vacuum and went at the floors like a maniac. But there were also hours spent lying in the guest bedroom, curled in the fetal position and trying to figure out what to do with myself. I didn't want this limbo to go on indefinitely. I needed some time, after the recent upheaval, but I'm also someone who is eager to get on with the next thing, whatever that is going to be.

And then one day, about six months after I'd left DHS and was planning my move from Susan's, I opened my inbox and found an email announcing that the National Coalition Against Domestic Violence was looking for an interim director. NCADV is a nonprofit that coordinates on behalf of victims, survivors, and advocates all over the country, mobilizing the collective power of many groups working to change the conditions that perpetuate domestic violence and to hold offenders accountable. (A lot of people assume, because of the name, that NCADV is the umbrella group for state coalitions, but that's the role of the National Network to End Domestic Violence.) NCADV was formed in the late 1970s, the decade that saw the flowering of what was called the battered women's movement, the period when I had watched my own life as a young wife and mother spiral into abuse and fear. It's odd now to think of those two facts in parallel— as though even as things were getting worse and worse for me, even as I was becoming increasingly lost to myself, there was a whole network of advocates and activists out there who were laying the groundwork for a system of support for women like me.

The 1970s were a decade of radical reimagining, and work on the front lines of domestic and sexual violence was still very grassroots—women were figuring it out on the fly, organizing through informal networks. The first official shelter for battered women was opened in 1974 by Women's Advocates in Saint Paul, Minnesota, though individuals such as Sandra Ramos were already turning their own homes into impromptu shelters. At one point Ramos had twenty-two battered women and their children living in her house in Passaic County, New Jersey.

Collectives formed. One of the earliest was Transition House in Cambridge, Massachusetts. Founded in the mid-1970s by two survivors, Transition House was run on the principle that decision-making was shared among the women who volunteered to help and those who sought services. Other early shelters, such as Casa Myrna Vasquez, started by a group of Latina women in Boston's South End, were operated as more traditional nonprofits. The founders of Casa Myrna wanted to empower themselves within the system rather than dismantle the system.

Discussion of domestic violence was beginning to emerge from the shadows. In 1976, *Ms.* magazine became the first national publication to run a cover story addressing the issue. Activist Del Martin published *Battered Wives*, the first book on domestic violence. The first state Coalitions Against Domestic Violence were founded in Nebraska and Pennsylvania, and Pennsylvania passed the first legislation enabling women to obtain protection orders.

Women of color were meanwhile drawing attention to racialized violence against women, and resisting the patriarchal culture of 1960s Black political movements. Founders of the National Black Feminist Organization, the Combahee River Collective, and other groups have become icons of Black feminism—artists, writers, activists, and politicians such as Audre Lord, Eleanor Holmes Norton, Florynce Kennedy, Margaret Sloan-Hunter, and Faith Ringgold.

Casa Myrna, Transition House, and Women's Advocates operate to this day, testaments to the grit and commitment of their founders and the many women who put in long hours for little or no pay to support those who had been battered. All of this energy, all these committed advocates—whether they were radical feminist separatists or community-based activists—were paving the way for the founding of NCADV.

It happened, the story goes, in a bathroom in Washington, D.C. In January 1978, a U.S. Commission on Civil Rights hearing focusing on battered women was held in the Senate Office Buildings. More than a hundred advocates attended from all over the country. The battered women's movement had been gaining momentum, and these advocates, many of them survivors, wanted to harness all the individual grassroots efforts from around the country into a stronger and more organized network. Because there was no space or time set aside for the women to brainstorm and strategize, they took to meeting in the bathroom, a couple dozen at a time, before and after sessions. Speakers stood on the sink in order to be heard. Female police officers broke up the meetings every time an outsider needed to use the bathroom. When the women were finally threatened with arrest if they continued to meet "unlawfully," the hearing organizers provided them with a meeting room.

NCADV was essentially born that January in the Senate Office Buildings bathroom. Eight months later, seventeen "founding mothers" signed incorporation papers in Portland, Oregon. NCADV's initial goals were to secure funding for shelters, serve as an information-sharing hub, and support research related to the battered women's movement. Although NCADV emerged from those meetings in Washington, its existence owes much to the organizing and hard work done over the years by feminists around the country.

There have been a lot of founding mothers. I will be eternally grateful to those women who blazed the trail with their ideas and demands, then considered so radical, at a time when there was essentially no acknowledgment or understanding of the problem of domestic violence. If this book is anything, it's an homage to all the women who broke the silence, and who did the hard work that those of us who came after have tried to build on. Not all of those names are inscribed in the history of the battered women's movement. Like every movement, this one has its army of unsung heroes. That is true to this day, something I came to realize more profoundly when I began to run NCADV and got to know the network of volunteers who are out there supporting the advocates and allies in leadership positions. They work incredibly hard for no other reasons than a passionate commitment to justice and a dedication to helping those who are suffering or in danger. They keep us informed, they keep us on our toes; they even poke us from time to time, in the best possible sense. Many are survivors, and whenever I interact with them—or get poked by them—I'm reminded of who it is I am out here fighting for.

The founders of NCADV were conscious, from the beginning, of inclusion and diversity. One of the founders was Matilda "Tillie" Black Bear from South Dakota, who was named cochair of NCADV. A Lesbian Task Force was immediately founded within the organization. At the first NCADV national conference in 1980, the Third World Caucus was formed in response to racism within the battered women's movement. (It was later renamed the Women of Color Task Force.) A Rural Task Force was also formed to address the unique needs of battered women and advocates living outside metropolitan centers.

That inaugural conference, held in Washington, D.C., was attended by more than six hundred women from forty-nine states. The following year, NCADV declared a national Day of Unity on the first Monday in October to connect advocates all around the country. By 1989, this had become Domestic Violence Awareness Month, when all of us in the field intensify our efforts to raise awareness and advocate for change.

By the time the call for an interim director of NCADV popped up in my inbox, the organization had long been headquartered right here in Denver.

The national office had moved from D.C. in 1992 at the time Rita Smith took over as director. Rita had been working in crisis shelters for about ten years before she came to NCADV. Now, after twenty-one years heading NCADV, she was stepping down.

I knew all about NCADV's work, of course. And I admit that on at least a couple of occasions I had looked at the organization and thought: *I could do that job. If and when the director leaves, I am someone who could step into that role.*

Well, here was my chance to find out if I was right!

I decided to apply for the interim position. It was the perfect stopgap, I thought, challenging but temporary, something I could do while I was figuring out what I was *really* going to do. At the interview I proposed that if I were given the interim director position, I would undertake a complete organizational assessment.

I was appointed for three months. Next thing I knew, I was diving in.

CHAPTER 12

Driving the Bus

A couple of months into my job as interim director at NCADV, I was coming to the conclusion that a complete cultural and infrastructure overhaul was needed. There was a core of members on the board who were good-hearted, strong advocates, passionate about the issues, and the former director, Rita Smith, was experienced and knowledgeable in the field. But it seemed to me that this was an organization that could be making much more of an impact than it was. There was a lack of consistency in a lot of areas of NCADV operations. We were trying to be all things to all people. There hadn't been a strategic plan in quite a while. Performance reviews were rare. There were no metrics in place that we could use to measure our external impact; nor was there much money in the bank. I just didn't get the sense of an organization with a clear mission and a staff and board who were trying, collectively, to achieve agreed upon goals.

Amazingly, for a national organization whose mission was to advocate legislatively and otherwise for victims and survivors, we had no one designated to work on policy and no permanent presence in Washington, D.C.

I was like, *What?*

There had been intermittent, ad hoc offices, especially during periods of VAWA reauthorization, but now whatever we had in D.C. from our last office—computer, supplies, bookshelves—was sitting in a storage unit there.

The board gave me the go-ahead to search for someone to establish our D.C. presence.

I had just begun to tap into policy networks when Rachel Graber's résumé popped up in my inbox, forwarded by someone at the National Task Force to End Sexual and Domestic Violence.

Rachel is from Iowa City. She had initially intended to be a rabbi, but after college decided she didn't have the right temperament. She then worked as a school counselor, and though she loved the kids she didn't feel the school setting was a good fit. So she went back to do a master's in Social Work, with a focus on Public Policy. She had found her calling. She's a news junkie who is still thrilled by the idea that ordinary people can make a positive difference at the legislative level if they work hard enough. She had come to D.C. without a job and was pounding the virtual pavement.

I interviewed her by phone as she was traveling in the car to New York City with her husband. Rachel insists now that I misread her résumé and believed she had far more experience than she did—thinking that some volunteer lobbying she had done with the Iowa legislature had been paid professional work. If I did, it was a lucky misreading. I could tell from our phone call that she had so much energy and exactly the policy perspective NCADV needed. The last question I asked her was "What's your philosophy about addressing domestic violence?" She thought for a moment, then said simply, "The patriarchy."

Rachel was my first hire. She's still with us today.

I was due to give the board my report at the end of three months, but I was still knee-deep in the assessment. I offered to stay on for another three months and complete what I was doing while they conducted the search for a permanent director. Of course I thought about applying for the job, but I wasn't sure that the overhaul I thought was needed was something either NCADV or I could withstand—or perhaps not the two of us together. The board agreed to an additional three months.

By then I had successfully shoehorned myself out of Susan's and moved into an apartment of my own. I was at home one day when I got a phone call—one of those calls you never forget. It was Lynn Rosenthal, whom I knew from the event in the East Room in 2010.

"Can you come to Washington?" she asked.

It was the twentieth anniversary of the passage of VAWA, and they were staging an event at the National Archives to mark it. I would speak briefly, then I would hand the podium over to Vice President Biden.

To step into the same river twice is to understand that you have changed.

Four years ago, I'd been an audience member at the White House, hearing President Obama tell my story. This time, I was being invited to Washington to make a speech myself, alongside the vice president.

I didn't hesitate. "Of course I can come," I said.

The arrangements were made, and within weeks I was sitting in the greenroom at the Archives. It wasn't just the obvious symbolic importance that marked the difference between this event and the one in the East Room—the fact that now I would be in full control of the narrative of my life, at least for those few minutes when I would have the podium. It was also the difference in the way I felt. I had been so nervous in 2010. All the imposter tapes were playing. But now as I sat waiting to be summoned to the podium, I felt . . . *accompanied*, like I had a whole bunch of sisters behind me, those I knew well and those I'd never met but to whom I wanted to say: *It's possible to come through this, and as long as I have this megaphone, I'm going to be calling on the powers that be to do everything they can to help you.* I had not only gained a voice and learned to use it with confidence; I was now being heard by people who could make a difference.

Admittedly, the vice president helped. In the greenroom, he put me at ease right away. He wasn't the least bit concerned about how I might perform or what I might say, and that allowed me to believe that I would be just fine. When I stepped up to the podium, I looked out over the audience. I was aware that I had before me a who's who of activists and advocates working to end violence against women. I hoped these allies who were hearing me for the first time would feel that I was doing justice to all the victims and survivors we were representing that day, and to the many, many women who had done the hard work long before anyone had ever dreamed of VAWA—those women who had braved the shame to speak publicly when no one was doing that, those who had turned their own homes into shelters for victims of abuse.

One of the things I focused on in my speech was how my own circumstances would have been different if VAWA had been in place when I was being abused, stalked, harassed, kidnapped. For one thing, my level of awareness about what was happening to me would certainly have been higher. There was no National Domestic Violence Hotline at that time. Law enforcement was underequipped, both in terms of their understanding and their ability to assist victims. Domestic violence shelters and services were under-resourced, and there were too few of them. Prosecutors and courts didn't have the personnel or skills they needed. Those who helped me did all that they could. My victim advocate was everything I could have asked for, and Jim McCord, the lead detective on the shooting case, was amazing, and committed to keeping me safe. But VAWA had changed the whole landscape for victims. Because of it, women now had many more sources of support to draw on.

When I was done speaking, I introduced the vice president. As I was handing over the podium, he gave me a big Biden hug and whispered, "I love ya, kid."

The vice president spoke about many aspects of domestic violence. The experience of victims—everything from cowering in your own home like a prisoner of war to feeling terrified that the 800 number you called was going to appear on the phone bill. He talked about how chronic stress from domestic abuse is literally toxic to the body, linked with so many long-term physical and mental health problems. He mentioned some of the changes VAWA had undergone in its subsequent reauthorizations. In 2000, dating violence was added. In 2005, a new training program for health-care providers to screen their patients for domestic violence. Just the year before, the 2013 version of VAWA had made the services it funded available to anyone regardless of their sexual orientation or gender identity, and it had addressed a loophole related to Native American enforcement mechanisms. Previously, Indian nations had been unable to prosecute non-Native abusers of Native women. At the same time, federal prosecutors weren't going onto tribal lands to prosecute them. As a result, abusers were getting away with their crimes. The latest VAWA had restored this authority to tribes to prosecute non-Indian abusers on their lands.

Finally, he thanked all of us who stand up and tell our stories, knowing that each time we do, it brings it all up again.

He was right. Talking about it is never easy. But that day in the Archives, I felt a long way from the days of my childhood, or the years I was married, when I was troubled and uncertain and just trying to survive.

———

I wasn't back long from that trip to D.C. when I was contacted by Marilyn Horsey, copresident of the NCADV board of directors, about becoming the permanent executive director of NCADV. I had not actually applied for the position, but I think the appearance with the vice president had caught the attention of many. I was a survivor who had a voice and connections within the administration. Domestic violence is the one issue on which I can speak with authority, and I had spoken that day in D.C. with conviction and clarity.

Marilyn reached me when I was dropping David off at his apartment. He was still shaky but had gotten a place of his own. I was standing in his living room when I heard Marilyn say, "We want you to know we'd love for you to stay."

As the call went on, David realized from the look on my face that it was something important—big news, either good or bad.

I accepted their offer. And when I hung up the phone, I burst into tears. I cried like I had cried when I graduated from college, like I cried when my first grandchild was born. Here was another milestone, a huge transition. I would be the CEO and president of a national organization.

And yet, even at 54, I could hear the old tapes whirring. Maybe the volume was lower, maybe it was easier to hit stop, but there it was: *You're not good enough. You're an imposter.* I was the woman, after all, who had lain in a hospital bed with gunshot wounds, a single mother with a GED, a woman who for years hadn't even known there was a name for what was happening to her. I knew I had worked hard since, and earned the good things that had come into my life, but even so, I was probably more stunned than anyone to see them happen.

Through tears, I told David. He was the first person to hear the news, which seems absolutely right to me. A lot had gone into this moment—all the work I'd done since the shooting to recover from my abuse and to educate myself, but also all the trauma and violence that had preceded that, which David had witnessed and frequently suffered himself.

He was so excited. He said, "Why are you crying?"

I said, "I can't believe this is happening."

I'll never forget how he looked at me and said, "I'm not surprised at all! If anybody can do this job, it's you."

David had never doubted my capabilities. Even as he worried about me, he had been my biggest champion as I moved into this field. When I was running the program at DHS, he used to say, "You're working way too hard. But I understand why."

I could feel in that moment that he believed in me. It was exactly what I needed. I thought, *Okay, I can believe in myself, too, then.*

Later that day, I called my mother. She was ecstatic. It wasn't about status, it was about succeeding at something I'd decided was my path in life. "I always knew you could do it," she said.

I called Albretta, too. Things were still strained between us, but we maintained contact because of David and were in a better place than we had been after Cedric's death. Her relationship to my line of work was obviously complicated. She was proud of me for working hard, staying strong, and making my way; those were things Albretta respected. But the whole reason I'd become an advocate in this field was because of her son's abuse and violence. She had a needle to thread, and to her credit, she had become fairly successful at threading it. She was thrilled about the NCADV news. She didn't have a great understanding of the dynamics of domestic violence—she had gotten away from Cedric's father pretty quickly—or of what an organization like NCADV was doing. But she liked the word *National*. It signaled prestige. Albretta's values were solid, but she did appreciate status.

Of course I called all my friends, too—Pam and Connie and Pat, and also the Usual Suspects. They were all remarkable. Every one of them responded with some version of *This is your place. This is exactly where you were supposed to end up.*

I was excited not only because the board had chosen me, but because they'd chosen a survivor. In 1982, the Battered/Formerly Battered Women's Task Force had been formed at the NCADV conference to ensure that survivors would continue to have leadership within the movement. But for a long time, as an outside observer, I had felt that NCADV had lost sight of its core philosophy: the centering of victims and survivors and their voices and perspectives. I was excited to bring that focus back to the work we did, and the fact that NCADV had now hired a survivor as its director sent a clear message that it was ready to do the same. It was a strong statement in favor of victims and against stigma and shame, and it was proof that survivors could become leaders. I was also a Black woman, and that sent an important message, too. NCADV would now have leadership that could speak from a point of view and a set of experiences that were too often missing from advocacy and policy-making.

My job would be to learn how to use the insights that grew out of my own life to advocate strategically for all those who were still trapped, as I had been trapped, who were trying to find safety, or trying to recover from everything they had endured. People in my field often say, "I don't speak for all survivors." I get that. No one should presume to speak for others. But from the beginning of my time heading NCADV I have felt that in a certain sense it is my job, and my ethical responsibility, to do just that. I have a duty to all victims and survivors, and I have a unique position and public platform. Of course I speak on their behalf.

———

The NCADV office today is a bright, sunny, wide-open space on the seventh floor of an office building in central Denver. But when I took over in 2014, we were housed in fairly grim quarters above a restaurant. The AC and heating often didn't work, and we shared our space with mice. There was a perpetual smell wafting up from the restaurant. The parking lot never felt entirely safe after dark. It would take some time and money to get us out of there, but the setting was a daily reminder of how a whole lot of change needed to happen.

None of the staff trusted me initially. They didn't know who I was or what I was about, and for the initial twelve months or so, there was a lot of pushback against my leadership. The first time I called a staff meeting, the reaction was like, *We're going to do* what*???*

One of my first firings was about five months in, a woman who had been challenging me at almost every turn. She was white, and I firmly believe she had difficulty taking direction from a Black woman. I can still remember the look she gave me as I was giving her the news that she wouldn't be working with us anymore—I thought she was going to hit me!

While I wouldn't tolerate racism, I didn't need people to like me. As women, we tend to want to feel good about the people we work with—and the field of domestic violence work is dominated by women. But I needed my staff to understand that no matter what their personal feelings were about me, I was the director now. That was what mattered. And much of the pushback *wasn't* personal, it was just resistance to change. One of the team members told me I'd get used to the way things were done: the unstructured, lackadaisical culture.

Ah, actually, no, I thought. *I'm not here to get used to that. I'm here to get rid of it.*

The old way of doing things, from top to bottom, was over. Forget about silos and sitting in your office with the door closed. Forget about wearing flip-flops to work. We have a schedule. We have clear deliverables for which you'll be held accountable. I was determined to put NCADV back on the map with other national organizations in the field.

The staff member who had been there the longest was Gretchen Shaw. Gretchen had been at NCADV for twelve years and had worked in various roles, overseeing membership, communications, projects, and events. At the time I took over, she was in charge of developing and managing our partnerships. Gretchen comes from Alabama, where she worked for several nonprofits, including the Alabama Coalition Against Domestic Violence. Eventually she had wanted to spread her wings beyond Alabama and had ended up in Denver. When I was appointed permanent director, Gretchen had been looking for another job. She was frustrated by what she felt was a lack of direction in the organization, its unfulfilled potential. But Gretchen was the institutional memory, and I saw how valuable she could be. I could also see that she was ready to work hard to make NCADV a more effective organization. She believed we had a place at the table, and that we needed to get our act together and claim it. I asked her to stay on. In 2016, I would make her my deputy, a position she still holds.

Gretchen remembers her first impression of me as stern. But also "a breath of fresh air."

A stern breath of fresh air . . . ? That makes me laugh!

The feeling she got from me was: *This is where we're going, you can stay on the bus or you can get off.*

Now she calls me a "badass." Which I believe is an improvement on stern!

Jacquie Gonzales, who is now our administrative assistant, joined the staff just before I did, though she had been volunteering with NCADV since 2010, so knew the ins and outs of the organization. She had worked mostly on the Remember My Name project, a national registry that NCADV created with *Ms.* magazine in 1994 to help keep the focus on victims. The registry records the names of women killed through domestic violence, along with information about the incidents; to date it contains more than ten thousand names. NCADV was a family affair for Jacquie: Her mother-in-law, Sylvia, had been our membership director for seventeen years.

I knew nothing about Jacquie when I started, but I sensed she had a story. I thought: *There's a reason she is here.*

As time went on, I learned Jacquie's stories, just as she learned mine. Jacquie's husband's cousin had been murdered by her estranged husband in 2004 when she was twenty-five years old. He had broken into her apartment, smashed her skull, and left her in a pool of blood. (The man was convicted and sent to prison.) Jacquie herself had experienced teen dating violence. She was seventeen when she had her son and nineteen when her daughter was born. She didn't want her daughter to go through what she'd been through. She wanted to learn whatever she could to break the cycle. In 2021 Jacquie's daughter graduated from high school with honors; as I write this, she is a freshman at the University of Colorado, the first generation in Jacquie's family to go to college.

Conducting an assessment of an organization is one thing. Putting those changes in place is a whole other thing. There were a lot of difficult conversations that first year about the direction of the organization. Of the five employees who were with NCADV when I began, Gretchen, Jacquie, and Rachel have remained. The other two didn't last. I got the board to dismiss itself, and we started a new board from scratch, one developed strategically.

I was working sixty-hour weeks, making many uncomfortable decisions. But it was invigorating. Aside from the actual focus of our work, which was something I cared passionately about, I loved using my education and experience to do change management. Change is always hard, and I needed to call on everything I had learned in my working life, from the odd jobs to my post-grad studies and of course all the years at DHS. I include in that my very first job at Der Wienerschnitzel. I worked at the hot dog chain briefly when I was about eighteen. I was on trash duty and had to clean the patio tables. I wasn't happy about that. But I needed a job, and dammit, if this was the job I had I was going to do it to the best of my ability! I would tie that trash bag just right and always drop it into the appropriate dumpster; I would make sure that not one of my tables had a single smidgeon of bird poop on it.

I was a long way from Der Wienerschnitzel now, but maybe some of those old tapes are helpful—the ones about tenacity and having a strong work ethic and taking pride in whatever you do, even the stuff you would prefer not to be doing. I was going to oversee a transformation that involved every aspect of how we worked internally and how we operated as an organization with a national platform. At the same time, I needed to support the others through these changes—those who were, as Gretchen put it, on the bus. I wanted everyone from the part-time accountant to the new board to our partners and allies to reimagine what we could achieve together, and to feel empowered by the possibilities. Our members needed to know what services they would get out of joining NCADV. We needed to clean up and clarify our fundraising efforts. I relished the practical side of all this. Thinking very strategically about change, but also that feeling that everything was going into a big tumbler and getting whirled around.

Walking through the door of that grungy little office every day was exciting, because there was so much to do. Naturally, it was also petrifying . . . because there was so much to do. I leaned on my friends a lot then, the Usual Suspects as well as other women in my life. They did everything you'd want friends to do—they were sounding boards who shored me up, but they also called me out if I was overdramatizing or indulging my self-doubt. They shepherded me through this major transition in my life, which was also a difficult time for me personally. I had taken on the job when my son was at his lowest point, and he was still trying to heal from that. It was also a period when I felt I'd lost my own bearings—I wasn't even living in my own house but in Susan's spare room. I think about that now and wonder if maybe it wasn't such a bad time to have taken a leap. Maybe if I had been a little less raw, a little less at sea, I'd also have been less likely to take a risk. We usually think of a new challenge as stepping outside our comfort zone, but in the fall of 2014, I'm not sure I even had a comfort zone. I didn't know how any of what I did at NCADV was going to play out—we usually don't know nearly as much as we like to believe we do—but I was quickly coming to feel the truth of what my friends had told me: This was exactly where I was supposed to be.

CHAPTER 13
Everything I Never Dreamed

One afternoon in February 2015, when I was still fairly new at NCADV, I got a call from my brother Brady. My mother was on her way to the hospital again.

My mother had always been a heavy smoker. For the final ten or fifteen years of her life, she suffered pretty badly with COPD, an inflammatory lung disease that can make breathing difficult. She had been in and out of the hospital a few times, and on those occasions I had traveled to Riverside to see her.

At first it seemed like this stay in the hospital was going to be routine, that she would get her lungs checked, and they would calm her breathing down and send her home again. Brady said he thought she was going to be okay, and I asked him to keep me posted.

Next thing I knew the phone was ringing again. The doctors wanted to put my mother on a breathing machine. This was serious. I told Brady I would get there as soon as I could. I hung up and started frantically searching online for a direct flight out of Denver that day. I couldn't find anything that would get me there quickly enough, so finally I called Southwest. A sympathetic woman took matters in hand and somehow found me a flight. I called Cindy, a dear friend and a member of the Usual Suspects, and she dropped everything, raced over to pick me up, and brought me to the airport. I made the flight, took my seat at the very back of the plane, and spent the trip bawling my eyes out. I knew there was no way my mother would want to be put on a breathing machine. I knew she was going to die.

It has taken me a long time to see my mother clearly—to the extent that we can ever say we see another person clearly. Until I was well into my forties, I just thought she'd made some really bad decisions in life—the awful husbands and boyfriends, the times she'd failed to be there for me, like never coming to see me in the hospital after I'd been shot. Because of how harsh she could be, she had no real friends. She had a way of insisting you do things her way, and if you refused she went straight into victim mode. But at some point I began to understand that my mother was not just a difficult person, she was clinically depressed.

She was just fifty-five years old when she retired in 1992. She had been working for the State of California as an "unemployment insurance technician," helping people to apply for their benefits and also doing job skills training, something she was very proud of. She had gotten a good retirement package, and I suspect she thought only of how set up she'd be and nothing about what her life without a job would actually look like. When she was raising all of us, the sheer chaos of a house full of kids probably kept her somewhat vital, or at least kept her head above water. But eventually we all grew up and left. And then she retired and had so much time on her hands. That was when her depression really deepened, and she began to exhibit much more obvious signs. She tended to isolate, and I knew there were times she just stayed in her room for days. She also grew even more brusque and cranky, and I couldn't find a way to shift that mood. My mother wasn't a person for hobbies, and mostly she just watched a lot of TV. But she was also restless. She couldn't stay in the same place for long; she moved to Ohio at one point, then back to California; there were various moves within California. It seemed she no sooner settled somewhere than she was off again. She had even made that brief attempt to live with me in Denver. She was trying so hard to find happiness, some rest for her mind, any place she could. I think of my mother as a very vulnerable human being, someone who had wanted all her life, more than anything, to be loved and cared for. Instead she'd had a string of unhappy, and sometimes abusive, relationships that had left her depleted.

Most of my mother's life after her retirement was spent alone. Her sixth husband, Reese, died in 1997 of a heroin overdose. Once I really began to understand that depression had played a big role in her life, I encouraged her to think about going on antidepressants. She was in her sixties by then. She told me that she'd tried them and they hadn't worked, but when I pressed her, she admitted that she had only given them a couple of weeks. Even late in life, even when she had nothing to lose, she was still headstrong enough to do things her way.

A few years before she passed away, we had a reckoning of sorts. I sat her down and said, "I know what life has been like for you, but I won't be the brunt of your anger anymore. I'll take care of you the best I can, but I can't put up with you being mean and nasty when I show up."

I also spoke about how let down I'd felt after the shooting. She was living in Riverside when I was shot, and I didn't see her for a long time after I got out of the hospital—at least several months. Too long for me to feel okay about. I didn't say I couldn't forgive her, but I did say that I wasn't able to forget that she hadn't come to be with me. She repeated what she'd said about how she hadn't felt safe—because no one knew where Cedric was—but beyond that she mostly just listened. She never wanted to go too deep; it unraveled her pain and made her feel like she had to take responsibility. And that was something she tried to avoid.

It was a hard conversation, and I thought there was a good chance she might declare that she was never going to speak to me again. But she did keep speaking to me, and our conversations after that were sometimes different. They were a little lighter, which I know didn't come easily or naturally to my mother, and she played the angry victim less often and a bit less adamantly.

Shortly after the event in the East Room of the White House in 2010, I visited her. When I got to her house in Riverside, there were three neighbors waiting there to meet me. My mother had invited them over. This wasn't the first time she'd alerted the neighbors when I was coming.

I've said that for much of my life I have never felt seen. But my mother did see something in me when I was a young girl. Then I had gotten pregnant, and she thought everything was over. Then I'd gotten shot, and God knows what kind of future she saw for me then. And then there I was, fresh off a visit to the White House. She couldn't hide how pleased she was. As she'd done on other occasions, she shook her head and said, "I knew it when you were younger."

I don't know, really, what was going through my mother's head and heart that day as she beamed at me in front of the neighbors. But over the years, as I'd become an outspoken advocate for victims, she had always been proud of me.

"I tell everyone about you," she said. "You're everything I never even dreamed of being."

When she first began to say that, I thought: *Is this envy?* But there was an aura of admiration when she said it. She had seen me navigating the highs and lows of my life, its promise and reversals, the violence she knew all too well, and the accomplishments she couldn't have imagined.

Her pride in me was part of our reconciliation. So were my own insights. When I was sixteen and pregnant, I'd looked at my mother and thought I knew more than she did. Life had since knocked the corners off me; it had also taught me empathy. I understood that my mother's allotment of resilience for this life had been used up raising her children and surviving the terrible abuse of my stepfather.

By the time the plane landed at Ontario airport in California and I got to the hospital, about five hours had passed. My mother was still alive. My brothers and their wives and kids were mostly all there. (Ric would arrive the next day.) There was a lot of crying going on. My mother was on a morphine drip and wasn't conscious—if she'd been awake, she would have been pissed off at the scene we were all making.

I sat on her bed, held her hand, and hoped that she knew I was there. I looked at her intently, trying to make an imprint in my mind of her before she was gone. I didn't want to forget.

She passed away about twenty minutes after I arrived. The machines were all shut down and it was suddenly quiet. The nurse pulled the curtain. I spent another several minutes with her by myself, wishing her peace.

I stayed in Riverside for a week after that, doing the practical things that death requires of us. Ric and I shared a hotel room for those days, which added a certain comfort and comic relief to the weight of our mourning. All but one of my mother's sons and their families were at the funeral—one of my brothers had become estranged from her. Albretta came to the funeral, too. She had a house in Riverside as well as Ohio, and just then she happened to be in Riverside. I had let her know about my mother's death, but I was surprised she came. She hung in through the whole thing, even going to the graveside. I could tell she felt apprehensive being there, worrying about what my brothers might be thinking about her, knowing that my mother disapproved of her, and of my relationship with her. My mother and Albretta had gotten into it when I was pregnant, and whatever Albretta had said to her about me, my mother never forgave her. That Albretta had turned up at the funeral in spite of all that, to show support for me and my family, said a lot about how she had grown.

She said, "I'm here for you, honey."

Our relationship was still fraught, and soon enough we would have our own reckoning.

As for my mother, I have never stopped honoring her resilience. She lived in a dark world, and always saw herself first and foremost as a victim, a stance that drained her strength. She had a hard life, and some of that was her own doing, but there were many things that were not under her control: the way she was brought up, her own mother's abuse of her, the limited avenues that were available to a pregnant, uneducated teenager—all those doors that close so quickly. She was just seventy-six years old when she died, but I felt a certain kind of relief for her, that she could rest now from all the darkness and the struggle.

I miss her to this day, sometimes terribly. My understanding of her is still growing. How many times I have said, *Oh, I get it now, I see what you were going through, because now I've gone through it, too*. Or I think of things she tried to tell me over the years that I dismissed too easily, and I think, *Yes, you were right*.

Raising David, of course, gave me more compassion for my mother, and what she faced raising all of us. There is a beautiful passage in Tarana Burke's memoir, *Unbound*, where she reflects on this evolution. "I was an adult with a child of my own and a trail of mistakes behind me before I could say with certainty that my mother loved me. That clarity came from being faced with my own limited capacity. No matter how deep my desire was to love my child, I was still encumbered by the ghosts I had tried to bury. I failed—often. If I hadn't had the experiences I had with my mother, I'm not sure I would have fought so hard to build my capacity."

I can say with certainty that my mother loved me. I can definitely say that I loved her. It was an extremely complicated love we shared, and one that was often a source of disappointment and pain to me. But I keep going back to her beginnings, the things I knew she had been scarred by, and the damage, too, that I know nothing about. We never know the full extent of another person's burdens.

When someone we've been close to dies, our relationship to them doesn't stand still but continues to evolve. My mother and I are no exception. We are a work in progress, an ongoing, unresolvable question. A mystery I keep making my peace with, again and again.

CHAPTER 14

Why We Do What We Do

Two steps forward and one back. And on the bad days, one step forward and two back. After eight years of an administration led by a president and vice president who took violence against women seriously and were leading in the direction of progress, the 2016 presidential election knocked the wind out of us. A man who had bragged on tape that he had sexually assaulted women swept into office.

It wasn't just the tape, of course. By then we knew multiple women had made allegations of assault and harassment against Donald Trump, including his first wife, Ivana, who accused him of rape in a divorce deposition in the 1980s. (She later changed "rape" to "violated," and Trump's lawyer Michael Cohen, apparently unaware that marital rape laws had existed in all fifty states for more than twenty years, said that Trump couldn't have raped Ivana because "by the very definition, you can't rape your spouse.") We knew that as the owner of the Miss USA and Miss Teen USA pageants, Trump would walk into the young women's dressing rooms unannounced. He had described this perk himself to Howard Stern: "And I'm allowed to go in because I'm the owner of the pageant. . . . They're standing there with no clothes. And you see these incredible-looking women. And so I sort of get away with things like that." In a *New York* magazine profile many years before, Trump had been quoted as saying about women, "You have to treat 'em like s***." A *Guardian* columnist looking at many of Trump's utterances over the years suggested he was conducting a "masterclass in rape culture," doing his bit for the normalization of sexual violence in society.

Just days after the release of that tape, when you might have thought Trump would present a contrite face, he doubled down instead. When Hillary Clinton was speaking at the next presidential debate, Trump followed her around the stage, staring at her, making faces. The media used words like "prowl" and "stalk" to describe what he was doing. Hillary said it made her skin crawl. A telling coda to the night was the way Hillary second-guessed her reaction, asking herself (and us) if she should have called him out in the middle of the debate rather than keeping her cool, engaging with the issues, carrying on: "Maybe I have overlearned the lesson of staying calm, biting my tongue . . . smiling all the while."

Not every misogynist is an abuser. But they inhabit the same spectrum. Chelsea Clinton called misogyny a "gateway drug" to worse. I'm not saying that everyone who voted for Trump did so *because* he was a misogynist. I'm saying that the fact that he was one, and wore it proudly—it was part of his brand—didn't bother people enough to not vote for him. His election proved that misogyny was fine; it wouldn't hurt your chances for a good job. One of the ways that children and adolescents develop beliefs about the appropriateness, or not, of behaviors is by noticing which actions are rewarded and which are denounced or punished. Well, the reward doesn't get much bigger than the Oval Office.

It's hardly surprising that we are still mired in misogynistic thinking. Women speaking out about violence and abuse, and organized efforts to combat them, really began in earnest only in the 1970s. Just five decades have passed since we started working to expose and eradicate millennia of entrenched ideas and practices. In the early 1990s, when Vice President Biden was drafting VAWA legislation, judges told him, off the record, that women would use the new laws as "leverage" in divorce settlements. (Well, yes.) Senate colleagues said the laws would bring about the "disintegration of the American family." Some characterized safe havens for abused women—shelters or transitional housing—as "indoctrination centers for runaway wives."

Indoctrination centers? What exactly were we being indoctrinated into? The belief that we deserved to be safe from violence?

The idea that there is actually anything wrong with beating your wife is a relatively recent one—and in several countries it is still not explicitly outlawed. Wives have historically been regarded as possessions, not partners, whom husbands were entitled to rule as they saw fit. The concept of women as property has been baked into our own legal system via English common law, on which much of U.S. law is based. The Puritans of the Massachusetts Bay Colony were the first in the world to enact laws expressly prohibiting wife-beating. That was in 1641. But the social stability of the colony took precedence over a wife's right to be safe from violence, and the laws were rarely enforced. For the next two hundred years, there was essentially no effort in this country to legislate against domestic violence, though courts in Europe and the U.S. gradually began to nuance the notion of permissible abuse, taking into account the reasons for a beating and the degree of physical harm inflicted. Harsher beatings were allowed if the wife was "responsible" for the abuse—by being a "nag," say, or committing adultery. The so-called rule of thumb expressly permitted a husband to beat his wife if the rod or stick used was not thicker than his thumb. One eighteenth-century French ruling gave the husband the right to punish his wife if it was limited to "blows, thumps, kicks or punches in the back . . . which did not leave marks."

In the latter half of the nineteenth century, some courts began to question certain long-standing assumptions, such as the rule of thumb, acknowledging that it was the degree of harm done that mattered, not the instrument used. But what continued to enable domestic abuse was the notion that it was a private matter and not the business of the courts. A ruling by North Carolina's Supreme Court found a husband's violence "excessive and malicious," but regarded that as largely beside the point: "We will not inflict upon society the greater evil of raising the curtain upon domestic privacy, to punish the lesser evil of trifling violence."

A beating, in the end, simply wasn't worth airing the dirty laundry over. And who decided that? Not the victim, whose safety was secondary to both society's right to turn a blind eye and the abuser's right to privacy.

Finally, in 1871, Alabama became the first state in the U.S. to rescind the legal right of husbands to beat their wives. Soon after, Maryland made wife-beating a crime. By the start of the twentieth century, numerous states had adopted such laws, but they were usually enforced only when injuries were severe enough to make punishment unavoidable. This started to change in the late 1970s, and states began to pass statutes creating specific new domestic violence crimes. In the 1980s, Congress authorized federal funding to states to support programs to prevent family violence and provide shelter and other assistance to victims. The Victims of Crimes Act was amended to explicitly add domestic violence as a compensable crime. By the end of the decade, there were statutes in all fifty states providing for restraining orders. Stalking eventually became a crime in every state, and certain adjudicated domestic abusers are now prohibited from purchasing or possessing firearms.

There are still loopholes in our domestic violence laws. But we've come a long way in recent decades. In many ways, policy and legislative progress have outpaced changes in attitudes and cultural norms. Beliefs so deeply ingrained, and enshrined in law for so long, aren't easily abandoned.

———

The 2016 election was a tough time for a lot of people, and certainly for anyone who had experienced domestic or sexual violence or was working in the field. I remember how traumatized my own staff were. I was supporting them as best I could, but I felt as though I were doing triage, and trying to maintain my own composure when I felt exactly as they did. I said, "Let's take a couple of days to mourn what we know is coming, but then we have to keep on with our mission. We can't let this overwhelm us." It actually took months, not days, to get over that initial shock.

We carried on in this new and nasty climate, horrified but also energized. Trump's administration quickly showed itself to be as dysfunctional and regressive as we feared it would be. There was one week, about a year into his term, when two of his staff resigned amid allegations of domestic abuse. The President, meanwhile, continued to insult his own accusers and to defend men accused of assault and harassment, such as Roger Ailes, Roy Moore, and Bill O'Reilly. But maybe it was his very embrace of awfulness that helped to trigger a countercurrent of *enough is enough*. More and more victims of sexual violence were speaking out—and being heard. The #metoo movement was on fire. The young gymnasts who had been abused by Larry Nassar, doctor for the U.S. women's national gymnastics team, were talking about it on major platforms such as *60 Minutes*. If we couldn't end assault and harassment right now, we could at least end the silence about it.

From a policy perspective, our work at NCADV continued to focus on the three legislative acts that are the pillars of federal response to domestic violence: the Victims of Crimes Act (VOCA), which established the Crime Victims Fund in 1984 to assist and compensate victims of all crimes, including domestic violence; the Family Violence Prevention and Services Act (FVPSA), another primary funding source dedicated to emergency shelters and other victim services; and of course VAWA.

We also got very involved in the development of the Fix NICS Act, a bipartisan effort that would become law in 2018. The NICS, or the National Instant Criminal Background Check System, is a computerized system that conducts a search of available records to help determine whether someone is disqualified from possessing or receiving firearms. But far too many states were simply not submitting the necessary records (including those related to domestic violence), and many adjudicated abusers were keeping their guns. To function as it was intended, the NICS needed relevant agencies throughout the U.S. to submit accurate and timely information. NCADV lobbied to improve submission of domestic violence records to the background check system. When the Fix NICS Act was passed, states were incentivized to improve their domestic violence record submissions, and a priority area for reporting of domestic violence convictions has been created under the NICS Act Record Improvement Program.

Rachel, our policy guru, was leading the way for us in D.C. My initial impression of her as being a detail-oriented critical thinker had proven correct. She was also a natural for D.C., and was building trust and relationships on Capitol Hill with people on both sides of the aisle. Whatever their policy disagreements, she could see who in Congress wanted the best for victims and survivors, even if they saw a different way of getting there. She was also continuing to strengthen our ties with key partners, namely the National Task Force to End Sexual and Domestic Violence (NTF). The membership of NTF is diverse, made up of civil rights organizations, labor unions, anti-poverty and immigrant rights advocates, racial justice organizations, and more, all of whom are approaching anti-violence work from an intersectional perspective. It's led by a steering committee, of which NCADV is a member.

It's rare that you get national, tribal, state, territorial, and local organizations working harmoniously together, but the NTF steering committee has a unified strategy and a level of mutual support that neither Rachel nor I have seen in other coalitions. It would be easy for NCADV's own identity to be subsumed or diluted within the Task Force, but we have an area of expertise—domestic violence and guns—and Rachel cochairs the firearms subcommittee within the NTF.

Working in partnership with three other organizations—the Educational Fund to Stop Gun Violence, Prosecutors Against Gun Violence (PAGV), and the Alliance for Gun Responsibility—we helped to launch Disarm Domestic Violence (disarmdv.org). Laws regarding firearm prohibition and removal vary from state to state, and the project created the first comprehensive website about domestic violence protection order firearms laws, a one-stop shop of information on a state-by-state basis. Disarm Domestic Violence is a critical tool for keeping people safe, but it has been underutilized so far because of the lack of resources to promote it and educate people about its incredible usefulness.

We also continued our long-standing financial education program for victims and survivors. Working with the National Endowment for Financial Education, we ran a series of webinars on financial literacy and economic independence, everything from budgeting to identity theft to credit. (It's amazing to recall just how recently women began to achieve legal financial independence. Before the Equal Credit Opportunity Act of 1974, banks could refuse to issue a credit card to an unmarried woman, and could require single, divorced, widowed, or married women to have a male cosigner.) The lack of financial independence, particularly when children are involved, remains one of the most common reasons victims stay with or return to abusers. Financial abuse—maintaining control over financial resources, withholding access to money, or preventing someone from working or attending school—is incredibly common within relationships where other forms of abuse are occurring. It is estimated that 94–99 percent of relationships that involve physical violence also involve economic abuse. I was fairly financially savvy when I left Cedric, and had always worked and had my own income. But even I had to think carefully about how to safeguard the money I had—some of which I'd hidden in a mattress—and in the end Cedric's friend cleaned out my bank account anyway.

In 2019, Santander Bank invited NCADV to work with them. Santander's approach to working with us could serve as a model for any business seeking to partner with a nonprofit. We are often contacted by individuals or corporations, but it turns out that the "partnership" they envision is more about building their own brand; they have no appreciation of the extra burden the relationship would put on us. Santander was a true partner in that they understood our limitations and treated us with respect. They also made sure other national organizations were involved, and supported the National Network to End Domestic Violence micro-lending program, which provided loans to survivors trying to build and repair their credit.

For Domestic Violence Awareness Month in 2019, Santander erected a stand-alone house in the middle of the Oculus, a New York City train and subway station in the financial district. Called "In Someone Else's Shoes," the project was an immersive exhibit spotlighting the financial hardships victims of abuse face, and the many factors that enable abuse and make leaving so difficult. The house was in many ways a "normal" home, furnished and full of personal effects, but it also contained elements peculiar to homes where there is domestic violence: a refrigerator dented from being punched, bullet holes in the walls, an interior door without a lock. Visitors to the house put on headsets, through which they could hear the words of many different victims describing their experiences.

I was in New York for the three days that the house was open to the public. It was amazing and powerful: to have so many people walking through that space, and seeing that every single person emerged from it moved or shaken. As a survivor, I found those three days exhausting, but as the head of NCADV, I was reenergized.

By then, our NCADV office had grown. I had hired Lynn Brewer to be our one-woman communications department. Lynn has her own story of abuse. She had left a relationship a few years before joining us. While she was with the man, she had told herself that she wasn't a victim of domestic violence because "that meant when someone slams your head against the wall." She had downplayed what she was experiencing as "just emotional" abuse. But six months after she left the relationship she was called to jury duty on a domestic violence case.

During jury selection, the attorneys asked for a show of hands, to weed out anyone who had either experienced domestic violence themselves or knew someone who had. About half the jury box raised their hand. Lynn thought this must be an atypical sampling. She also began to realize that there were ways of answering certain questions that would get her out of serving. But a gut feeling told her this was where she needed to be.

As the trial unfolded and details came out about the relationship prior to the defendant's strangling of his partner (the woman lived and testified in court), Lynn recognized the pattern. Her boyfriend hadn't hit her, but she could see that they were "on the same road, just a mile or two behind." It was then she began to understand that she'd experienced multiple kinds of abuse—financial, coercive, sexual—that tend to be precursors to physical abuse. She and her boyfriend used to "joke" about the possibility, in fact. One day he raised his voice angrily, then she pretended to cry. They were testing the neighbor, seeing if he would respond. *He's going to call the cops*, they laughed, *he'll think it's domestic violence!* All the while Lynn was thinking: *I can't be a victim of domestic violence because I'm a feminist.*

Though the evidence was clear and jury members were all in agreement on the verdict, they felt bad about convicting the man. He was only twenty-one and they thought, *If only he could get some help instead of going to prison.* It was only after they'd delivered their verdict that they learned that this was his *fifth* charge related to domestic violence. Prosecutors were now going to file with the state for habitual offender status in order to get a harsher sentence.

Shortly after the trial, Lynn's ex-boyfriend tried to reconcile with her. But by then she'd had her "awakening." No way, she said. She never saw him again. When she came to work at NCADV, she was dealing with the challenges that anyone faces who's suffered abuse and gone on to work in the field. You're immersed all day every day in material that can trigger reminders of your own trauma. With my staff, no less than with myself, I have to strike a balance between acknowledging the pain that still exists and remembering that I'm there to do a job. We aren't robots; we don't leave our emotions at the door. I want my staff to feel they can give voice to certain things, and I never want to create an atmosphere in the office that encourages repression around trauma or avoidance of certain subjects—that's exactly what we are struggling against in society. At the same time, if we're going to struggle successfully, then we need to practice self-care, and understand at what point we have to put aside what's happening to us personally and do the work. It isn't for everyone, and I don't fault survivors who aren't able to take on the trauma of others. Lynn is navigating that road, as many of us have. She's been with us now for six years.

I had learned a certain amount about leadership when I was at DHS and in charge of the domestic violence program. But heading NCADV was different. We were a small organization, and there was a kind of intensity to our work relationships that you just don't have in a large state agency. I wanted to be the best possible mentor I could to these women who were dedicating themselves to the anti-violence cause. I had my mental bullet points. Lead with compassion. Don't indulge subpar work. Allow each member of my staff to step into her own empowerment. Don't pretend that isn't a risk. Help them to understand what the risk involves. Open the door to that, and hope they'll walk through. Make it as safe for them as you possibly can. And don't shy away from the hard conversations.

———

Among the most difficult challenges I've faced during my time at NCADV was the financial crisis that hit us in 2019. NCADV is the only national grassroots organization focused solely on domestic violence that doesn't currently take government grants. We run on donations and membership dues: a whopping 87 percent of our donations are for $100 or less. We never say never with regard to government funding; it's not a policy set in stone, and if a grant aligned with our mission and didn't stop us from doing our work freely, we'd go for it. In fact, there was a time we took federal funding. But in 1986, NCADV voluntarily returned a grant for more than half a million dollars that it had received from the Department of Justice (DoJ). Certain conservative groups had voiced their opposition to members of Congress about the grant because NCADV was made up of "pro-lesbian, hard-core feminists." As a result, twenty-four members of Congress signed a letter to the DoJ, protesting the funding of NCADV. The DoJ then demanded to see the résumés of all NCADV board members; they wanted to make sure the funds wouldn't be used for "lesbian-related advocacy." When NCADV refused to hand over the board's résumés, the DoJ insisted that the word "lesbian" be taken out of our mission statement. (Who knew that lesbians could strike such fear into the heart of our government!) After an all-night debate, the board voted to return the grant money rather than allow the DoJ to meddle in the affairs of the organization. It wasn't unanimous—the chair of the board resigned over the decision.

In many ways, our independence from government funding is one of our strengths. It gives us a unique position from which to address the issues, free from conflicts of interest. Many federal grants come with the explicit proviso that you can't use any of the money for lobbying efforts to influence government policy. By remaining independent of that source of funding, we're able to do lobbying and policy work other organizations can't. It also helps us to retain a grassroots perspective.

But it can make doing our work difficult. Eliminating a significant and potentially consistent source of funding leaves us somewhat vulnerable. If a recession hits, we really feel it. And there is very little room for error. In 2019, we had a perfect storm of financial stressors. We found ourselves overstretched. It was on my watch, and I thought the right thing to do was to offer my resignation to the board. There are two schools of thought about such situations: either you bring in new leadership or, if you still have faith in the leadership you have, you get them to walk you back out of the crisis. The board wouldn't accept my resignation. They basically said, *No, you go figure it out.*

It was painful getting us back on track. I had to think about cost-cutting measures, what we could let go of and still carry out our mission. We had gotten a bit of extra short-term funding that had finally allowed us to move from our dark little space over the restaurant to the bright airy office we have today. I looked at everything from leaving our new premises to cutting office supplies to laying off staff. (Our office employed eight people by then.) I trimmed everywhere else I could, but in the end I had to let three members of our staff go. In the past, when I was new to NCADV, I'd had to let people go for other reasons, including because they weren't doing their jobs or were not contributing to a good environment. That didn't bother me so much. But when it was cost-cutting and things I knew I was responsible for, that felt terrible.

What kept me afloat, what has always kept me afloat, is being reminded of why we do this work. Sometimes the reminders are subtle, and you have to go looking for them, to inject yourself with a bit of fight for the day. Other times they come straight at you.

A couple of years ago, I was at our annual conference in Washington, D.C. It was at the end of our Lobby Day—when we train advocates in lobbying and educating their representatives, then set them loose on congressional staff—and the room where we'd debriefed was very crowded. The woman who worked her way toward me practically had to shout. "This is my second conference," she called out, "and I want you to know that I've got all the strength and support I need to fight my case." She explained that she was a victim of domestic violence and also sexual assault; the sexual assault case was going to court. There were a lot of people milling around, and she reached toward me over someone's head. She held her hand up and I grabbed it, and she was squeezing my hand and crying. "Thank you so much," she said. Then the crowd shifted, and other people came up to me. She let go of my hand, and when I looked out over the sea of heads, I couldn't see her anymore. To this day I wonder who she was and what happened in court and how she's doing now. I will always be grateful to her. She gave me the gift of allowing me to see that we were living out our mission. That we were needed.

All of my staff have stories like that, moments when everything feels suddenly less abstract and you get a glimpse into individual lives. Jacquie remembers a certain phone call she happened to pick up at work one day. We aren't a direct service provider, but people in crisis still call us. Sometimes they just want to talk, sometimes we're where they go when they have exhausted all their other options and haven't gotten the help they need and they're justifiably angry. On this particular day, Jacquie answered a call from a woman who lived on a farm. She was trying to flee her home, but she didn't want to leave the farm animals behind. I don't know whether this was for economic reasons or because she thought her husband would slaughter them to punish her. (This would not have been an unreasonable fear. Some abusers target pets. Anti-violence activist Gretta Gardner recalls a man who snapped the family dog's neck, then told his wife: "I'll do that to you next time.") Jacquie contacted a nonprofit in Colorado Springs that supported domestic violence victims and said they could help move the farm animals. The woman later phoned Jacquie back and told her that both she and the animals were leaving and were going to a safe place. It was an unusual call, like the one I had picked up from the woman who wouldn't leave her marital home without the antique desk her mother had given her. Jacquie didn't attempt to talk the woman out of trying to bring the farm animals with her. She heard what was being asked of her and she was able to help. Some days, you can help.

Fighting sexual assault and domestic violence does at times feel like one step forward and two steps back. Other times it feels like things are standing still. But I think about it this way: What would our country, and our world, be like if nobody was standing up for victims or survivors? If nobody was there to help? Instead of just dwelling on the progress we have yet to make, I also remind myself that if we hadn't come as far as we have, more lives would have been lost, more victims would still be living in terror, more of us would be suffering unnecessary shame, and all of us would be living in a much darker silence.

CHAPTER 15
Making Peace

One thing I have come back to in my life, again and again, is the power of the individual. There are big cultural currents that wash over us all, and then there are the folks who fill our lives, helping to steer its course and shape who we are. Albretta was one of those people for me. Our beginnings hadn't exactly been promising. And we had lost decades because of Cedric. He cast a long shadow, and it took years for us to emerge from that. It happened, finally, in the space of a single day.

It was 2017, and Albretta was staying with me in Denver. She was in town to see her granddaughter, Ida—Cedric's daughter—graduate from college. My relationship with Albretta had evolved over the decades. She had disapproved of me from the start, and when Cedric and I got married and the violence started, she knew about it but either denied the reality or minimized its severity. When he died, she blamed me—for having driven him to such a desperate state. At Cedric's funeral we were barely on speaking terms. I will never forget how, when I arrived at her brother's house that day, the first thing she did was give my head a furtive once-over, looking for evidence of my *supposed* gunshot wounds.

But a couple of years later, we met up. She had lost her only child and she didn't want to lose her grandchildren. I had no intention of separating her from David. "As long as you don't badmouth me," I said, "I would never keep him from you." Our contact grew more frequent as time passed. We had long phone calls, and when Albretta came to Denver to see her grandkids, she often stayed at my condo. When I went to the White House the first time, I called my mother immediately afterward, but I also called Albretta.

Albretta's own relationship to the past was strange. She would introduce me to people as her daughter-in-law but not let on that her son was dead or how he had died. She was class-conscious and didn't believe in airing dirty laundry, and she was still very traumatized and angry about what had happened. There was a lot we had never talked about.

At four-foot-eleven, Albretta was tiny—but she was formidable. I think of her as a mighty little package. Petite, dark-skinned, a clotheshorse and a fashionista, Albretta walked with style. As she got older, her hair falling out from the years of chemical treatments, she never went out without an expensive wig, and often a hat. But Albretta also had substance. She was one of the toughest and most engaged women I have ever known. She'd worked two jobs while raising Cedric on her own. She had been an usher at her church for thirty-seven years. She had also been active in several organizations, including the NAACP African-American Historical Society in Riverside, the Martin Luther King Senior Citizens Club, the National Council of Negro Women, the Elks Club, and more. She had even worked on Democratic campaigns in California and Ohio, and had canvassed for President Obama. (She got to meet Obama at one of his campaign stops and had a framed picture of the two of them hanging in her house.) Albretta prided herself on being a go-getter. She started at 6 a.m. and didn't stop till midnight, and she could out-shop, out-church, and out-work anyone I knew. I think the frenetic pace protected her emotionally; if she stopped, the facts of her life, and of Cedric's death, might overwhelm her.

Like my mother, Albretta had suffered domestic violence, though not nearly as severely. She had left Cedric's father, Ernie, when Cedric was just a few years old because Ernie was unfaithful and abusive. Ernie went on to abuse his next family. I knew this because Ernie had been in the news a couple of years before. He was long dead by then, but Darryl, his son and Cedric's half brother, was running for the U.S. Senate. The *Denver Post* had dug up an assault charge that Ernie had lodged against Darryl in 1983, when Darryl was eighteen years old. After some initially conflicting answers to the *Post*'s questions, including a denial that the person named in the arrest report was him (he even suggested it might be Cedric), Darryl had issued a statement. He explained that his father had hit his mother, and he'd gotten between them to try to protect her. "This was not the first night my father attacked my mother, and maybe more sadly, this wasn't the worst time it happened—not even close." Darryl said when you grow up in a violent home, all the fights and pain begin to blur together, and you block out as much of it as you can. Since the *Post*'s story had come out, he and his mother had spoken about the night in question for the first time in thirty-two years. As painful as it was to revisit it all, Darryl said he felt blessed, because he'd gotten free of the violence. "When I got older, as a father, I did everything I could to raise my children with a father that loved them, protected them and made them feel safe."

I felt sad reading that, knowing that Cedric had also suffered at the hands of Ernie, and that he hadn't gotten free of the violence, hadn't been a husband or a father who had made his family feel safe.

In a strange twist, my friend Connie wrote a letter to the *Denver Post* in support of Darryl. She wanted people to understand that it wasn't at all surprising that Darryl had blotted out the memory of the violent incident or the arrest that followed. That was how children who grew up with batterers tried to survive, by putting the trauma behind them. She hoped that people would view with compassion the actions of an eighteen-year-old who was trying to protect his mother.

I adore Darryl. Our politics are worlds apart, but he's a good man. One day in 2019, he messaged me on Facebook to tell me that he had become one of the directors at TESSA, a nonprofit in Colorado Springs that supports victims of domestic and sexual violence. Darryl was now their chief legal services officer.

Everything I had ever seen of Ernie, his treatment of Cedric and his predatory attitude toward me, made me very glad for Albretta that she had gotten away from him. She had clearly saved herself a lot of pain and abuse, but Ernie had left his mark on both Cedric and Darryl, if in different ways.

It was a beautiful May morning, the sun streaming into my living room. I told Albretta to sit in the recliner while I made us something to eat. Her health wasn't good. For the last few years, she had been living with a brain aneurysm. Her blood pressure was high. I could tell she was tired, worn out, and in total denial about her failing health. I poured her a cup of coffee, put her breakfast on a tray, and brought it over to her. We started shooting the breeze about Ida's graduation and whatnot. I noticed she wasn't eating much. Eventually, we got on to the subject of David. I had told her before about David's drug addiction, but this was the first time she'd asked about it. She was very forthright in her questions—*How long? What drugs, exactly?*—and if you didn't know her, you'd have heard it as accusatory. That was how we got onto Cedric. I said that David had struggled ever since he was a child.

"Do you understand how abusive Cedric was to David and to me?" I asked.

And then the floodgates opened.

I told her that I'd had to begin my own reckoning with the past by taking responsibility for my denial about what David had experienced with his dad. "I think David tried to tell you about the abuse," I added. "I think you should ask him."

As we began to talk about Cedric and me, she said something that floored me.

"My understanding was that you were cheating on him."

"*What?*" I said. Cedric had carried on with other women during our marriage—Ida was living proof of one such relationship—but I had never cheated. "Is that what he told you?"

"Yes," she said.

I shook my head. "Do you remember when he called you and insisted I was out of control, and you told me to stop being hysterical? You thought I was overreacting?"

She nodded.

"Well, I wasn't overreacting," I said. "I was terrified, for good reason."

Her questions came tumbling out then. I recounted specific instances of violence, and I didn't spare many details, even about the worst of it. I shared more details about the kidnapping, and everything I could remember about the day of the shooting.

She shared with me more things Cedric had said about me that were completely untrue, the worst of which was that I wasn't a good mother to David. She kept saying, "I just didn't know." More than once she said,

"You know he was my only son." She wasn't justifying. She sounded apologetic. She wanted to hear the truth from me, but she also wanted me to understand the choices she had made.

On one of her previous visits I had said to her, "I know you think Cedric's death is my fault, but it's not." I'd told her then that I wanted to make things okay between us. I said that I had been going to counseling on and off for a long time, and I thought she should get some help, too. To my surprise, she agreed to do it. Maybe it was because of the counseling that she had decided to seize this moment—a rare time when the two of us found ourselves totally alone—to get her questions answered. Or maybe her failing health had something to do with it. Maybe, too, the fact that she'd really begun to care about me meant she needed to make sure that I was genuine, that I was actually who she thought I was.

She'd had her reasons for blaming me for Cedric's death. She believed I had been unfaithful to him. I had left him. I had turned David against him. But her denial about Cedric had extended to his suicide as well. For years, Albretta had believed he hadn't killed himself but had been shot by the police. There was never a doubt in my mind though. I knew Cedric was going to kill himself. There was no way he was going back to prison, and he had often threatened suicide. I had also seen the autopsy report.

The conversation in my living room that day brought Albretta out of denial—not just about Cedric's death and why he killed himself but about our whole history. As painful as it must have been for her, I also sensed a feeling of relief. A change in her demeanor to something more relaxed, like *Thank God we finally got all this out.*

I could see the day passing in the slant of the sunlight. I had hardly dared break the spell by going to the bathroom or stepping out for a cigarette. Every hour or so, Albretta would say, "Girl, we should stop talking and get out." But then before you knew it, we were deep in conversation again.

At one point I said, "I always knew you didn't like me."

She said, "That's so not true. Your mom started that."

I shook my head. "I never felt until the last few years that you cared for me."

"I've always cared for you," she said.

I didn't believe her. I think she came around to caring. I certainly hadn't always cared for her. Cedric forced us to grow on each other, and gradually, as his death had receded further into the past, we had worked ourselves out of our trauma bond and into something that was more about us.

Sitting in my living room, she said, "You know I love you."

"I know you do," I said. "And I love you, and I've always looked up to you." It was true. Going way back, I had admired her. From my mother I got pure and unadulterated strength. Albretta guided me in other ways. She showed me how to move in the world as a Black woman. She taught me how to cook and dress and watch my money. She taught me about family. If my mother was the bedrock of my life, Albretta gave me the pieces for building a life.

That day in Denver was a deep reckoning of events, cathartic in the best sense. We talked for six hours, and by the time we got up it was 4 p.m. and we were still in our pajamas.

There are people I've had to forgive in my life, and Albretta is one of them. Forgiving isn't easy (now there's an understatement!), but I can do it. I think the capacity began when I was young and wanted desperately to be loved. When you're a kid, you figure out that if you accept someone's "apology" you're more likely to get what feels like love in return. As I got older, that impulse evolved into something more like empathy, trying to understand what made the other person behave as they did, which can be a starting point for forgiveness. But it has also been about my own needs and survival. If I had never learned how to let go and forgive, I would be miserable—hurt and sad and angry all the time. I remember my therapist Barb telling me when I was in my thirties, "Don't let other people eat you alive." She was right—there were certain feelings I just couldn't afford. I had enough to contend with in the day-to-day of what was actually happening. Why would I want to hold on to feelings that had a bad impact on my well-being? Over time it became second nature for me to ask myself: *If I can move past this hurt and anger, what are the positives for me? For the other person?*

So I made my peace with Albretta. And with my mother. Cedric was obviously the hardest, and also the most significant in terms of moving on with my life. In one way I had it easier than other survivors because of Cedric's death. With Albretta, I was lucky enough to make the peace while she was still alive.

In 2019, about a year and a half after that visit to Denver, Albretta died in her house. She was alone. Her husband, Mannie, had recently passed away. I'd been scheduled to visit her. The day before she died we had been speaking on the phone. She told me she wasn't feeling well, and I offered to fly to California immediately. "I can get on the next plane," I said. But she wouldn't have it. She had a doctor's appointment in four days. I was due to be at her place in three days. "Okay," I said, "I'll be there to take you to your appointment."

The following night while she was setting her house alarm, her aneurysm burst, and she collapsed.

At her funeral, there were people I'd never met who knew who I was. Unlike my mother, who often told me she was proud, Albretta only once said she was proud of me, but she would give people my business card. The day of her funeral, strangers came up to me and said, "Oh, *you're* Ruth!"

"Yes," I would say. "I'm Ruth."

I know that of all the things that simple statement entails, all the versions of myself it comprises, I owe part of who I am to Albretta.

CHAPTER 16

Solidarity Among Survivors

In mid-September 2021, along with millions of others, I watched four young women testify to a Senate Judiciary Committee hearing on the FBI's failure to properly investigate sexual abuse perpetrated by Larry Nassar, the former team doctor of the U.S women's national gymnastics team. The outrage wasn't just that Nassar had abused hundreds of girls—including the majority of the 2012 and 2016 Olympic teams—but that USA Gymnastics, the U.S. Olympic & Paralympic Committee (OSOPC), and the Michigan State Athletic Department had turned a blind eye to the abuse for decades, prioritizing medals over the safety of girls. As superstar Simone Biles pointed out, this wasn't a case of one bad apple: an entire system had enabled and perpetuated Nassar's abuse. USA Gymnastics has complaint files on fifty-four coaches from 1996 to 2006, some of them very high ranking, for crimes including rape. When the FBI finally was called in on the Nassar case, their bungling of it meant that Nassar was able to molest more than seventy additional girls.

This wasn't the first time gymnasts had spoken publicly about their former doctor. In 2018, during Nassar's seven-day sentencing hearing, 156 of them delivered victim impact statements. Rachael Denhollander, who was the first to come forward and who is now a lawyer, had the last word. She spoke for over half an hour. Judge Rosemarie Aquilina called her "the bravest person I've ever had in my courtroom."

Nassar's victims have been frank about the additional trauma that coming forward involves. Aly Raisman said that people asked them why they were only coming forward now. "Because it's terrifying to come forward," she said. "The fear of not being believed, but also because it affects us so much. And sometimes it's impossible just to say the words out loud." Aly told the Senate that there were times, years after the abuse, when she had been so sick from what happened that she was brought by ambulance to the hospital. She said it might take her months to recover from the Senate hearing. "I just wanted to make that clear."

I just wanted to make that clear.

This reckoning, so long overdue, was a watershed moment for survivors of all kinds of sexual violence, and I would say for survivors of domestic violence, too. (We all live within systems that continue to prioritize the reputations, jobs, gun rights, and freedoms of abusers over the safety of victims, and any words or actions that challenge those systems are on behalf of us all.) Hundreds of victims spoke truth to power—and to their abuser. Nassar is now serving what amounts to life without parole. The head of the FBI apologized, calling his agency's mishandling of the case an "inexcusable" failure. In December 2021 victims agreed to a $380 million settlement with USA Gymnastics and OSOPC, one of the largest ever in a sexual abuse case. For many of them, the money will no doubt go toward helping to pay for treatment for the mental health problems they continue to suffer. The settlement also contains a list of nonmonetary provisions designed to dismantle the structures that enabled the abuse and keep future athletes safe. One of those provisions is that at least one seat on the USA Gymnastics board will be held by a survivor.

If these outcomes seem like no-brainers (and of course they are), it's worth bearing in mind that they wouldn't have happened—in fact, didn't happen—twenty or even ten years before. Things are changing, and in large part because so many survivors have dared to break a silence that seems as old as time itself. In the past few years, they have spoken out with greater honesty and less apology than ever before. We owe a debt of gratitude to them all, and a special debt to Tarana Burke. In 2006 Tarana, a Black activist from the Bronx, began using the phrase "me too" to empower girls and women of color who had been sexually abused, assaulted, or harassed. Then, in 2017, prompted by a friend's suggestion, actor Alyssa Milano invited everyone on Twitter to add "me too" if they'd been sexually harassed or assaulted. The hashtag #metoo went viral, and we all watched in astonishment as victims spoke out and numerous powerful men lost their jobs and reputations because of sexual violence and workplace harassment. Almost overnight, it seemed, something that had been talked about only among women, only in whispers, became a national and international conversation. Power shifted from predators to victims. And while sexual harassment and sexual assault have by no means vanished, assumptions have been upended, people have been held accountable, and a silence has been broken. A foundation was laid for continued work.

Tarana has since gone on to cofound Survivors' Agenda, a collective advocating for survivor justice and ensuring that survivors are the ones shaping the conversation on sexual and domestic violence, harassment, and coercion. There are numerous survivor groups all over the country, some broadly based and others focusing on the needs of specific survivor communities. Survived and Punished is dedicated to ending the criminalization of survival and the incarceration of people for self-defense or the "failure to protect," something a parent can be charged with if they are perceived as having failed to shield their child from abuse. There are survivor-led organizations focused on the well-being of the LGBTQIA+ community, on people of color, immigrants, Native women, and more. Trauma can be extremely isolating, and the solidarity among survivors that has taken shape in recent years has not only made our collective voice stronger, it has given us access to new sources of compassion and therapeutic alliance. The more survivors can speak openly, the more we will normalize the discussion of domestic violence and demystify the dynamics of it.

I spend a lot of my workday thinking about how we can change cultural attitudes about domestic violence. Language is an obvious starting point. We have to talk about domestic violence in ways that ensure we are supporting survivors and placing responsibility for abuse where it actually resides. Educator and anti-violence campaigner Jackson Katz likes to demonstrate how, by linguistic sleights of hand, we shift focus from the abuser to the victim—and not in the right way. Drawing on the work of Julia Penelope, Katz compares the sentence "John beat Mary" to "Mary is a battered woman." (John is now nowhere to be seen.) It reminds me of the headline following my husband's attempt on my life: *Woman, 32, shot in head* . . . I could have shot myself in the head, for all the reader knew. Even the term "violence against women" gives no sense of who is committing this violence, as though we don't actually know, and lends weight to the notion that domestic abuse is a "women's issue," something men can comfortably ignore.

Within the domestic violence field, we continue to reassess the language we ourselves use. How can we most authentically and respectfully represent the experience of victims and survivors? How can we avoid dehumanizing both victims and abusers? Are "victims" and "abusers" even the best terms to be using? In November 2021, NCADV hosted a webinar called "Why Aren't the Abusers Held More Accountable? Flipping the Script on 'Why Doesn't the Victim Just Leave?'" It attracted our biggest audience ever—between the website and Facebook Live, we had 1,800 participants. When the panel talked about what forms accountability could or should take, we kept coming back to language. There seemed to be two things we were in broad agreement on.

The first and most obvious was that language should never diminish the seriousness of violence and abuse. We have all seen examples of this. I remember a *Vanity Fair* journalist writing in 2014 that the near-decapitation of O.J. Simpson's ex-wife Nicole "had *crime passionnel* written all over it." The term "crime of passion" has always sounded suspiciously complimentary, as though the perpetrator loves with such intensity that the laws of ordinary mortals can't contain him. When a seventeen-year-old boy in Maryland fatally shot sixteen-year-old Jaelynn Willey in the head after their relationship had ended in 2018, the Associated Press referred to the shooter as a "lovesick teen." More generally, so many newspaper reports on domestic violence cases use words like "dispute" and "argument," both of which imply mutuality and equal power.

The second thing those of us on the webinar seemed to agree on was that we didn't want to use labels for those who abuse that permanently relegate them to the realm of criminal, perpetrator, abuser. Neither did we want to let them off the hook. If domestic violence is a choice perpetrators make, then we also need to believe that they can make different choices, and we need to put systems in place that support them in doing that. A lot needs to happen for an abuser to change their behavior, something I'll talk about in Part IV, but we're contradicting ourselves if we say, on the one hand, that abuse is a choice, and on the other hand use labels that suggest that people can't change.

Many people are leery of the word "abuser" as they feel it reduces a person to their worst acts; it makes abuse innate to who they are. Just as I am more than the victim of Cedric's violence, Cedric was more than those acts of violence. He was a human being. But I'm leery of soft-pedaling the reality. Someone has abused someone else. Someone has caused harm. I was abused for thirteen years. I speak of Cedric as my abuser. Other people label their experiences differently. I keep an open mind about these things. Language is ever evolving, and I'm still learning.

There is another problem with the word "abuser." When people hear it, who and what they envision is too often informed by preconceptions and stereotypes about race, lifestyle, class, and economic status. Whatever images "abuser" brings to mind, they are unlikely to include a white doctor who is a pillar of his community or a handsome and successful Hollywood actor. When we fall back on stereotypes, we leave out whole groups of victims, and we let whole groups of offenders off the hook. So in thinking about the language we use, we also have to consider societal perceptions of those words.

We're at a crossroads now with language. The anti–domestic violence movement began as the "battered wives" movement, a term that didn't cover the gamut, either of forms of abuse or those who suffer it. Many people now use "intimate partner violence." So far, I've chosen not to. I'm not comfortable with that use of the word "intimate," as though it isn't violence or abuse unless the victim is having sex with the perpetrator. I may not be intimate with my abuser at all. Perhaps we were intimate partners in the past, perhaps we never were. Domestic violence may be hidden, it may be a secret, but I don't like confusing it with intimacy. I'm also not entirely happy with the term "domestic violence"—it suggests that the abuse is confined to a shared house, and we've spent years hammering home the message that that isn't true—but it's the term that, for now, I'm most comfortable with.

As far as being called a "survivor," I am 100 percent good with that. No one is stronger than survivors, and I don't want anyone to take away from me what I went through. Others don't want their identity tied to "victim" or "survivor," more labels that they feel box in and define them. When I speak to victims and survivors, I'm conscious of the fact that I have to operate on two levels. If I'm having a personal interaction with someone who has experienced abuse, I have to listen to the language they use and, unless I feel it's harming them, reflect that language back. But I'm also a public advocate. I work within a number of systems, and I have to try to do justice to people's experiences as broadly as I possibly can. There are legislators and media people I speak to whose understanding of the dynamics of domestic violence isn't deep or nuanced. They get the terms "victim," "survivor," "abuser," and when I'm dealing with them, those may be the most effective words I can use as a starting point for a discussion.

I'm very proud of the fact that NCADV is led, advised, and staffed by survivors. I mentioned before what it meant in terms of the message NCADV was sending when they hired a Black survivor (and a victim of gun violence) to be the CEO. But as time has gone on, the importance of that as reflective of our mission has been brought home to me again and again. I am not just the manager, I'm bringing an underrepresented perspective to the table, whether I am with partner organizations, funders, the media, legislators, or other victims and survivors. Women and men who are not survivors can be incredibly passionate and effective allies in this field, and I am grateful every day for their commitment. But if you are a victim or survivor seeking support or looking for a reason to believe that life goes on, that things can get better after even the worst forms of abuse, then it helps to see yourself reflected in the movement's leadership.

And it isn't just me at NCADV, it's our whole organization. Our bylaws require that more than 50 percent of our board identify as survivors, and over half of our current staff identify as survivors of domestic violence. One of our advisory board members is retired police officer Mark Wynn, who now trains prosecutors, judges, legislators, service and health-care providers, and victim advocates all over the world on aspects of family violence. Ten years of Mark's childhood was spent in an incredibly violent home with a stepfather who abused Mark's mother and all of her children. There were broken bones, two miscarriages, his mother pushed out of a speeding car. This was Texas in the 1960s, and there were no shelters for families in trouble. Nor was there much sympathy. Once when the police came to the house they told Mark's mother, "If we have to come back here one more time, everybody's ass is going to jail." Mark was five years old, clinging to his mother's leg, which was trembling. The family eventually escaped one night with the clothes on their backs. Mark is a testament to the fact that violence does not always beget violence; sometimes it fosters deep empathy for other victims.

———

In the summer of 2020, I was invited by a member of candidate Biden's team to record a brief speech for the 2020 Democratic National Convention. I was conscious of a certain risk—not everyone in the domestic violence world, and not all victims and survivors, are Democrats. I didn't want to alienate anyone. But I felt that Biden was a friend to the cause, and I could not say no to the chance to speak about this problem before an audience far larger than any I had ever addressed.

The message I recorded ran along with those of Mariska Hargitay of *Law & Order*, and Carly Dryden, a young survivor and activist from It's On Us, which works to prevent and address college sexual assault. I talked about that day in the parking lot, when Cedric left me for dead. I said that at the time I didn't even know the name for what was happening to me, but that since then I've made ending domestic violence my life's work. I knew exactly what my message needed to be. First, we have to do something about domestic violence. Second, if you are a victim or survivor, you can make it.

The speech was both a thrilling milestone for me and a cause of pain. David was so proud. He taped it and watched it repeatedly, and told everyone about it. But it was a traumatic trigger for him, too. Even as he appreciates what it takes for me to be out there telling my story, and respects me for doing that, it brings back everything that happened. David went through a lot of pain, much of which he is still struggling to deal with, and I never want to add to that pain. But our past is a shared past, and I also have to do what I do; my work as an advocate has allowed me to rebuild myself and help others. I imagine that just about everyone who has spoken out about domestic abuse or sexual violence has had to navigate that tension between public advocacy and the wish to protect those they love. There is no right answer to the question of how to strike the balance. There is only doing the best you can, proceeding responsibly and with compassion.

The DNC appearance was virtual because of the Covid pandemic, which had resulted in nationwide lockdowns beginning the previous March. The lockdowns had led to a predictable rise in domestic violence, but also to a heightened awareness in the general public of some of the tools of abusers, especially control and isolation. I think a lot of people who hadn't given much thought to what it was like to be trapped at home with an abuser were suddenly imagining that. The lockdown didn't turn someone into an abuser, but it created the conditions that made abuse easier and that made accessing support or safety much more difficult. Victims had no privacy to call hotlines, and shelters often had to reduce their capacity in order to comply with the need for social distancing.

By now we have a lot of data that gives an idea of what was unfolding during what the UN called the "shadow pandemic." Domestic abuse rates shot up around the world after January 2020, rising an estimated 25–33 percent globally compared to the previous year. In the U.S., various metrics—including arrests for domestic violence, calls to helplines, and calls to the police—reflected that rise. Many abusers use some form of tech to track their partners, often downloading stalkerware or spyware apps on their phones, and tech abuse also rose dramatically in 2020. Antivirus companies reported that by June, there had been a 780 percent increase in the detection of monitoring apps and a jump of 1,677 percent in the detection of spyware.

A study conducted at Brigham and Women's Hospital in Boston compared wounds and organ injuries consistent with domestic abuse from March to May 2020 with those from the previous three years. The researchers found that although the overall number of people reporting domestic violence had decreased during that period, the incidence of physical injuries involving strangulation, weapons, stab wounds, and burns that doctors were seeing was higher, and the injuries were more severe. The findings suggested that victims were reaching out to health-care providers at the last possible minute, in the later stages of abuse.

Every aspect of support services and the criminal justice system was scrambling to adapt to the new conditions. One particularly harrowing scene, which went viral, involved a Michigan court proceeding on Zoom. Coby Harris had been charged with assaulting Mary Lindsey with the intent to "commit great bodily harm less than the crime of murder" and had been released from jail as his case was pending. At a certain point in the hearing, Mary tipped off the prosecutor that her alleged abuser was actually tuning in from within her apartment—in direct violation of the no-contact order. The prosecutor, the judge, and the police all acted swiftly, and the police arrived at the apartment and arrested Harris, likely adding witness intimidation to the charge he was already facing.

In ordinary times, the courtroom would not have been closed but would also not have been broadcasting to the world. In an effort to maintain judicial transparency, the courts had unwittingly retraumatized Mary. The whole episode gave the public a rare view of the kind of intimidation that is so incredibly common in domestic violence cases. The video was removed from the court's own streaming channel, but it is still viewable online, with Mary's face obscured. As I write this, it has been viewed 14 million times.

Like so many organizations, NCADV recovered from the shock of that first wave of the pandemic and figured out how to get on with our mission. Rachel had been working closely with the National Children's Alliance and other groups, both within and outside the NTF, for more than a year to change a federal law related to the Victims of Crime Act (VOCA). The Crime Victims Fund, set up by VOCA, is the largest pool of federal funding for victims of crimes, providing grants for victim compensation and assistance programs. The Fund has been particularly useful for victims of domestic violence and sexual assault.

Money for the Fund comes not from tax dollars but mostly through federal criminal fines, the bulk of which are from white-collar crime. By 2020 deposits into the Fund had dropped to a historically low level—from over $6 billion in the mid-2010s to about $500 million. The decline was largely because the Justice Department was increasingly entering into deferred prosecution and non-prosecution agreements, and the penalties from those went into the general treasury instead of the Crime Victims Fund. The result was big cuts in funding to our field.

Along with our partners both within and outside the NTF, we lobbied hard for a change in how the Fund was financed, and in July 2021, the Senate unanimously passed a bipartisan fix to VOCA that redirected those penalties from the deferred and non-prosecution agreements into the Crime Victims Fund. Other stipulations in the new law include offering states additional flexibility to provide compensation even when victims have not interacted with law enforcement. It will take time for the Fund to be fully replenished, and in the meantime programs are still facing cuts, but we expect the law to make a huge difference for victims and survivors of domestic violence. By September 2021, we had already seen an extra $224 million deposited into the Fund.

It was a victory for victims and survivors, and a testament to the hard work of all those advocates. The fight to see VAWA reauthorized was more protracted.

Since its original passage in 1994, VAWA has been reauthorized four times; the third of these lapsed in 2018, and for the next three years, VAWA programs received their annual funding through the appropriations process. Finally, in February 2022, a bipartisan group of four senators—Diane Feinstein, Dick Durbin, Joni Ernst, and Lisa Murkowski—announced an agreement on proposed legislation to reauthorize VAWA through 2027. On March 15, the VAWA Reauthorization Act of 2022 was signed into law by President Biden. I traveled to Washington, D.C. and delivered the opening remarks in the East Room of the White House before the President took the podium to celebrate the signing.

The reauthorization enhances and modernizes VAWA, particularly in its recognition that survivors are a varied group with a wide range of needs and life circumstances. It includes key provisions that focus on rape prevention and education and the reduction of dating violence; the enhancement of judicial and law enforcement tools; holding non-Indian perpetrators accountable when they commit domestic or sexual violence on tribal lands; and specific services for marginalized communities, such as LGBT survivors.

What the bill does not do is close the boyfriend loophole, which has excluded certain people convicted of stalking or abuse from laws limiting the ability to obtain firearms. (Existing law applies to a limited range of relationships, such as when the abuser and victim are married or have cohabited or had a child together.) All four of the bill's sponsors wanted to see the loophole closed, and NCADV and our partners have long felt strongly about this. Approximately half of female homicide victims in this country are killed by current or former male partners, and female victims of domestic violence are eleven times more likely to be killed by their male abuser if that person has direct access to a gun. But the bill was unlikely to receive the needed votes in the Senate if it closed the loophole. It was a big disappointment, but I will continue to work hard to ensure that everyone who has been subject to abuse is protected from gun violence, including from dating partners. If someone is pointing a gun at you, it doesn't matter what your relationship to that person is—the damage the bullet will inflict is the same.

———

Shortly after I appeared at the Democratic Convention, there was a voicemail left on my phone that didn't quite make sense to me, a man I had never met saying something about the convention. I promptly forgot about it. I get a lot of strange calls. Then an email appeared in my inbox, which I didn't realize was from the same man, and which I also ignored. Like everyone, I get more email than I have time to read. And then the man wrote a second time, and I noticed that his email address was Simon & Schuster. He wanted to talk to me regarding writing a book about my life.

As the idea settled in, and then later, as I began to work on the book in earnest, I noticed my anxiety level rising—a feeling that was broadly familiar but also new and distinct from other periods of anxiety I've had. Over the last thirty years or so, I've often challenged myself. *Let me poke the bear*, I'd think, *and see what happens.* Followed often by, *Oh my God, the bear is awake, what am I going to do now?!* The book felt like the biggest bear of all. The old tapes in my head were revving up. *Who do you think you are?* I began to say to myself, *Hm, maybe I've poked the bear one too many times . . .*

What was going on? I have told my story more times than I can count, to more audiences than I can recall. But in my speaking role I feel I'm serving as an educator, working for the good of all survivors, to try to create a society that is more just and compassionate toward them and that takes seriously the abuse they've suffered. Writing a memoir has been different. It's been a process of peeling away layer after layer of feeling, trying to recall and describe the emotional and psychological effects of years of abuse; I've had to excavate some difficult relationships. Instead of just laying out the events, as I do when speaking, using the main plot points of my story to shine a light on a larger problem, I was now teasing out my deepest feelings about those events, in order to present them to anyone who might care to look. And all the time the question nagging at me: *Will anyone be hurt by this?*

It was easier to revisit some memories than I had imagined it would be. Other things caught me off guard and left me with a fresh sense of mourning. It turned out I didn't always know where I was most raw. But even at sixty, I'm still looking for growth. Maybe it was never knowing my father. Maybe it was that neighbor who stopped me on the street when I was a new mother and said, in so many words, *You'll never amount to anything*. Maybe it was Mrs. Malcolm telling me the opposite. Or my mother, in her own complicated way, believing in me.

This book is not meant to be a record of how I got all better. I'm not 100 percent okay. Who is? Sometimes I crash and burn. I isolate more than is healthy, and friends have to nudge me out. I just want to make that clear, as Aly Raisman said about the consequences of her own abuse. As much as I applauded those young women for calling out their abuser, ensuring that he was held accountable, the immense courage it took to come forth, I also appreciated their honesty about the ongoing struggle of healing from abuse. We like a narrative of recovery, triumph over adversity. I'm all for triumphing over adversity, but there is often an expectation that when survivors come forward, when they've gotten free of an abusive situation, they're going to have all the answers and carry on with extraordinary strength. We are still human, though, and we've been marked by the things that have happened to us. And for every case that gets media attention, there are millions more survivors who quietly keep going, even when they don't feel strong or feel like they have any of the answers. I take heart from other survivors, and I know that it's okay to be triggered. I go through it, and I move on. What happened to me doesn't rule my life. So what I hope this book *will* be is proof of what's possible, that we can accept that some struggles continue but that the bad days always end, and that there are so many things to feel joy about. Because I also love life. I can be gregarious. I laugh a lot, loudly, and dance in the supermarket aisle if the music is right. I *have fun*. I drink wine with the Usual Suspects and I am dedicated to my six grandkids and three great-grandkids, and I'll keep poking the bear for as long as I'm able.

PART IV

Designing Solutions

The first time my husband beat me, I was hurt and disappointed—but I wasn't surprised. It was what I had seen growing up, and what I had absorbed from the culture. For a number of years, I essentially resigned myself to psychological and physical abuse. *I guess that's just the way things are*, I thought. But domestic violence isn't *just the way things are*. It's the way that we, as a society, have *allowed* them to be.

More than 10 million adults in the U.S. experience domestic violence annually, the vast majority of them women, and the effects ripple through our society. Domestic violence takes a huge economic toll in health-care costs and lost productivity. It is a problem that the legal and criminal justice systems have not been able to successfully address, and it is horribly bound up with the problem of gun violence.

We need to provide the best possible support for victims and survivors of domestic violence—emergency shelters, appropriate interventions from law enforcement and the judicial system, and longer-term social services. But intervention is a Band-Aid, a response to a problem that shouldn't exist in the first place. We have to get beyond treating the effects of violence and start addressing its causes.

If I had all the money in the world, one of the first things I would support is more research into why men abuse. We need to have a much larger conversation about that, and about how violence is accepted (and even encouraged) in a culture that equates masculinity with dominance, that devalues women, and that continues to shift responsibility for violence from perpetrators to their victims. We cannot assume that violence inevitably begets violence—it is a factor, but many perpetrators don't come from violent homes and many people who do grow up with it never go on to abuse. I challenge us to think outside the box about why violence happens and what we can do to prevent it. Only when we have a better understanding of the reasons behind domestic abuse can we focus on those interventions most likely to disrupt the progression toward violence and establish an evidence base for what works.

In the pages that follow, I discuss domestic violence from a range of perspectives: understanding its causes and how we might prevent it, intervening to stop its escalation, supporting victims and survivors, and holding offenders accountable. I look at the changes we need to make—both in the legal and policy realms and in terms of pervasive cultural attitudes—if we are to reduce and eliminate domestic violence. How can we more effectively support victims as they try to find safety from their abusers, navigate systems, and regain their autonomy? How can we hold perpetrators accountable in a way that isn't simply punitive but serves to disincentivize them and others from continuing to abuse?

The discussions around these issues are complicated; we won't solve them tomorrow. Our understanding of how to prevent and respond to domestic violence evolves alongside other changes in the way we think about our cultural, judicial, and policing practices. There will continue to be disagreements in my field, which is not an unhealthy state of affairs. Some things we know—that the presence of a gun significantly increases the likelihood that a woman who is being abused will be killed. But there is much we still don't know, particularly about changing the behavior of those who abuse and meaningful alternatives to incarceration. We have to keep trying to find out what works, then scale up those approaches that evidence shows to be most effective. I don't have all the answers. No one person or organization does. But I have hope. More and more people are joining the conversation about sexual and domestic violence. Victims and survivors are speaking out and being heard. Men and boys are becoming increasingly involved in prevention efforts. The more allies we have, and the clearer we are about keeping survivors at the center of whatever we do, the greater the possibility for change.

CHAPTER 17

Causes and Prevention

Who Is Violent and Why?

We cannot begin to address the problem of domestic and sexual violence until we are honest about the perpetrators. In virtually every category of violence throughout the world—from school shootings to genocide to serial killing to gang warfare to rape—men and boys vastly outnumber women as perpetrators. Men in the U.S. murder at at least seven times the rate women do. Of the murder-suicides involving an intimate partner in the U.S., 95 percent of the murder victims are women. Approximately 80 to 85 percent of domestic violence victims are women.

Yes, there are people who abuse and murder all along the gender spectrum. There are certainly male victims of sexual and domestic violence, as well as trans and nonbinary victims. And of course, most men are not abusive or violent. I can't state those things emphatically enough. But the same systems and cultural attitudes that produce men who abuse and murder women are also producing the men who abuse and murder men and boys. We are so deep in the matrix of male violence that we regard it as natural or inevitable. If we don't challenge this status quo, we are abandoning not only the many female victims of male violence but also the boys and young men who are enculturated into it, and whose lives are ruined by or lost to violence. Hamish Sinclair, who has worked for decades with abusive men, has described our reluctance to name the perpetrators as a kind of meta-violence, in that the silence only serves to perpetuate the conditions that enable violence.

When we talk about the reasons for domestic abuse, we need to be clear about the difference between risk factors (or correlations) and more fundamental causes. We have to be careful about justifying domestic violence by finding "explanations" for it. There *are* risk factors—several applied to my own husband. They are not an excuse, but we need to understand them.

Those who study the causes of domestic violence, such as Leigh Goodmark, have described various social and economic risk factors that have been found to correlate with an increased likelihood of domestic violence. Household income is one of the strongest of these. While women of all socioeconomic classes experience domestic abuse, the lower a woman's income, the more likely she is to be a victim. Underemployed and unemployed men are more likely to be perpetrators of domestic violence. Low-income neighborhoods have higher levels of domestic violence.

Another risk factor is substance abuse. It is estimated that men are eleven times more likely to commit violence when they have been drinking, and that up to 70 percent of men who use violence are abusers of alcohol. But the relationship between alcohol and domestic violence is complex. Some research has shown that the association between drinking and re-assault disappears when male attitudes of dominance change—that is, rather than drinking being the driver of violence, the heavy drinking and the violence may both be symptoms of the same underlying attitudes.

The presence of a gun is a risk factor in terms of increased lethality, something I'll talk about more later in relation to the need for more effective gun laws. We know that if an abuser has direct access to a firearm, it is eleven times more likely that he will kill his partner. Race also correlates with domestic violence. In 2019, Black females were murdered by males at a rate more than twice that of white females. Femicide is actually the leading cause of death in the U.S. among Black women between the ages of fifteen and forty-five. Where the relationship could be determined, 91 percent of those women knew their killers, and 93 percent of the homicides of Black females were committed by Black men. Perhaps one of the most talked about correlates for domestic violence is childhood exposure to violence or direct experience of it. It is estimated that nearly half of abusive men grew up in homes with an abusive father or stepfather.

Me at thirteen years old.

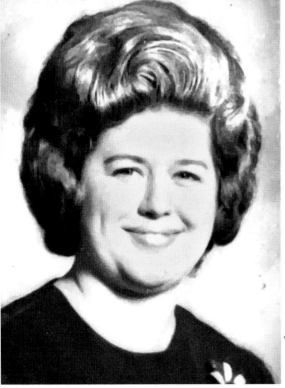

Mrs. Malcolm, 1970.

David and me, 1980.

Mom and me, 1990.

David and me at my graduation party, 2001.

My graduation from University of Denver, 2001.

Pam and me, 2000. We decided we would take a studio portrait to commemorate our friendship.

Regi and me today.

The Usual Suspects, 2014. Many have come on board and a couple
have departed since this photo, but all are wonderful!

Women's March with my friends Cindy and Ann, January 2017.

Gabby Giffords and me at a gun violence
prevention event, 2015. I adore this woman.

Courtesy of the White House

President Obama and me at a CNN town hall
on firearms, 2016. I was so very honored.

Angelina Jolie, Zahara Jolie-Pitt, and me being
greeted by President Biden, 2022.

A brief chat with President Biden in the Green Room before celebrating
the Reauthorization of the Violence Against Women Act, 2022.

Mrs. Malcolm today.

Me today.

Finally, there are some psychological correlates. Certain mental health issues, such as antisociality and insecure attachment, have been linked with the likelihood of domestic violence. Psychiatrist James Gilligan, who has worked extensively with prison populations, has written about the interplay between respect, shame, and violence. Gilligan notes that the less self-respect people have, the more they depend on respect from others, and that this desire for respect spurs many men to violence. "Violence occurs when people see no means of undoing or preventing their own humiliation except by humiliating others; indeed, that is the underlying purpose of inflicting violence on others." While domestic violence is a particular kind of violence, the demand for respect is certainly an element in many abusers' mindsets.

What Domestic Violence Isn't

Myths about domestic violence abound. Before we go any further, we should put them to rest. Domestic violence is not primarily a problem of anger management or a loss of control. As Lundy Bancroft, author of *Why Does He Do That?*, writes, "When people conclude that anger causes abuse, they are confusing cause and effect. . . . Abusers carry attitudes that produce fury." In my case, it was not that Cedric wasn't angry with me—his fury the evening of the shooting was such that he could hardly speak straight—it was that his anger was so disconnected from any legitimate cause. I had left him, and for that he would kill me. From Cedric's point of view, *his* anger was not the problem. The problem was *my* anger, that I had dared to express it. What had driven him to a murderous rage was his realization that he had lost control of me, not of himself.

If domestic abuse were an anger management problem, then those who abuse would be lashing out all over the place. But the majority of abusers are able to target their anger. Cedric reserved his abuse for me—and, less frequently, David. He didn't get into fights at work, or in bars, or in the grocery store. He didn't hit his mother. (Bancroft, who works with abusive men, describes the response he invariably gets when he asks them if they've ever treated their mothers the way they treat their partners. The very idea appalls them. The implication is that you *can* treat your wife or girlfriend like that, as long as you have a good enough reason.) Abuse isn't the result of out-of-control feelings or emotional problems that can be addressed through ordinary psychotherapy, conflict-resolution workshops, or couples counseling; the latter can actually be dangerous for victims, as they may feel safe enough in the therapy room to speak freely, only to suffer the consequences later when they are alone with the abusive person.

Another myth is that batterers lash out because they are unable to express their feelings, and if we just helped them become better communicators, the violence would cease. But domestic violence is not evidence of a man's inability to express his needs or feelings; it is actually the *means* by which he expresses them.

If abuse is a choice, as I firmly believe it is, then the question is not which circumstances "caused" someone to be abusive, but why someone is choosing, in response to any circumstance at all, to abuse. At what point do risk factors and cultural norms give way to personal responsibility? We should certainly support the creation of jobs and the kind of wages that enable people to provide for their families and to enjoy the self-esteem that comes with that. And we should work to create safer homes, neighborhoods, and communities. But just improving economic or social circumstances isn't going to address what's happening at a deeper level, which is the idea that a reasonable and legitimate reaction to life's stressful challenges is the subjugation, harm, and abuse of the person you claim to care about.

We need to get at this deeper level, because we cannot always eliminate risk factors. We have no control over what happened in our childhoods. Jobs come and go, financial security can fluctuate. (Women lose jobs all the time—in fact, domestic violence has a terrible impact on women's livelihoods and ability to retain jobs—and they don't turn to abuse; many men lose jobs but don't make their partners pay for the bad feelings that triggers.) If we don't root out the belief that abusing another person is a valid way of gaining respect or re-establishing self-esteem or masculinity, then we are still only at the level of secondary fixes.

The "P" Word

Domestic violence has complex roots that date back to long before someone actually begins abusing. But underneath all the risk factors and correlations lies a more fundamental cause: very deep-seated attitudes about women that enable and encourage domestic and sexual violence.

The desire for power and control that underlies domestic violence arises from an interplay of cultural norms, values, and beliefs that tells men they *should* enjoy power and control, that their dignity depends on it. (One of the reasons lethality rises dramatically after someone has left an abuser is that the abuser is reacting to that loss of control and trying desperately to regain it.) These norms also imply that when that power and control are threatened or denied, men are justified in re-establishing it—often through violence. We call this set of beliefs and values *patriarchy*.

Patriarchy refers to a social system organized along the principle of male supremacy and power. This power structure is embedded, overtly or subtly, in all aspects of public life—political, social, cultural, religious. But it is also embedded in personal relationships and domestic settings. Patriarchy is a zero-sum game. It values male power and control at the expense of women and children, who are human beings of lesser value. It also drives violence between men.

Entitlement is one of the best lenses through which to view the whole spectrum of violence against women (as well as institutional forms of sexual violence, such as we've seen in the Catholic Church). Sexual harassment, exploitation, trafficking, rape, domestic abuse, femicide, incels—all manifestations of a sense of entitlement run amok: I am entitled to enjoy your body, to profit off it, to imprison it, to render it black and blue. Entitlement as a driver of sexual harassment was highlighted when #metoo broke and many men were unmasked as abusers of their power. In 2018, the *Washington Post* reported that television journalist Charlie Rose had allegedly physically and verbally sexually harassed women who worked for him over several decades[‡]. One of the thirty-five women who came forward was Sophie Gayter. Sophie said she was twenty-two when she was groped by Rose, who was at least seventy years old at the time. "I had been there long

---

[‡]   Rose issued a statement saying that although he did not believe all of the allegations were accurate, he did admit that he had "behaved insensitively" at times. "I always felt that I was pursuing shared feelings, even though I now realize I was mistaken."

enough to know that it was just the way things went," she said. "People said what they wanted to you, people did what they wanted to you."

I can't think of a more concise description of entitlement than that.

Allied with entitlement are possessiveness and ownership, both things with which victims of abuse are all too familiar. The abuser's idea that he has the right to do with you as he wishes only grows stronger as a relationship progresses. This belief, taken to its extreme, shows up again and again among abusers who kill their victims, or attempt or threaten to kill them. In the police recording of Natasha Trethewey's mother speaking to the man who would soon murder her, he says, "I said I was gonna kill you when I got home. And I would ask myself why, and I would say because if I can't have her, nobody will."

We can define sexism as gender prejudice plus power, and misogyny as dislike, contempt, or hatred for women added to that ingrained prejudice. The organization Men Stopping Violence has described the cascading effect: sexist cultural norms and messages about women lead to personally held beliefs about women, which in turn lead to expectations men have for their female partners; men are then able to rationalize their abuse when women act with autonomy rather than according to the men's wishes. The point is not that sexist or misogynist norms and beliefs force men to choose abusive behavior, but rather that they provide the justification from which those choices can flow.

Finally, I want to say something about guns. There is a lethal connection in this country between ideals of hypermasculinity and gun use. One of the worst mass shootings in the U.S. was in Newtown, Connecticut, in 2012, when twenty first-graders and six adults at Sandy Hook Elementary School (as well as the shooter's mother) were killed. Nine families sued Remington Arms, alleging that their Bushmaster assault rifle was marketed recklessly and inappropriately to civilians, especially troubled young men. (The lawsuit was settled for $73 million in 2022, and Remington agreed to allow the families to make public thousands of pages of internal company documents obtained during the suit.) The promotional campaign included one advertisement that showed the Bushmaster along with the tagline: "Consider your man card reissued." It doesn't get much more blatant. Not every gun owner is a danger to society, and the vast majority of men with mental health issues are not violent. But if boys in this country grow up being told they should dominate, and if weapons manufacturers tell them that to walk the earth without an assault rifle is unmanly, it will all keep ending in tragedy for a lot of people.

So the answer to the question of why men seek power and control may be twofold. One reason is that they are taught they are entitled to it. The other is that power has its own rewards. In the domestic realm, these perks include financial control, the prioritization of an abuser's needs, the certainty that he will get his own way, and the intrinsic satisfaction of exercising power.

Intersectionality of Causes

Conversations in my field continue to revolve around how systems of oppression interact to perpetuate conditions that condone violence against women and children. On a recent NCADV webinar, a colleague noted that addressing domestic violence is truly anti-oppression work. When we confront the problem of privilege that is at the heart of oppressive social and economic systems, we are doing anti–domestic violence work; this is because all systems of oppression, from colonialism to the Jim Crow South to workplace harassment, tend to share certain characteristics—intimidation and control of those without power, erosion of autonomy and personhood, blame of the powerless and derogatory distortions about them, and so on.

At NCADV, we believe that domestic violence involves an individual using force or threat to achieve and maintain control over another person, and that responsibility for abuse lies ultimately with the abuser. But we also know that violence is fostered and condoned by society-wide abuses of power and domination such as sexism, racism, homophobia, classism, anti-Semitism, able-bodyism, ageism, and other oppressions—belief systems created by human beings that do not, by design, distribute power equally. Some groups have always had more power than others, and domestic violence is one manifestation of this inequality. Domestic violence also feeds back into so many social problems, making the conditions of women's lives worse in the form of homelessness, mental health crises, lost wages and poverty, and other costs.

Stories and Allies

In the last few years alone, there has been an explosion of story-telling, kicked off in large part by the #metoo movement. To those of us working to end domestic violence, #metoo has been both inspiring and disheartening. On the one hand, it is evidence that attitudes can change and that we have the potential to dismantle abusive power structures. On the other, #metoo and the massive media coverage it generated were largely silent on the subject of domestic violence. The #WhyIStayed movement, initiated by Bev Gooden, didn't gain similar traction; neither did NCADV's own social media campaign using the hashtag #survivorspeaks. I still have faith in them, and we will continue to promote them to ensure that those who share their stories there are heard.

The reasons for the different fates of the two movements shed a lot of light on the challenges we face if we are going to reduce and prevent domestic violence. One big reason is the difference in context. Domestic violence tends to be a private and even hidden matter, with only the woman and her abuser (and sometimes children) present when abuse occurs. By contrast, workplace harassment and even workplace assault are more public, likelier to be witnessed by others and experienced by more than one person in a given setting; a woman who reports them can have her story corroborated. Certain high-profile men exposed by the #metoo movement were accused by several women, and women found credibility in numbers. Law professor and activist Catharine MacKinnon has noted that while keeping track of cases of campus sexual abuse over decades, she found that it typically took three to four women testifying that they had been violated by the same man in the same way to begin to make a dent in the man's denial, which meant that a woman, for credibility purposes, was one-fourth of a person. We take this situation so much for granted we hardly blink, but imagine if you'd been mugged and the police told you that it would really help your case if you could find three other people who'd recently been mugged by the same person. That we unthinkingly approach cases of sexual assault or harassment this way only underscores the depth of our society's distrust of women.

It may be true that within the #metoo movement, domestic violence was hiding in plain sight—that some women who used the #metoo platform *were* victims of domestic abuse but didn't say that specifically, because so many women still live in fear of retaliation. In 2018, the National Domestic Violence Hotline and its youth outreach arm, "love is respect," saw a 30 percent increase in contacts from the previous year, something Katie Ray-Jones, the CEO of the Hotline, attributed in part to #metoo. Victims of domestic violence, she said, were identifying with the national conversation, but felt safer speaking confidentially than on public platforms.

One thing that became clear at the outset of #metoo was the power of story-telling. As the movement gained momentum, many men who would have regarded themselves as aware of the dangers and harassment women face confessed to being stunned by what they were hearing. People would be equally stunned to hear what women have to say about domestic abuse and to see just how many of their coworkers, friends, and family members have suffered it. By telling our stories to the wider community and bringing domestic violence out of the shadows, we can destigmatize abuse and create understanding in those who may be largely unaware of it but who can become allies.

There are different ways of acting as an ally. One of NCADV's advisory board members is Aaron Steed, who cofounded Meathead Movers with his brother in 1997. Aaron noticed early on that some of the calls they were getting were from women fleeing abuse, so they began to provide their moving services to victims of domestic violence at no cost. They have since officially partnered with several domestic violence shelters in California, and Aaron continues to encourage other businesses to get involved in supporting victims and survivors.

Another great supporter of survivors is Ben Talei, a California-based plastic and reconstructive surgeon. Ben worked with NCADV's Cosmetic and Reconstructive Surgery Program, which helped survivors who needed surgery to treat injuries sustained through abuse. In 2017, he and his brother undertook a cross-country marathon drive from New York to Miami to Los Angeles to raise money and awareness for NCADV and the pro bono Face-to-Face Surgery Program. Like Aaron, Ben is focused on finding concrete ways to support survivors. Both men have said to us what every nonprofit wants to hear from business owners or individuals eager to help: "We won't ask a lot of you, we just want to serve."

Recently I read about another ally named James Smith-Williams. One day in 2019, when James was a student and football player at North Carolina State, he was among about four hundred male athletes who went to hear Brenda Tracy speak. Standing up in front of this huge crowd, Brenda described the night in 1998 when she says she was drugged and gang-raped by four men at a party, two of them football players at Oregon State University. Brenda contacted the police anonymously and they collected evidence from the scene. Four men were arrested and charged with a range of crimes, including sodomy and rape. But in the end, Brenda dropped the charges—in part, she says, because she received death threats from people who didn't want to see football players get in trouble. She subsequently endured several years of despair and suicidal ideation. (The two OSU players were each suspended for a single game.) When James heard Brenda's story, he decided he wanted to get involved. He soon began to work with her and her nonprofit, Set the Expectation, which focuses on prevention of sexual assault and domestic violence.

James now plays in the NFL for the Washington Commanders and still works with Brenda. When it was revealed by the *Washington Post* that there had been widespread sexual harassment and misconduct from former male employees of the team, he put out a lengthy statement on Twitter. "I believe that being silent on things you know to be wrong is almost as bad as committing the act yourself," he wrote. (The NFL fined the team $10 million for fostering a workplace culture where sexual harassment, bullying, and intimidation were common.)

Brenda has talked about the ripple effect of story-telling. "Anytime I go anywhere to share my story or work with any group of people, no matter how big or small the room is, I might not change the world, but I might inspire the person that does." Since 2016, Brenda has visited more than one hundred college campuses and spoken to some fifty thousand athletes, talking to them about violence against women and how silence, even among good men, is complicity.

I would not tell anyone that they have a responsibility to share their story publicly. But those of us who feel comfortable can do that. Emotion has a role in changing attitudes. Even if we had infinite government resources and all the best programs in the world, if we don't tell our stories, we can't convey the scale of the problem, and we can't connect on a personal level. Without that connection, and the empathy it enables, it's very hard to bring about change.

Education and Prevention Programs

Charlie Stoops, cofounder of the Chicago-based Center for Advancing Domestic Peace, wrote recently that we should consider approaching men's domestic violence as a behavioral and public health issue, similar to smoking, and address it through large-scale, adequately funded prevention and intervention efforts that are covered by health insurance. This view seems both radical and self-evident. The anti-smoking campaign didn't focus its efforts on getting passive smokers to change their behavior or quit their jobs in smoke-filled bars or offices; it focused on those doing the damage and worked on changing *their* behavior. It made smoking, to a large extent, socially unacceptable, and tens of millions of Americans gave up a highly addictive drug. Could we achieve a similar change in attitudes and behavior with domestic and sexual violence?

Ideally, we need to start educating people about violence, and about equality and respect, when they are young. We need to dismantle the norms that legitimize domestic and teen dating violence, and teach young people to recognize it and have the courage to call it out. I'm not talking about assumptions that only boys grow up with; girls and young women absorb them, too, and we need to help them understand that they are not responsible for someone else's behavior (or for fixing it), that they have the right to feel safe and happy, and that it is not their job to remain hopeful of change in damaging or dangerous situations.

Author Leslie Morgan Steiner said of her first marriage, "I would not have told you, at that time, that I was a battered wife. I thought that I was a smart, strong, independent woman in love with a troubled man, who I was trying to help." If a Harvard-educated professional can believe that it's her responsibility to nurture someone who she says literally held a gun to her head, how can we expect vulnerable girls and young women in troubled environments to recognize harassment or abuse and extricate themselves? We have to help them. This means going into schools and teaching girls to recognize controlling or abusive behavior, empowering them to get away from abusers, and imbuing them with the confidence they need to become autonomous, independent people with a solid sense of their own boundaries. It means teaching them to not just say, "Stop calling me," but to say, "I won't allow that and I'm breaking this off with you because your behavior is wrong."

There is a lot of emphasis now on "healthy relationships," and I'm all in favor of those, but I think we aren't doing enough for individuals, to ensure that boys and girls and teens, whether they're in a relationship or not, understand their right to safety and respect and understand what it means to be respectful of others. If we can work on this from the time boys and girls are toddlers, teaching them about the value of other human beings, particularly those who have been historically marginalized, then maybe we have a chance.

I recall vividly a talk I gave to a group of teenaged girls who'd been identified as high risk. During my talk, a pager belonging to one of the girls was going off repeatedly. Suddenly it dawned on me what that was all about, and afterward I spoke with her. Just as I'd assumed, it was her boyfriend. She told me that he was paging her all the time because he cared about her so much. I shook my head. "Don't mistake that for love," I said. "Anyone who needs to check on you every ten minutes to know where you are—that's not love, that's control." I was once a sixteen-year-old girl on the brink of a relationship with a controlling young man. What if I'd had the tools and the confidence then to recognize those behaviors and attitudes of Cedric's that had caused me a niggling sense of discomfort? I might have walked away sooner.

Teen dating violence is depressingly prevalent and a risk factor for domestic violence later in life. One-fifth of female high school students and over 13 percent of male students report being physically or sexually abused by a dating partner. The trauma is significant: Half of students who report dating violence and rape also report having attempted suicide, as compared with 12.5 percent of non-abused girls and 5.4 percent of non-abused boys. To add to the tragedy, just a third of those who say they have experienced dating abuse ever tell anyone about it, suggesting not only the presence of fear and shame but also a lack of confidence in adults to deal effectively with the problem. One area we could expand on in our prevention efforts is looking at more comprehensive approaches—for instance, how prevention of teen dating violence could be part of strategies to reduce other forms of violence and abuse, such as bullying, cyber abuse, and suicide.

Young people live their lives online, which raises two immediate concerns—one is cyber abuse, and the other is ready access to pornography. The vast majority of young people have viewed online porn, either intentionally or unintentionally, often before they are in their teens, and the messages they're internalizing are unhealthy—for starters, that sex is something men do *to* women rather than *with* them. A study in 2020 found that 45 percent of heterosexual scenes on Pornhub depicted aggression (including choking, gagging, and slapping); in 97 percent of these scenes, the target was women, and their response to the aggression was most often either neutral or positive. Pornography has become the de facto sex education, for boys especially, shaping assumptions and expectations that encourage abusive behavior in the real world. Research is showing that perceiving porn as an accurate depiction of intimate relationships is associated with an increased risk of sexual aggression.

We need to counter the forces—media, entertainment, pornography—that are warping our children's understanding of intimate relationships by discussing these issues with them and investing in educational programs that teach healthy manhood, female empowerment, and respectful relationships.

Such programs should also inform teachers about how to recognize signs of teen dating violence and what steps they can safely take to intervene. The National Domestic Violence Hotline provides comprehensive education and support to young people through its "love is respect" project. A confidential helpline, live chat, and text services operate 24/7, but the project also provides practical resources such as training, tool kits, and curricula for educators, counselors, and other service providers, with the goal of promoting healthy relationships and preventing abuse. There are similar curricula being rolled out elsewhere, and we need to mainstream these programs into our educational systems.

One of the things that allows violence against women and girls to persist, and even enables it, is the silence of men and boys who witness their peers behaving abusively. Imagine if, instead of viewing sexual and domestic violence as inevitable dangers women must do their best to avoid, we saw them as problems men needed to solve. Individuals such as Aaron Steed, Ben Talei, and James Smith-Williams, and organizations like Men Stopping

Violence, Wica Agli, and A Call to Men, are critical to our anti-violence work. Many men and boys who abuse may be more responsive when confronted by other men rather than by women. We need men's involvement if we are ever going to change the socialization of masculinity and the aspects of it that contribute to the ongoing epidemic of violence. We need to move on from the old definition of male strength as power over others, and commend the strength of men and boys who take a stand against violence. As Jackson Katz has written, "It is ironic that men who speak out against men's violence against women are often called wimps, when they actually have to be more self-confident and secure than men who remain silent in order to fit in and be one of the guys."

There is growing evidence that engaging boys and young men in dating abuse prevention programs such as Safe Dates, Green Dot bystander intervention training, Peace Over Violence, and Coaching Boys Into Men can reduce violence and give young people tools to intervene. Coaching Boys Into Men, developed by Futures Without Violence, leverages the influence that athletic coaches have with young men. A study published in 2019 by Elizabeth Miller of the University of Pittsburgh looked at its effectiveness with middle school boys. Miller followed nearly one thousand male athletes in forty-one middle schools in Pennsylvania over a two-year period. Coaches used guided conversations to promote attitudes of gender equality, and to talk about respectful behavior toward girls and regressive ideas about masculinity (the glorification of male superiority, the prioritizing of men's needs in relationships, and so on). They discussed physical and verbal aggression, online abuse, and consent, and also taught positive bystander behavior.

By the end of the sports season, the boys who went through the program reported being much more likely to speak up when they witnessed other boys behaving disrespectfully. A year later, those who were dating had 76 percent lower odds of abusing a romantic partner than nonparticipants. They were also better at recognizing abusive behaviors.

Finally, we have to think about the communities where we live and raise our children. If our communities truly held offenders accountable—sending the message that abuse is not tolerated—and stood up for and protected victims, we could end domestic and dating violence. Evidence on community-level approaches to prevention is just beginning to emerge, and I'll talk more about the role of communities in Chapter 20, but we know that certain neighborhood characteristics correlate with increased risk of domestic violence (poverty, high unemployment, the presence of violence), and it seems likely that community characteristics such as social cohesion within neighborhoods and the presence of support for those experiencing domestic violence can serve as protective factors.

CHAPTER 18

Intervention

Encounters with Police

On August 12, 2021, police in Moab, Utah, pulled over a white van that was speeding. Inside was a young female passenger, in tears, and a male driver. Gabby Petito and her fiancé, Brian Laundrie, were on a cross-country road trip. About three weeks later, Laundrie would return home to Florida alone. Petito's remains were subsequently found at a campsite in Wyoming. She had been strangled to death. Laundrie's body was discovered in October at a nature reserve in Florida. He had died of a self-inflicted gunshot wound. In January 2022, the FBI announced that Laundrie had admitted to killing Petito in a notebook of his that was found with his body.

Gabby Petito's case got huge media coverage, and that became its own story, what Gwen Ifill once called the "missing white woman syndrome," in reference to the disparity between the media attention given to white women who go missing and brown and Black people who suffer the same fate. (Indigenous women experience the highest rates of domestic violence and homicide in the U.S., and in the past decade missing Indigenous people have been about 100 percent more likely to be missing after thirty days than white people.) But Petito's case is also remarkable in that we have over an hour of body cam footage from that police stop. The video is excruciating to watch, especially when we remember that these are the last images Petito's family have of her. As an advocate, I have to hope that the clip becomes a training tool for police.

The encounter seems to start out well enough. I believe these officers had good intentions. They see that Petito is upset and they immediately separate her from Laundrie; they speak to her gently and empathetically. But as discussions with the young couple progress, the police completely misread the situation. Despite Petito's obvious emotional distress ("At no point," one officer will later write, "did Gabrielle stop crying, breathing heavily, or compose a sentence without needing to wipe away tears . . ."; she was also reported to be hyperventilating), and Laundrie's jokey, friendly demeanor, the police decide that Petito is the "primary aggressor" and that Laundrie is the "victim." They take care to photograph small scratches on Laundrie's arm and face. They eventually decide that what they are seeing is a mental health crisis—Petito had mentioned her OCD and stress, and blamed herself for the turmoil—rather than a domestic violence incident. They separate the couple for the night, arranging for Laundrie to stay at a hotel and, after suggesting that a shower might help her relax, sending Petito off in the van, still in tears.

By this point, Laundrie has thoroughly charmed the officers. He fist-bumps one as he departs, and in the police car on the way to the hotel, he and another officer chat about various things, including women and their anxieties. Laundrie had earlier told the officers, in that *you-know-women* sort of way, that Petito was "crazy." One officer says, "She seems a lot like my wife." In the car, the officer tells Laundrie how medication really helped his wife to calm down.

The stereotypes are beyond depressing. Much of that bias was likely something the officers viewed as harmless, not understanding how it was affecting their reading of a domestic violence situation—their tendency, for instance, to see a hyperventilating woman not as terrified or traumatized by her partner but as suffering from her own self-generated mental health crisis. (Smile and roll your eyes. *Women are so emotional!*) There was a female Park Service ranger on the scene as well, who spoke to Petito on her own and warned her that her relationship with Laundrie had the signs of something "toxic." She implored Petito to view this moment as a chance to make a change in her life. The ranger later said she wished that she had found the right words to help Petito see that she deserved better. "This wasn't a good day for anybody," she added. "We thought we were making the right decision when we left them."

Unfortunately, the kind of missteps and misinterpretations that took place that day are far too common when officers respond to domestic violence calls. They simply don't understand what they're looking at.

More than a month after the traffic stop, audio of a 911 call was released. The caller had phoned 911 shortly before the police pulled the van over. He reported having seen Laundrie "slapping" Petito in the town. "They ran up and down the sidewalk. He proceeded to hit her, hopped in the car, and they drove off." (This caller was a model bystander: He saw something, promptly said something, and provided the police with a description of the van and a license plate number.) A statement was never obtained from the 911 caller, something that came out in a review of the handling of the case that was released in early 2022. The review recommended more domestic violence investigation training and legal training. The city of Moab has committed to hiring a trained domestic violence specialist.

Police have come a long way since the 1970s and 1980s, and some of our best and most enlightened trainers of police are officers or retired officers. Mark Wynn, who has trained three or four generations of officers, describes the change in attitudes as night and day. There are more women in policing, and male officers talk about domestic violence differently than in the old days. (It should be noted that rates of domestic violence are higher for police than for the general public, an obvious problem if we are trusting officers to respond appropriately to domestic abuse calls.) But we need to keep educating police. Domestic violence calls can be incredibly volatile and dangerous to them, and if police aren't trained to understand the dynamics and the history of a situation, frustration with victims can result. Officers may assume, naturally enough, that if a woman is being harmed and calls 911, she will want the abuser arrested, not realizing that an arrest is no guarantee of her safety and may even place her in greater danger. They need to understand what can happen in those few moments between the call—made when the victim was desperate to stop the violence—and their arrival on the scene: that she has begun to fear that she will lose her children; that she's afraid her partner will lose his job if he's arrested; that she fears even worse retaliation if he's arrested and then released. Many victims know that when bad things happen to their partners, worse things happen to them. In the face of a complex, dangerous, and traumatic situation, victims employ immediate survival strategies, which may appear irrational to police who haven't been properly educated about domestic violence.

I want to touch on a couple of points I think are key about police response to domestic violence calls. One is the human element of the encounter. The arrival of police may be the first brush with the system a victim has, and it will shape what she thinks she can expect if she asks for help in the future. If she feels that she has been treated well, that she has been heard, that she hasn't had her fears trivialized or her decisions criticized, then even if she doesn't leave that day, the encounter has planted a seed that there is something out there for her, systems in place staffed by people who understand what is happening and whose primary concern is her safety. Ideally, a police response would also involve a victim advocate who appears on the scene once it's safe. A good advocate helps the victim assess what is best for her safety, makes sure she has what she needs, and can support her later in moving on to the next step when she's ready. Many police departments have domestic violence units, which work closely with victim advocacy groups on responding to domestic violence calls.

The other critical piece of a good police intervention is knowing that traumatized victims require specialized interview techniques. Trauma can impact the brain in many ways, shutting down higher-level cognition and allowing the more primitive parts of the brain, which are far better at recording sensory details than factual details, to take over. People working in criminal justice long thought that inconsistencies in a victim's statements indicated lies, when in fact inconsistencies are entirely normal for someone who has been traumatized. (In addition to the psychological trauma, many victims of domestic violence have sustained traumatic brain injuries.) Evidence-gathering techniques have been developed that take into account what we now know about how the brain responds to trauma and the physiological reactions to a crime, such as trembling, flashbacks, nausea, terror, and the recall of sounds and smells. As one commentator remarked about the Gabby Petito video, her extremely distressed state was more telling evidence than a scratch on Laundrie's arm. The police certainly noticed her distress; they just didn't know what it meant.

Protection Orders and Guns

A key piece of domestic violence intervention is the protection order (PO), sometimes called a restraining order. POs are civil court injunctions limiting or prohibiting the contact that an abuser is allowed to have with a victim. POs in the U.S. can cover dating violence, sexual assault, and stalking, as well as domestic violence. Anyone who feels threatened can file for a PO, and police often file for emergency protection orders when called to a scene. Emergency orders last for a few days to two or three weeks, depending on the state. During this time, a hearing with a judge will be scheduled, and the judge may issue a final PO, lasting for about a year in most states, often with the possibility of renewal when the order expires. It is very rare that lifetime POs are issued, and many states don't have statutes allowing for them. Violation of a PO is a crime, and the consequences can include prosecution, imprisonment, and/or a fine.

For various reasons, the impact of POs on victim safety is mixed. Some studies have shown that women with final POs experienced an 80 percent reduction in physical abuse compared to women with none. Women with only emergency POs, however, may be more likely than women without them to be psychologically abused. In addition, while POs can be critical for stopping harassment and nonlethal assault, they may be less effective in stopping an abuser whose intent is to commit murder, and they may even be a catalyst for retaliatory violence.

There is also the challenge of enforcement. A PO is simply a piece of paper, and violations are common. As Cedric said to me, a protection order won't stop a bullet. It is believed that around 40 to 50 percent of domestic abusers violate the orders, with even greater rates of violation in cases of rape and stalking. A PO or bail condition violation is a strong indicator of further violence. The risk of violation, and the corresponding danger to victims, is greatest soon after a PO is issued: About one-fifth of murders committed against women by intimate partners occur within two days of an order; one-third occur within a month.

But because there is ample evidence that POs are associated with reducing or stopping domestic violence, we have to ensure that they are effectively deployed and enforced. Procedures for obtaining them should be as clear and comprehensible as possible for survivors. Given ongoing changes in the laws, the many types of POs, and the different jurisdictions in which they are granted (including tribal orders that cross jurisdictional lines), everyone involved in issuing and enforcing POs must be provided with up-to-date training. Critically, we must insist that POs be better enforced. Inconsistent enforcement raises the level of danger for survivors by giving them a false sense of security, sends a message to abusers that they can behave with impunity, and may discourage victims from seeking help in the future. One study out of Johns Hopkins showed that nearly half the women with a PO who were killed by intimate partners had already had multiple POs. We also have evidence that enforcement improves compliance. It has been found that abusers who are arrested for violating POs are about 30 percent less likely to assault their partners again than those not arrested.

Linked to POs is the issue of access to firearms. A 2015 study found that 92 percent of women killed with guns in high-income countries were in the U.S. Every country in the world has an abuse problem. But ours is the only high-income country in which abusers have ready access to firearms. The mere presence of a gun within a relationship is a terrifying tool of control, but it also leaves a victim at much higher risk of death. The statistics on this are clear. More than half of domestic violence homicides involve a gun, and when an assault involves a firearm, the victim is eleven times more likely to die. Domestic homicides rose by 26 percent between 2010 and 2017, and this rise tracked with gun ownership: between 2010 and 2016 the number of guns manufactured in the U.S. doubled. (In this same period, domestic homicides committed by means other than a firearm decreased.) States with the highest rates of gun ownership (the top quartile) have a 65 percent higher rate of domestic homicide involving a firearm than states with the lowest rates of firearms ownership.

In the mid-1990s, two major statutes came into force related to domestic violence. They prohibited the purchase or possession of a firearm by anyone who was either subject to a PO or had been convicted of a misdemeanor crime of domestic violence. Since then, several states have passed laws that match or elaborate on the federal statutes. Laws vary from state to state—for example, whether law enforcement must confiscate firearms when responding to domestic violence calls; whether officers are allowed to search for guns; whether any gun confiscated must have been used in the present incident, and so on. Neither of the gun prohibitors is permanent. The first lasts for the duration of the PO. In the case of misdemeanors, in most states, if you do not re-offend you are eligible to have your conviction expunged or set aside, which allows you to possess firearms again under federal law.

Studies have shown that limiting access to firearms for people subject to POs under state and federal law reduces gun-related intimate partner homicides from between 7 and 16 percent. In forty-six of the largest U.S. cities with state statutes that reduce access to guns for individuals under POs, intimate partner homicide risk from firearms decreased by 25 percent between 1979 and 2003. Unfortunately, prohibitions are often not consistently enforced—because law enforcement officers either lack a process for recovering firearms held by domestic abusers or are unsure of their exact legal authority, or because judges are reluctant to impose the prohibitions or simply lax in doing so.

There is such a thing as responsible gun ownership. But if you use a firearm to hurt or terrorize someone, if you are a known abuser, then you have relinquished your right to possess a deadly weapon. Over the last several years, understanding has improved among the public and legislators about the links between domestic violence and firearms (as well as about domestic violence as a warning sign of mass violence). Just about everybody now accepts that firearms place victims in greater danger, but there are disagreements over how to address this.

We can improve our enforcement in several ways. The Fix NICS Act, passed in 2019, is helping to ensure that domestic violence gun prohibiting records are entered into the background check system. We could go further, screening all POs for evidence of firearms and requiring the surrender of them, as was done in a pilot project in two California counties that recovered hundreds of guns. We should also close the various loopholes that allow abusers to retain their firearms. The so-called "boyfriend loophole" (which means that someone who is or was dating the person they abused, but does not live with them or share a child, is not subject to the gun prohibition) needs to go, as does the Charleston loophole, which allows abusers to purchase guns without a completed background check if the check isn't finished within three business days. No one should be able to purchase a firearm without a background check.

Finally, to those who might suggest, as many have, that the answer to domestic violence is for women to arm themselves, my view is absolutely not. Support for the idea of arming victims has come from various quarters. In 2016, a bill passed in Virginia that would allow anyone over the age of twenty-one who is protected by a PO to carry a concealed handgun without a permit or training for forty-five days. The owner of a firearms store in Baton Rouge offered free concealed-carry training to women with POs after a local sheriff said women should shoot their abusers in the backyard, before they could get into the house.

After Cedric shot me and fled, and no one knew where he was, some people tried to convince me to get a gun. It isn't that I never thought about harming Cedric. I had my thoughts of revenge and relief. I just never wanted to use a gun. I was terrified of them; they were what he used against me. I didn't want to kill anyone, and I didn't want to end up hurting myself by accident. And if you have a gun and decide to use it against your abuser, you had better make sure you kill him. Because if you don't, you could be facing some really terrible consequences.

Aside from my personal aversion to guns, there is a practical reason why I don't think arming victims is the answer: Guns don't make us safer. Studies have shown that purchasing a handgun is associated with a woman's increased risk of homicide. Women who were murdered were more likely to have purchased a handgun in the three years prior to their deaths. Victims and survivors have to make their own choices, of course, but unless you understand the dynamics of domestic violence, I think it's very dangerous to be telling victims to arm themselves. And of course there are numerous cases where women have ended up in prison for killing their abusers. There is no guarantee that if you shoot him in the backyard, your troubles will be over.

But possibly the most important reason why I don't think it makes sense for victims to arm themselves is because it's a "solution" of more violence. We need to disarm those who are violent and abusive, not adopt the tools of violence ourselves.

Preventing Escalation

We know that domestic abuse tends to escalate over time in terms of its severity and lethality—whether that takes days, months, or years—and that a misdemeanor domestic violence offense is a strong predictor of more serious violence. The earlier we intervene, therefore, the greater chance we have of saving victims from harm. A few steps have been taken to this end, including the use of mandatory arrests, lethality assessments, and even dangerousness hearings and pretrial detention.

Mandatory arrest laws began to appear in the late 1970s and became more widespread in the 1980s following the first big study of the effect of arrest on domestic violence, which found lower rates of re-assault if the police arrested the perpetrator when responding to a domestic violence call. It was common for activists at the time to support stronger arrest policies as, up to then, police had consistently failed to take domestic violence as seriously as other crimes. Many states now have some form of mandatory arrest laws, which require police to make an arrest when responding to a domestic violence call, regardless of the victim's preferences, if there is probable cause to believe violence has occurred. These policies are also called pro-arrest or preferred arrest policies if officers are encouraged but not required to arrest an offender.

Since that first study, a more nuanced picture of the costs and benefits of mandatory arrest policies has emerged. For one thing, they seem likely to deter some offenders much more than others (those who are married or employed and have more to lose through arrest), while offenders who already have a higher number of prior arrests appear just as likely or even more likely to engage in repeat violence regardless of another arrest. In many cases, arrest can actually leave victims *more* vulnerable to retaliation by abusers with a prior history of violence. Mandatory arrest may also be disempowering for victims by taking away their ability to decide what is best for their own situation and handing that power over to the police. But again, each victim and each situation is different; victims have also reported feeling that the policy relieved them of the responsibility of pressing charges, and the law can result in offenders receiving treatment they otherwise would not have gotten, protection orders being issued, and harsher penalties for repeat offenses.

I have my own misgivings about mandatory arrest. If the police on the scene lack adequate training in the dynamics of domestic violence, they may not be able to identify the primary aggressor. (The Gabby Petito case was a tragic example of the primary aggressor being misidentified.) Police unable to tell who is at fault have often arrested both parties. Arrests of women increased dramatically under mandatory arrest policies, without evidence that their use of violence had correspondingly increased. And of course any law can be used against a population if you have racial or other biases. Black Americans are legitimately leery of involvement with the criminal justice system, and from the outset saw that mandatory arrest policies were likely to have a disproportionate effect on communities of color. In that sense, these policies may actually disincentivize certain women from reporting domestic violence—Black women, but also undocumented immigrant women whose status, or that of their partners, would be endangered by an arrest, and who are not willing to risk deportation.

We have learned over the last few decades that domestic violence is not a problem we can arrest our way out of. Arrest and detention are sometimes necessary to protect victims, but they are not long-term solutions. They should be used as part of a coordinated, broad-based strategy to prevent further violence.

Arrest shouldn't be a blunt instrument wielded indiscriminately. We now have tools that can help us use arrest more selectively. Preferred arrest models—which encourage officers to arrest under specific circumstances, such as in the case of injury, the use of a weapon, or violation of a restraining order—allow police to retain discretion and recognize that not all victims have the same needs. Danger assessments can identify those aggressors at highest risk of re-offending, while also assisting victims in devising the most appropriate safety plans. Originally intended for use by victim advocates or health-care professionals to assess risk of femicide, danger assessments are now widely used to also predict nonlethal domestic violence escalation. The assessments, which were created by Jacqueline Campbell in 1985, are a statistical (rather than clinical) prediction of future violence, based on domestic homicide record reviews and known risk factors. Non-fatal strangulation, for instance, is associated with a significantly higher risk of subsequent homicide. Controlling behaviors, amphetamine and alcohol use, and forced sex are other indicators that lethality is likely to increase.

Over time, danger assessments have been modified, and versions have been created that are situation-specific—for example, one for immigrant women and short forms for use by first responders in the emergency room or police at the scene of a domestic violence call. The Lethality Assessment Program, developed by Campbell and others in 2005, is an intervention as well as a risk assessment strategy. Police inform victims of the assessed risk, then immediately offer to connect those at high risk to domestic violence services. The best risk assessment tools include the victim's own perception of danger and a clinical evaluation, as well as the actuarial results. The picture that emerges can then be used to make decisions about incarceration, probation, or court-ordered offender intervention.

There was no risk assessment carried out when Cedric kidnapped me. No one even used the term "domestic violence." Within hours of having been arrested for holding me at gunpoint and threatening my life, he was out on bail. Should he have been? Denying bail is rare in non-capital cases, though some jurisdictions in the U.S. have adopted provisions for denial in certain domestic violence cases on the basis of dangerousness. Pretrial detention is a legal mechanism that has to be used carefully in order not to infringe on constitutional rights. But where there is strong evidence to support a charge, and the domestic violence offender is deemed dangerous and very likely to re-assault or even murder if released, preventative detention could keep a victim alive. Dangerousness hearings, now used in some states, can assess risk factors for severe violence, utilizing danger assessments and other tools. Such a hearing would have shown that Cedric was very likely to re-offend and that I was almost certainly in grave danger. He had a long history of abuse and stalking; he had threatened my life multiple times and with a gun; he had threatened to commit suicide; he was abusing drugs and alcohol; he had already violated one protection order (issued immediately after I left him and he tracked me down at the apartment I had rented). All of those factors would have indicated that violence was likely to escalate. I was lucky to survive being shot in the head. Had Cedric been detained following the kidnapping, I would not have had to rely on luck for my survival.

Focused Deterrence

Most crimes that police respond to are single-incident, but domestic violence tends to be multiple incidents over a period of time, a history of behaviors, not all of which leave physical evidence or qualify, legally, as criminal. If police and first responders know how to talk to victims and which questions to ask, and understand the many forms abuse can take, they can build that history. They also need access to a strong universal reporting system and databases. One of the obstacles to assembling a clear picture of an abuser's past is that crimes are often not properly recorded. If a domestic violence "enhancer" has been removed (an enhancer is an add-on to a crime that can increase the penalty), it is impossible to build an accurate picture of previous crimes, histories of abusive behaviors and violence, and patterns of interactions with the system. Domestic violence should be viewed as a fundamental element of a crime, not a trivial add-on to it, and if we don't know it happened we can't protect victims or hold perpetrators to account.

The kind of background data that can tell us whether this is someone's first interaction with police for domestic abuse or his tenth is all the more important in light of promising new approaches to intervening earlier with abusers, before the pattern becomes ingrained or lethal, and targeting harsher responses at habitual offenders.

In 2011 law enforcement in High Point, North Carolina, embarked on a program of "focused deterrence," a crime reduction strategy developed in the 1990s in Boston to combat gang gun violence. For years, High Point had had the highest rate of domestic violence in the state. Despite the po-lice department's use of protection orders, a pro-arrest policy, and active prosecution, they weren't making progress either keeping victims safer or controlling the most violent abusers. So they partnered with researchers, anti-violence advocates, prosecutors, and community members to roll out a strategy of focused deterrence, which concentrated on ensuring genuine and predictable consequences for offenders. The approach is something like a lethality assessment and is intended to direct resources at chronic offenders while keeping criminal justice involvement to a minimum for those deemed less dangerous and less likely to re-offend.

In the High Point model, offenders are placed in one of four categories, with each category having its own sanctions, ranging from going on a watch list for those with no previous charges who aren't arrested (category D) to aggressive prosecution of those with a history of domestic violence (category A). The two interim categories can involve meetings (sometimes in jail) with police, community members, and domestic violence service providers, in which specific sanctions (e.g., bringing new charges, raising bail, tightening the conditions of probation) are laid out as the consequences if the offender continues to abuse. But the offender is also offered certain services such as job skills training. Victim advocates work in tandem with police and ensure that victims' needs and safety are looked after and that they are also offered specific services at each class of intervention, from information about services at the D-level to safety planning after offender arrest at the A-level.

High Point's trip-wire system has led to reduced intimate partner homicides and a decrease in cases where victims are injured. Versions of it have been rolled out in other police departments around the country.

Batterer Intervention Programs

The first batterer intervention programs, or BIPs, were founded in the late 1970s, in parallel to the beginning of the shelter movement, and often at the behest of women who called on men to begin working with other men. As new statutes were put in place in the 1980s, arrests of men for battering rose, and the courts began to use BIPs as a sentencing option. Consequently, the demand for them grew, and the programs became more aligned with the criminal justice system.

BIPs typically place men in psychoeducational groups led by either male or female counselors. The counselors aim to teach abusers about the causes of their violent behavior and the consequences of it for others, as well as introduce them to strategies for interrupting the dynamics of their own violence, resolving conflicts nonviolently, and changing the attitudes used to rationalize and justify abuse.

Although BIPs have become a primary response to domestic abuse, the evidence for their effectiveness has been mixed, with little proof of anything beyond very modest results. There are a number of challenges for those of us trying to understand what works and what doesn't. Accurate information on re-offending is hard to get, as both offenders and victims tend to underreport abuse. Response rates are low for all follow-up data, and largely reflect only those men who have finished programs—an incomplete picture given the high drop-out rates in BIPs.

In order for abusers to change within BIPs, they have to be ready to relinquish the deep sense of entitlement that tells them they have the right to bully, control, and batter. Many opt not to do the work. But I don't believe we should give up on these programs. Research on them has grown more sophisticated over the last ten to twenty years, and we are gaining insights into which aspects of BIPs are more effective and how the programs might work better.

One critical element is ensuring that there is timely referral through the courts, followed by monitoring and swift, clear sanctions for failing to comply with the requirements of the program. Edward Gondolf, who has studied BIPs extensively, found that men who entered a program under pretrial referral (within a couple of weeks after arrest) and who had to reappear in court periodically to confirm their participation in the BIP had far fewer no-shows and much higher completion rates. He also found that noncompliance among those referred was the single strongest predictor for re-assault.

People I know who work in BIPs stress the need for these programs to be longer than they usually are. Many say that a very small percentage of abusers will come into a BIP horrified by what they've done and genuinely hoping to make changes, but that the vast majority are full of justifications, denial, and excuses. As I was writing this, I happened to read an update on Zac Stacy, the ex–NFL player captured on a home surveillance video in November 2021 in which he appeared to be brutally beating his former girlfriend in front of their infant son. Stacy, who was arrested and released on bail, allegedly slapped, punched, and threw Kristin Evans across the room into a television. Despite the video of the assault having gone viral, the evidence there for all to see, Stacy subsequently claimed that Evans "staged" the beating, because she was bitter about his not wanting to be with her anymore. Echoing Brian Laundrie, Stacy also questioned his victim's mental stability, suggesting that she was suffering from postpartum depression. Whether Evans was suffering from postpartum depression or not, she didn't throw herself across the room. In my opinion, Stacy has a long way to go if he is going to emerge from his denial. Beliefs and behaviors so ingrained aren't going to be rooted out in twelve or thirty-six weeks, when people are attending programs for an hour and a half each week. Most offenders need sufficiently strong external motivation—in the form of sanctions for noncompliance—that can tide them over until, hopefully, they internalize the motivation.

One thing that has become clear is that batterers are not a homogeneous group, and BIPs should therefore not take a one-size-fits-all approach. We need to carefully assess each person and their history in order to identify the most appropriate intervention, a process that takes time. Too many people are lost within those first weeks when we are trying to get at the specifics linked to their abuse. A key to tailoring interventions to motivate behavior change is understanding what motivates abuse. Is someone abusing simply because he's sadistic? Is he controlling because he has severe abandonment issues brought on by trauma? Or has he just gotten the message growing up that he, as a man, should be in charge? These aren't excuses, they are factors that need to be taken into account and addressed. It still comes down to power and control, but there are different motivations for wanting to achieve that power and control.

Juan Carlos Areán, who directs the Children and Youth Program at Futures Without Violence, has been working with domestic violence offenders for many years. He has begun to use fatherhood to motivate change, as he found that many abusers were more affected by the realization of the impact their violence had on their children than on their partners. Empathy for children isn't the end point of the BIP but a starting point for developing an abuser's understanding of the harm he has caused. (A word about couples counseling. Although some people argue that it can be helpful for a carefully identified cohort, especially as an adjunct to batterer intervention programs, I would be very cautious about this. Couples counseling is intended to address issues that are mutual, and battering is not a mutual issue. And the presence of abuse negates the possibility that the counseling sessions can take place on a footing of equality for both partners.)

Alongside tailoring interventions for the batterer there must be ongoing monitoring of risk to the victim. Survivor voices and survivor safety should always remain at the center of any BIP approach. Risk assessment and risk management are complex, and questions remain about which risk assessment tools are best under which circumstances, who should be conducting the assessments (court psychologists, victim advocates, probation officers, BIP staff) and at what points, and who is best positioned to oversee risk management. Risk is less a fixed category or static condition than a dynamic state that requires ongoing assessment and planning, along with a coordinated response from a range of services.

Practitioners in the field of offender treatment, such as Juan Carlos, speak of the need for consequences *and* change. "There is a lot of fear that if we focus on trauma people will use it as an excuse," he says. "People who use violence will use almost anything as a justification. We know that. But it doesn't mean you don't talk about trauma, culture, religion. You must give it the weight it deserves while not letting people use it as an excuse." He puts great emphasis on connecting with offenders as human beings, supporting positive change and addressing barriers to making healthier choices—but alongside strong consequences. For a long time, there was a focus on shaming in BIP programs, and we've essentially realized that shaming doesn't work when you're asking someone to change. It is also true that feeling ashamed is not the same as accepting responsibility and being open to working toward change. As much as we fight for victims not to be shamed, we need to refrain from shaming batterers. Juan Carlos and others practice compassion without collusion. Keeping strong accountability—both inside and outside the legal system—and also empathizing with and supporting an offender. Meeting them where they are and finding out what will motivate them to change.

If we are going to get men involved in anti-violence programs before they reach the stage of arrest or come to the attention of police, we have to create an environment that makes perpetrators feel comfortable enough to come forward, even anonymously on helplines. We can do more at the level of school and community education to encourage help-seeking, much as we do for substance abuse. In the UK, the Respect Phoneline for perpetrators has been operating since 2004, and Sweden, Australia, and Nova Scotia all have helplines for abusers. A Google search here in the U.S. for violence prevention hotlines will turn up several options for victims but virtually nothing for offenders. In 2021, the 10 to 10 Helpline became the first such hotline in the U.S., serving western Massachusetts. A project to create a national Violence Prevention Hotline in the U.S. does exist, modeled along the lines of the National Suicide Prevention Lifeline, but so far it is only a plan, and a great deal of research and discussion will have to go into any such project.

CHAPTER 19

Serving Victims and Survivors

Service Provision and Deterrence

In the early days of VAWA, services for victims tended to be about immediate safety. Getting a woman into a shelter was often the beginning and
the end of the support on offer. Much has changed since then in terms of
the availability and range of services to help survivors rebuild their lives,
but there are still significant gaps in service provision, most glaringly in
the area of post-shelter housing and legal services. If we are going to better
serve survivors, we need to minimize the barriers that prevent or discourage
them from contacting services and provide for their needs once they do
reach out for help. All the services we provide—whether housing, medical
care, legal advocacy, or financial support—should be informed by an understanding of the dynamics of domestic violence, and the particular kinds
of trauma it causes. They also need to be grounded in an understanding
that different cultures and groups—such as immigrant, Indigenous, and
trans populations—will have specific vulnerabilities and needs.

There has not been as much study done of the effects of victim services
on violence prevention as there has been of the effects of arrest. Evaluating
victim service programs has always been complicated. Most services are
delivered confidentially, and providers must ensure that any data collection
will not endanger a victim's safety or overburden someone still in crisis.
Service provision is also fluid; some victims might avail themselves of services for a night or two, while others have more long-term engagement. But

one study out of the University of Maryland looked at 2,221 victims and survivors over a sixteen-year period and compared the violence-reduction effects of three responses: reporting of domestic violence to the police, the arrest of the suspect, and the victim receiving services from agencies other than the police. The researchers found that while arrest had virtually no effect on reduction of future violence, simply reporting an incident to the police (with no resulting arrest) reduced revictimization by 34 percent. The deterrent effect may have to do with the stigma associated with police intervention and the practical problems someone faces if they are actually arrested. What had an even greater impact, however, was the use of victim services: It reduced revictimization by 40 percent. The impact of these two deterrents (calling the police and availing of services) could be linked, as officers on the scene may inform victims of their rights and options, and urge them to undertake domestic violence risk assessment and safety planning—actions that are often part of police response protocols.

Ironically, the availability of victim services seems to benefit male abusers as well. Domestic violence homicides began to decline in the 1970s (in 2014 they started to rise again, driven by an increase in firearms homicides), and several studies have found that much of the overall decrease was due to fewer women killing their male partners; male-perpetrated domestic homicides declined much less sharply. What this suggests is that resources that support women leaving abusers—such as protection orders, domestic violence shelters, and more liberal divorce laws—have enabled them to escape relationships before a killing occurs. Killing an abuser is generally a last resort for a victim, and having accessible services and legal supports may save not only her life but the abuser's as well.

Transitional Housing and Legal Protections

When we hear of someone suffering domestic abuse and wonder why she doesn't *just leave*, the answer might be because she has nowhere to go. Domestic violence is one of the leading causes of homelessness for women and children in the U.S.—between 22 and 57 percent of them who are in that situation are there because of it. A shortage of both emergency shelter options and affordable housing is regularly cited by survivors as the main barrier to being able to escape an abuser. In one nationwide study in 2020 it was found that 57 percent of more than 11,000 unmet requests for services from domestic violence victims on a single day were for emergency shelter and housing. We need to improve enforcement of legislation specific to domestic violence and federal housing, and strengthen existing laws to ensure that victims and survivors can quickly access stable and affordable housing, as well as flexible funding to cover things like security rental assistance or security deposits; they must also be protected against housing discrimination and the penalties they often suffer based on the behavior of abusers.

Often a victim's first experience of safe refuge outside her own home will be at an emergency shelter. Shelters offer immediate short-term safety, and can be lifesaving; they also offer victims help with seeking longer-term accommodation and accessing social services. But because they are only a temporary solution, and because affordable housing is in such short supply (it can take ten months or more to find stable and permanent accommodation), victims may hesitate to leave their homes for a shelter, knowing that when their thirty or sixty or ninety days there are up, they may wind up back home (with their abuser), or on a relative's sofa, or even homeless. We need to increase funding for emergency shelters, a first stop for many survivors, ensuring that we use coordinated interstate systems to locate the best options for shelter when those are not close to home, while also strengthening bridges to independent living.

Transitional housing is one such bridge, conceived around the unique needs of survivors for safety and confidentiality. Transitional housing is usually offered for a period of six to twenty-four months. The sites are operated by domestic violence service providers and include support services such as childcare, financial assistance, transportation, therapy, safety planning, and job counseling. The programs also link to wraparound services such as family law advice and health care. The units may be at a single location or at scattered sites. In some cases, residents may be able to transition in place to permanent housing. Transitional housing is a critical stepping-stone to independence. The U.S. Interagency Council on Homelessness has reported that on average 88 percent of participants in transitional housing funded under VAWA have a lower perceived risk of violence upon exiting these housing projects, while 74 percent exit to permanent housing of their choice.

An alternative to transitional housing is rapid rehousing, an approach to alleviating homelessness that offers accommodation for a shorter period of time (usually about six months). People are assisted in finding affordable permanent housing and provided with funds for things like moving assistance, security deposits, and household essentials. There has been a push lately to use rapid rehousing more often with domestic violence survivors. Six months is a very short time to expect someone who has left a traumatic and possibly violent home situation to transition to permanent independent living, and there are legitimate reasons to be wary of this approach for those fleeing domestic abuse. However, rapid rehousing can work for survivors provided certain conditions are in place. The process should be survivor-led (survivors identify the housing options they need and the resources needed to access them, and define safety for themselves), and advocates should focus on community engagement, educating landlords, police, local government, and housing councils on the dynamics of domestic violence and survivors' unique needs. Flexibility within the programs is critical, as rapid rehousing was not initially conceived with survivors of domestic violence in mind. Rapid rehousing programs must take into account the barriers unique to stability for survivors and tailor services accordingly. Some survivors may need only brief financial support to tide them over, while others will need support and housing that goes beyond a six-month window. The early months of independence from an abuser can be particularly precarious; a survivor may need to attend multiple court hearings, for instance, or to relocate due to threats to her safety, both of which can threaten job and financial stability.

In trying to secure affordable housing, victims often find themselves punished for the violent actions of their abusers. They can be unfairly evicted, and those living in public housing can face denial of housing benefits. Victims and survivors may have damaged credit, little to no savings, or insufficient employment history, particularly if they have been subjected to financial abuse. Because of "nuisance ordinances," which require property owners to evict tenants in the case of repeated police or emergency service calls, they may be evicted because they sought protection from abuse or stalking, whether or not the perpetrator lives on the premises. Property owners are often required to take action under nuisance ordinances, and end up evicting tenants, refusing to renew their leases, or telling them not to call 911. The result of these various measures is that victims are often forced to choose between abuse and homelessness.

VAWA reauthorizations have included provisions to protect victims from discrimination in federally subsidized housing—letting them remain in their houses while accessing criminal or legal procedures or when the subsidy is in the abuser's name; allowing for early lease termination; enabling public housing agencies to prioritize victims for housing; and forbidding those agencies from denying victims housing or evicting them on the basis of domestic violence alone. All states should pass laws that protect victims from eviction or from being refused rental accommodation based on domestic violence, and from penalties if they break their lease for their own safety.

Finally, there is an urgent need to fund the creation of more affordable housing stock. Since the mid-1980s, the amount of available low-cost housing has decreased significantly, while rents have continued to rise and wages for low-income people have been stagnant or grown too slowly. Lack of affordable rental options is a particular challenge in rural communities, where homeownership is the norm. What is true in general about the homelessness crisis is also true for survivors of domestic violence: There simply isn't enough affordable housing. All the eviction protections in the world mean nothing if you don't have a roof over your head.

Financial Support

Survivor safety is inseparable from economic security. One nationwide study found that about half the victims of domestic violence surveyed listed not having enough money or resources as the biggest barrier to leaving their abuser. Increasing access to resources that allow survivors to gain financial security is critical to enabling them not only to escape abuse but to engage in longer-term financial rebuilding. If they are to avoid returning to an abusive home or becoming homeless, survivors need job security, employment protections, and ready access to cash, utility, and food assistance. Financial independence not only keeps survivors safer, it empowers them, so that they can approach negotiations or legal proceedings from a stronger position.

We need to take a flexible approach to financial support. Not all survivors who leave their homes are financially dependent on their partners. In my case, despite the fact that Cedric had never wanted me to better my career prospects by becoming educated, I had always worked, so I was able to secretly save money to move into my own apartment and support myself and my son. But even someone in my position might need temporary financial assistance in order to leave an abuser—for instance, help paying off credit card debt (perhaps run up by the abuser) or paying for a security deposit on an apartment. And even though I was financially independent, I had to take leave from work after the shooting. I was fortunate that I had a job to return to. If I hadn't had certain job protections, I might have suddenly been out of work, trying to find employment and support David and myself while recovering from a traumatic injury and years of abuse.

Economic security for survivors means the same thing it means for everyone: the capacity to meet basic needs (housing, childcare, food, transportation, and health care) in the short term while saving for emergencies and the future. At least some of the legislation related to survivor support, employment, and assistance depends on individual states. We should ensure that all states enact statutes that remove economic insecurity as a barrier to leaving an abuser and that federal job-protection legislation, such as would be provided in the Healthy Families Act, is passed. The critical areas of focus include:

- Improving and extending paid and job-protected leave policies. "Safe leave" provisions allow employees to take job-protected time off for safety reasons—for instance, if they are the victim of any act or threat of domestic violence or stalking. Employees can use safe leave to attend to issues related to the violence they've experienced, including court hearings, medical treatment, relocation, and counseling.

- Making unemployment insurance available to anyone who has to leave a job in order to stay safe, by requiring states to include reasons relating to domestic or sexual violence on the "good cause" list for unemployment insurance.

- Providing job skills training, financial literacy, and education support. A survey by the Institute for Women's Policy Research reported that 83 percent of domestic violence survivors said that their abusive partners disrupted their ability to work. Many survivors will need support making up lost ground, particularly as they may now be sole earners.

- Ensuring that anti-discrimination measures are in place that prohibit survivors from being fired or not hired because they are currently experiencing or have experienced domestic violence.

- Making micro-grants more widely available for needs such as gas money, clothes for a job interview, or even a down payment on a house.

Trauma-Informed Care

All services need to be provided from a survivor-led perspective—survivors are the experts on their experiences and their decisions should be respected—and from within a trauma-informed framework. The trauma-informed approach means that anyone providing services should understand the physical, mental, and emotional impacts of domestic abuse. Trauma-informed care views survivor behaviors not as pathological but as ingrained adaptive reactions to having lived in an abusive, and perhaps life-threatening, environment. It also takes into account collective or historical trauma, which is critical when working with marginalized communities or immigrant populations.

It isn't only those who are working in direct service provision for survivors who should employ trauma-informed care. Health-care providers can also be trained to recognize the signs of trauma related to domestic violence and screen for evidence of physical abuse, reproductive coercion, and so on. Sometimes one of the few places an abuser permits a victim to go is to the pediatrician's office with the children. We should ensure that doctors are educated and equipped to support a victim safely if she does report abuse.

Immigrant populations face their own challenges, and abusers will often exploit a victim's immigration status in order to compound their isolation. If it is the abuser who is at risk of deportation, he may use that as a way to pressure a victim not to contact police. The situation leaves many victims having to choose between living with abuse and risking deportation or separation from family.

From the outset, VAWA has included provisions for reducing the vulnerability of victims to deportation, and subsequent reauthorizations have strengthened those provisions. But recently anti-immigrant sentiment has grown (and been stoked by political leaders), while local law enforcement has become increasingly entangled with federal immigration authorities. We need to redouble efforts to protect vulnerable immigrant victims of domestic violence. The most pressing and obvious way of broadening protections is to eliminate the cap on U visas. A U visa is for noncitizens who have suffered substantial physical or mental abuse and who are or will be helpful in the investigation or prosecution of that crime. U visas represent an avenue to safety for victims and survivors of domestic violence. The problem is that the U.S. government issues only ten thousand of these each year. About 85 percent of U visa applicants are approved, providing recipients with protection from deportation and permission to work. But more than thirty thousand applications are received on average each year, and the wait for approval is often five years or more.

A new policy came into force in 2021 to address the backlog. Applicants who have applied for U visas are now eligible to receive an interim "bona fide determination," which will allow them to work and protect them from deportation. This is very good news, but is insufficient. Congress should lift the cap on U visas to keep tens of thousands of immigrant victims of domestic violence safe.

Immigrant victims are often dealing with layers of trauma—the state violence they have fled in their home country, the abuse they have experienced in their own homes in the U.S., and the fear and uncertainty of living without full documentation. Abusers will often use misinformation about documentation and immigration status to instill greater fear and increase their control over victims, who are often not proficient in English. Service providers can empower victims by informing them of their legal rights, and also by doing broader outreach within the community to let people know that they do not need documentation to receive services.

Legal Representation

Imagine having to represent yourself at a court hearing. Now imagine that the person who has spent months or years terrorizing you, and perhaps your children, is sitting just a few feet away. Imagine that what is at stake is whether you and your children will be kept safe from that person through a PO. You have no legal training, no money to hire a lawyer, and you are in severe psychological distress from chronic abuse. Nevertheless, you have to make your case convincingly, without coming across as unhinged or hysterical, unable to reliably narrate your experience of abuse. You need to prove that you're traumatized enough by your abuser to need protection from him, but not so traumatized that you lose custody of your children. This is the situation in which hundreds of thousands of victims find themselves every year.

In a recent case in Connecticut, a young woman named Adrianne Oyola was trying to extend a PO because she knew that her baby's life was in danger from the father. But Adrianne had no lawyer; nor did she have any knowledge or experience of courtroom advocacy. She therefore didn't sufficiently detail the nature and frequency of the threats the baby's father had made. And there was no one to cross-examine the father. The judge saw no risk of "imminent harm" and refused to extend the PO. One week later, the father threw the baby from a ninety-foot-high bridge into the Connecticut River. He is now serving a seventy-year sentence for murder. We have laws (often problematic) that allow for parents to be jailed when they fail to protect their children from an abuser. In Adrianne's case, a young woman was *trying* to protect her child. It was the legal system that failed—by leaving her to fend for herself in the courtroom.

There are many dedicated agencies that support pro bono representation for low-income victims, but there are too few lawyers, and they sometimes have not been properly educated about the dynamics of domestic violence. Until recently, New York was the only state that guaranteed court-appointed representation for low-income victims in civil PO cases. In the wake of Adrianne's case, the governor of Connecticut signed into law a measure that provides lawyers to low-income domestic violence victims seeking POs. Pushback against funding legal representation in civil domestic violence cases comes mostly from those who believe it would be too expensive. But many studies have shown that the cost of providing legal counsel is much less than the costs incurred by continued abuse—including medical and mental health care, foster care when children are removed from violent homes, and absenteeism from work.

We know that having an attorney dramatically raises the probability that a PO will be obtained. One study found that 83 percent of victims who had representation obtained a PO, compared to only 32 percent of those without one. Access to legal representation can therefore reduce the likelihood of future violence.

So we can agree: A lawyer is a good thing to have. But not just any lawyer. As with every link in the legal or criminal chain, lawyers who represent victims must be trained in the specific dynamics of domestic abuse and the tactics used by abusers.

People whose safety, or even life, is in danger are being left to fend for themselves in courts all over the U.S. We need more lawyers. We need to fund representation for victims—it isn't just the humane thing to do, it has the added practical benefit of saving our society additional costs. If being able to obtain life-saving protection from an abuser is not dependent on the legitimacy of your claim but the availability of good counsel, we don't have justice.

Supporting a Loved One Who Is Being Abused

Many people have asked me over the years how they can help when someone they care about is being abused. The first thing to bear in mind is that the victim's safety is the most important consideration. Human nature dictates that when we see a friend or loved one in trouble, we want to rescue that person—this is commendable, and evidence that we care. But as difficult as it is, we have to resist the instinct that says we should tell them to leave their abuser. They likely know that, and have a clear understanding of the obstacles and dangers related to that decision. Insisting they leave before they are ready can backfire. Say instead, "Let me know if and when you are ready to leave, and I'll be here to support you." Tell them you are concerned for their safety (and that of any children), and make sure they know how to contact their local domestic violence program as well as the National Domestic Violence Hotline (800-799-7233 and TTY 800-787-3224). Offer whatever concrete forms of assistance you can, whether it's some cash, picking up prescriptions, collecting the kids from school, or providing a sofa to sleep on—whatever it is you can safely do.

We encourage discussion of a safety plan as a first step. There are detailed instructions on the NCADV website for devising a safety plan with someone who is being abused (https://ncadv.org/safety-plan-friends -and-family), so just a few broad points here. Listen to the victim, carefully, not just because you want to be supportive but because you may be called on at some point to back up their story. Assure them that anything they tell you stays in confidence. Try to get a clear understanding of what is happening, what kind of abuse your loved one is experiencing, and how they are managing their own safety. For instance, a good idea is to identify a code word that they can use when speaking to you that will let you know to call the police. Assure them that no one deserves to be abused, and it is not their fault, but that there is a good chance it will get worse. If they *have* decided to leave the situation, try to make sure that they don't tell the abuser, or anyone who might tell him, in advance. If you know where they are when they leave, don't reveal that location to anyone.

The second really important thing you can do is to refrain from judging the victim. Nothing about the situation, or the victim's choices, may seem rational to you. But judging won't help. By the time a victim opens up to you, they have likely experienced a great deal of humiliation, control, embarrassment, and shame. In sharing the truth with you, they are experiencing yet another level of vulnerability. Reassure them that you're there for them, that you aren't judging them, that you want to help. Absolutely resist the urge to say, *How could you let that happen to you?* or *Why do you put up with that?* The message you're sending when you say that is: *I would never let myself get into that situation.* I once read that when someone confides to us a painful or shameful experience, we should never respond with the phrase *I can't imagine*, because even if we're trying to honor their pain or acknowledge the severity of their trauma, the statement erects a wall between ourselves and the person confiding in us. It's not a big leap from *I can't imagine* to *I don't want to try*. Of course we don't know what certain things are really like unless we've been there. But we have to try to imagine. The refusal to do so leaves survivors of sexual and domestic violence stigmatized and isolated, cut off from the empathy and support they so desperately need.

CHAPTER 20

Accountability

What Accountability Is—and Isn't

Accountability isn't simply punishment, though it might include some form of that. It may mean, for a survivor of domestic abuse, that someone surrenders unearned power and privileges within a relationship. Or it may mean prison. But it is more than a simple apology or a sentence served. It involves an active reckoning on the part of the abuser with his behavior, a process by which a person who has harmed another, or others, commits to healthier behaviors and accepts that those others are entitled to hold him responsible if he fails to follow through on his commitment.

If our goals are to change behavior and keep survivors safe, then the most effective approach to accountability seems to be early intervention from a coordinated and holistic perspective. Any penalties for domestic and sexual violence should be firm, consistent, and proportionate to the crime. The devil, of course, is in the details. Who gets to decide on what is proportional and at what stages of the process? And how do we balance any punitive actions with the worst aspects of the carceral system: its dehumanization, its failure to deliver behavior change, and its history of discrimination against communities of color and other marginalized groups?

There is no shortage of examples to illustrate what the absence of accountability looks like. The prevalence of sexist and misogynistic attitudes causes our justice system and our society to take crimes of domestic and sexual violence far less seriously than we should; these attitudes also result in people focusing their empathy and concern on perpetrators rather than victims.

Brock Turner is one of the most obvious recent examples of this. Turner was a Stanford student convicted of sexually assaulting Chanel Miller. Turner's father became infamous during the trial for his line about his son's conviction having been a "steep price to pay for twenty minutes of action," but there was so much that was offensive about Dan Turner's statement on his son's behalf. Brock, he said, had been "deeply altered forever"—as though, having assaulted an unconscious woman, his "happy go lucky" life should continue unchanged. His son shouldn't go to prison, he argued, because he was completely committed to educating other college students about "the dangers of alcohol consumption and sexual promiscuity" and about how society can break the cycle of "binge drinking and its unfortunate results." Dan Turner clearly didn't get it. What happened was not an example of "promiscuity," which can be completely consensual. It was the result of one person acting violently upon another.

Judge Aaron Persky decided that a prison sentence would have a severe impact on Turner, and sentenced him to only six months in jail. (Turner was released after three months.) Persky, who was subsequently recalled by California voters following the sentence, remarked in the aftermath—and with no apparent irony—that there was "an underlying deep frustration among actual victims of sexual assault and women in general about the criminal justice system not taking sexual assault and domestic violence seriously. It's a very genuine and important problem. The passion is authentic, the end is justified, let's increase sexual assault reporting." Persky seemed oblivious to the fact that inappropriately lenient sentences such as the one he handed out to Brock Turner are a huge reason that it's so hard to increase reporting of these crimes.

The statement made by Turner's father reminds me of something that was written in the aftermath of Oscar Pistorius's trial for the killing of his girlfriend Reeva Steenkamp, whom he claimed he had mistaken for an intruder. Pistorius is now in prison for murder, though he got less time for killing Steenkamp than he would have gotten for killing a rhino. As Suzanne Moore remarked in the *Guardian*, "Women are not an endangered species, after all." The day before Moore's article ran, *Guardian* columnist Simon

Jenkins had published a piece in which he argued that, although Pistorius was clearly guilty, imprisoning him would serve no purpose. "Men such as Pistorius have had their lives ruined, their failings exposed and chance enough to reflect on their crimes and what they can do to atone for them. . . . Finding why he behaved as he did, and working to prevent others doing likewise, would be the most useful outcome of his crime." Tellingly, Jenkins does not once mention Steenkamp's name. It's all about the fallout for Pistorius.

The problem with this sort of "logic" is not that someone convicted of murder is incapable of remorse or of working to prevent others from committing such crimes. We know that this is possible. The problem is Jenkins's suggestion that Pistorius's experience of having had his failings exposed is somehow equivalent to Reeva Steenkamp having lost her life. The problem is also the fact that Jenkins presumes to know enough about Pistorius's inner reflections to declare that they entitle him to freedom. And the problem is the idea that sentencing Pistorius to prison negates the possibility of also looking at the causes of domestic violence.

This sleight of hand, which suggests that if we just use incidents of domestic violence as teachable moments, we don't really need to hold perpetrators accountable in any other way, ignores the fact that part of the ongoing problem of domestic and sexual violence is that so many perpetrators are never held to account. How can we claim to be taking such violence seriously if all we require of perpetrators is, as Dan Turner and Simon Jenkins suggest, that they give speeches or hold workshops? When we don't hold perpetrators of domestic and sexual violence accountable, the effects of that go far beyond that one case. We send a message that these crimes are not serious enough to warrant punishment, and we discourage other victims from coming forward.

The two cases I just discussed involve well-to-do white men. The differential application of justice across classes and races is a terrible stain on our criminal and legal systems. Many men who wind up before the courts, or in prison, or in batterer intervention programs come from communities where schools, infrastructure, housing, and medical care are subpar, and where they are likely to have witnessed violence from a young age. These men, if they have abused, also need to be held accountable. But simply feeding them into the carceral system hasn't worked to disincentivize violence or change behavior. It may keep a victim safe, but only for the period of incarceration. There are vital discussions going on now, some of which I'll talk about in this chapter, that are re-examining how we hold domestic abusers accountable and whether there are forms of accountability that would better serve survivors, offenders, and communities at large than those forms we have been relying on in the decades since we began to take domestic violence seriously as a crime.

Let's Stop Blaming the Victim

Tondalao Hall was nineteen years old when she brought one of her three children to the hospital after discovering that his legs were swollen. Soon after that, Hall and her boyfriend Robert Braxton were arrested on child abuse charges. Braxton had been abusing Hall, as well as two of their children (one had suffered several broken bones). He pleaded guilty to child abuse, and was handed a ten-year suspended sentence; he was released on probation after serving two years in jail. Hall pleaded guilty to enabling child abuse. Although actual abuse charges against her were dropped, she was sentenced to thirty years under Oklahoma's "failure to protect" laws, which state that enabling child abuse is a felony that can carry the same penalties as child abuse.

Eventually, the ACLU took up Hall's case, and she was freed in 2019, having served fifteen years behind bars. Her lawyer noted that she knew of at least fourteen other women in Oklahoma who had been imprisoned under that law and been given a longer sentence than the actual abuser in their case.

Of the various things we can do in the service of holding perpetrators of domestic and sexual violence accountable, we have to start with this: Stop blaming the victim. Stop scapegoating victims for their "failure" to control the behavior of abusers. Sometimes the misplaced blame is absurd and overt, as in Tondalao Hall's case; other times it's subtle. Often it begins with the way we speak about victims and perpetrators.

In 2010, an eleven-year-old girl was gang-raped in Cleveland, Texas, by a group of males who took pictures and video of the assault. A *New York Times* piece on the case revealed just how far we still have to go in our victim-blaming culture. The problems begin with the headline: "Vicious Assault Shakes Texas Town." *What?* How about: "Eighteen Men and Boys

Arrested for Gang-Raping a Child"? But the headline actually reflected the article's content, which focused on the effects that a vicious rape had on the townspeople, including the perpetrators. "It's just destroyed our community," one woman lamented. "These boys have to live with this the rest of their lives."

Apart from the mention of local churches holding prayer services for the victim, there was no mention at all of the effect of the horrific ordeal on her; she was spoken of only in terms of what she might have done to trigger the attack. The journalist noted that among the questions the locals were asking themselves was how their young men could have been "drawn into such an act"—implying that the victim had seduced them. "They said she dressed older than her age," he reported, "wearing makeup and fashions more appropriate to a woman in her 20s. She would hang out with teenage boys at a playground, some said." There were also questions raised by one of the interviewees about the victim's mother—Where was she?—but no questions about the fathers of the middle-school boys who participated in the rape. Where were *they*? And what exactly had they taught their sons? Nor was there any attempt in the story to provide context for the comments of the locals, or to interview an expert in sexual assault who might remind readers of how such attitudes harm survivors and help to perpetuate a culture in which rape is permissible, or at least not the fault of the rapist.

Victim-blaming taken to its extreme enables perpetrators to justify misogynistic violence. In March 2021, eight people were killed at three spas in the Atlanta area. Six of the victims were Asian women. A man in his twenties, who pleaded guilty to four of the murders and has been sentenced to life without parole, told police that the women were "temptations" he needed to "eliminate." This young man had a history of hiring sex workers, something of which he was reportedly very ashamed, and had been treated for sex addiction. He told police that he had considered killing himself but had decided that he could help other men by targeting the spas. There have been a number of cases in which men have killed women they blame for having "tempted" (or rejected) them, and there is a thriving online culture that encourages these beliefs. Murders such as those in Atlanta are the inevitable outcome of the toxic blend of victim-blaming and misogyny.

In the case of domestic violence, victim-blaming is often more insidious. Compare domestic homicides with mass shootings—which are often preceded by acts of domestic violence. The annual number of domestic homicide victims far exceeds the number of people who die in mass shootings, but they get only a fraction of the attention. Part of this is because of the sensational nature of mass shootings. Another factor, though, is that victims of mass shootings are often randomly chosen, and the killings occur at places any of us could frequent: grocery stores, movie theaters, churches, synagogues, schools, and college campuses. *That could be me*, we think. *That could be my children.* Domestic violence, on the other hand, is something that, unless we've experienced it, we tend to believe couldn't happen to us. It happens to certain kinds of women, women who make bad choices or who are too weak to leave their abusers, women—in other words—who are in some way responsible for what is happening to them. If we can succeed in convincing ourselves of this, then we can deny the unsettling possibility that abuse can happen to any woman (and to many men). We can focus on what one woman did to have gotten herself into such a mess rather than focusing on larger and more difficult questions about societal attitudes that enable and encourage male violence. It's like hammering away at the fact that the victim of a mugging was in a bad neighborhood rather than asking why we have neighborhoods, whole communities and sections of cities, that are impoverished and dangerous and best avoided. You could avoid those neighborhoods for your whole life, but that wouldn't actually solve any problems.

The message the culture sends to victims of domestic violence—that you should walk out immediately—fails to take into account all the things a woman has to fear when she leaves, and that I've talked about throughout this book: an escalation of violence, loss of custody of her children, the loss of wages or a job if she's forced to seek shelter, and so on. It holds women responsible for the abuse they suffer, and it ignores the insidious effects of chronic abuse. We've spent far too long trying to figure out what is wrong with victims and survivors of abuse, looking for some pre-existing psychopathology, and not enough time learning about how abuse is damaging to someone's psychological and emotional health, affecting their capacity to think and function—and plan a safe exit.

Family Courts

When we seek to hold perpetrators of domestic violence accountable through legal means, we are talking about family courts and/or criminal courts, and the systems with which they interact, including probation and batterer intervention programs.

Family courts are special civil courts designed to deal with family issues such as adoption, divorce, and child support or child custody disputes; they can also issue protection orders against abusing partners. The original idea of family courts was that it was preferable to solve family problems via discussion and negotiation than in criminal courts. But the family court system is often a nightmare for survivors of domestic violence and their children. (Garland Waller at Boston University has done great work documenting how family courts have failed survivors egregiously over the years.) A big problem with family courts is that they operate in a way that provides abusers with numerous opportunities to manipulate and coerce both survivors and the system. In many cases, family court is the only remaining form of access to a survivor that an abuser has, and he will try to make the most of it—often by drawing the process out. In most areas of law, final judgments and settlements end litigation, but verdicts in family court are open to frequent modifications (e.g., because someone's financial situation changes), which creates a situation that is easy for abusers to exploit. Each time an abuser files a motion, he has another opportunity to force the survivor to return to court, and he continues to reach into her life, harassing and controlling her.

The area of family courts that is most susceptible to this sort of manipulation is child custody. Abusers often want custody as a form of revenge against a woman who has left them, or simply for the sake of staying involved in the victim's life; abusers are in fact *more* likely to contest custody than men who don't abuse. A report by the American Psychological Association on violence in the family found that violent and abusive fathers sought sole custody twice as often as nonviolent fathers. Despite laws that require judges to consider domestic violence in their custody decisions, many still prefer to give some degree of custody, often unsupervised, to abusers.

Why does that happen? For one thing, there is a long-standing belief that shared custody is in the best interest of children, despite the fact that no studies have shown that joint custody results in better outcomes for children in families with a history of domestic violence. There are also ways that abusers can come off looking better in court than their victims. Custody disputes require that both parents take psychological tests. If a mother has been subject to prolonged abuse, she may actually do worse on such tests than the father, despite being the more loving, safe, and responsible parent. The father may also be better off financially, particularly if there has been financial abuse in the relationship, and so he can afford to engage in costly court battles that are beyond the mother's means.

I don't believe that the people who work within the court system are "siding" with the abuser—I actually think that most people are working from good intentions. But the system simply isn't set up to serve victims and survivors, and domestic abusers have been able to manipulate it to serve their own ends and to retraumatize those they have abused. We need a complete rethink of family courts if we expect those overseeing them to avoid making the same mistakes over and over again. Here are a few of the main issues we should address:

- Mandate training for family court judges to educate them in the dynamics of domestic violence and the specific means abusers use to manipulate the judicial system to their advantage (including accusing victims of "parental alienation syndrome" in order to gain custody); such training would also educate them on how the trauma of abuse affects a victim's psychological state, which is often used by abusers in court to score points in legal battles.

- Minimize in-person contact between abusers and victims in cases of shared child custody.

- Ensure that any visitation plans are carefully thought through to guarantee the safety of the child(ren) and the mother—for instance, more active monitoring of child-parent visitations and greater safeguards for mothers at visitation centers (e.g., to ensure they aren't followed after picking a child up).

- Immediately hold abusers in contempt of court on the first instance of failure to pay child support, bearing in mind that an abuser may avoid paying in order to prolong a court case and force the victim to initiate additional proceedings.

- To the greatest possible extent, cases involving a family should be heard by a single judge in order to minimize court appearances, reduce the risk of conflicting court orders, and ensure that decisions are based on full knowledge of the issues affecting that family.

Prosecuting Domestic Violence in Criminal Court

Domestic violence is notoriously difficult to prosecute. Many of the most damaging forms of abuse fall outside the categories of physical violence and threats of violence, those things now considered criminal acts. The unique dynamics of domestic violence complicate attempts at prosecution. Victims are often terrified of what their partners might do if they engage with the legal system. In some cases, they continue to love them, and hope that the abuse will stop and the relationship can be repaired.

The landscape for prosecution of domestic violence has evolved over the last several decades. More proactive prosecution strategies came into effect in the late 1980s as a reaction to high rates of dismissal in domestic violence cases. The standard practice had been for prosecutors and judges to dismiss cases in which a victim was unwilling to testify against the defendant. No-drop policies gave prosecutors the power to continue with a case even if the victim had withdrawn a complaint or refused to testify. A strictly enforced no-drop policy stipulated that all cases be filed and that no case be dismissed once charges were filed.

Proponents of no-drop polices argued that they removed long-standing justifications for inaction by prosecutors and made the possibility of prosecution credible to abusers. They felt the policies were victim-friendly, in that they didn't allow a batterer to pressure a victim into withdrawing charges through intimidation or control. Early evidence suggested that while mandatory arrest on its own was not a deterrent, the combination of arrest and prosecution could reduce recidivism and lethality. One study released in 2001 by the National Institute of Justice that compared outcomes from domestic violence court cases in the years prior to and following the advent of no-drop policies found a large increase in guilty pleas and a corresponding reduction in dismissals following introduction of the policies. The proportion of cases brought to trial rose tenfold, and there was also a large increase in convictions.

But problems with no-drop policies have become evident over the years. As with mandatory arrest, it's clear that an approach meant to protect victims and survivors can wind up placing them in greater danger as perpetrators retaliate with more violence. (The abuser could also lose his job, putting financial strain on the survivor and her children.) The victim often knows better than the legal system what will keep her safe. It makes no sense to issue a subpoena to a woman whose abuser has threatened her life if she comes to court. Because dismissals and acquittals resulting from cases taken under no-drop policies can embolden an abuser, the policy can serve as yet another deterrent to victims to contact the police. Finally, prosecuting all cases regardless of the chances of a successful conviction is costly and uses resources that could be employed in better ways.

With the growing recognition that police and court systems should move forward *with* survivors rather than *in spite of* their wishes, rigid no-drop policies have fallen out of favor, though recent cases such as Rachael Feazell's in Indiana make clear that there are risks to abandoning evidence-based prosecutions completely. Feazell had been in a relationship with an abusive man. Police were called at least twice—on one occasion, she declined to press charges; on another, she filed formal charges but then asked that the case be dropped. Feazell subsequently left her abuser and was living in a new home with a new partner. But in November 2021 her former partner sought her out and killed her, before turning the gun on himself. Had prosecutors proceeded with the case, against Feazell's wishes, she might be alive today.

Many advocates feel that, despite the risks, stripping a victim of autonomy still isn't the right path, and may not guarantee safety in the long run anyway, particularly if an abuser is acquitted. I feel strongly that in cases where there is sufficient evidence of abuse, escalation, and potential lethality, going ahead with a prosecution—even without a victim's agreement—can be justified. Once the abuse has reached the point where a victim's life is very likely in danger (and we have tools now to help us assess danger), a prosecution can rely on things like 911 calls, witness statements during police interventions, body cam footage, photos of injuries, cell phone and internet records, history of involvement with the police related to the abuse, the testimony of neighbors, and so on. The prosecution can proceed with the victim remaining safely out of the picture.

It is estimated that up to 80 percent of survivors recant or change their testimony before a case reaches trial. I've never liked the term "recanting victim," which makes it sound as though all the blame for lack of legal follow-through lies with the victim. The question we should be asking is: How are we making it safe for someone to go forward with a legal action? I certainly didn't feel safe when I showed up for a hearing and Cedric threatened me right there on the steps of the courthouse. If we push ahead without prioritizing victim safety, we are just replicating the conditions of abuse.

Prisons and Domestic Violence

The other school of thought about prosecuting domestic violence says that what we actually need to do is take it out of the hands of the criminal justice system and look more to communities and practices of restorative justice to change abusive behavior and protect survivors. This rethink about alternatives to criminalization that is going on in my field and among anti-violence activists is in line with a growing awareness that mass incarceration generally has not solved any of the problems it was meant to address, and has even exacerbated them. Rates of incarceration in the U.S. were essentially stable between the 1920s and the early 1970s, but since then the incarcerated population has increased by 500 percent. One out of every three Black boys, and one in six Latino boys, can expect to go to prison in his lifetime; for white boys, the figure is one in seventeen. Every year, 650,000 people are released from prison back into their communities, where they encounter nearly fifty thousand federal, state, and local regulations that serve as obstacles to reintegration. I am not an advocate for prison abolition. But mass incarceration has been a disaster, disproportionately targeting low-income people and individuals and communities of color, and serving little or no rehabilitative purpose.

Decades ago, there were reasons for believing that prosecution and imprisonment might be the answer to domestic violence. By the time VAWA passed in 1994, there was among victims, survivors, and those who supported them an enormous amount of pent-up anger and frustration about the failure of police and the courts to take domestic violence seriously, a situation that was putting women's lives at risk. There was a belief among many that if only the criminal justice system were doing its job, we could make real headway toward reducing abuse. The focus of the anti-violence movement at the time was therefore very much on holding perpetrators to account through the criminal-legal system. From the start, however, there was a divide along racial lines, as women of color were pretty sure that turning to the carceral system for solutions wasn't going to work for their communities.

VAWA was an incredible step forward in our country's acknowledgment of the problem of domestic violence and the beginning of efforts to support survivors and hold perpetrators to account. It is impossible to say with certainty how much VAWA has led directly to a reduction in domestic violence. A statistic often quoted says that rates of domestic violence dropped by more than 60 percent between 1994 and 2012. But we should bear a couple of things in mind with regard to that figure. One is that violent crime generally decreased at roughly the same rate during that period, and the other is that the figure is based on self-reporting; each year, the Bureau of Justice Statistics and the Census Bureau conduct a Crime Victimization Survey, in which a representative sampling of people are asked about victimizations experienced over the previous year, both reported and not reported to police. In addition, because the figure is based on victim interviews, it does not include homicides. In the years since 2015 there has been an uptick in domestic violence, as there has been in violent crime generally, and domestic violence homicides rose 19 percent between 2014 and 2017.

The fact is, domestic violence remains a huge problem, and the criminal justice system has not been the panacea that many hoped it would be. Laws are enforced erratically (e.g., those related to protection orders and gun possession) and there are numerous obstacles to prosecution. But a big reason criminal and legal systems haven't solved the problem is that arrest, prosecution, and incarceration all kick in after a crime has been committed; they aren't designed to address underlying causes of violent behavior, either at the level of structural inequalities and cultural norms or in terms of individual attitudes and histories. The legal system is based on the principle of separation in cases of domestic violence rather than behavior change. Arrest and incarceration make many problems correlated with domestic violence worse, such as poverty and unemployment, and it isn't clear that prosecution has a deterrent effect, especially in the absence of close monitoring through probation. When we do send a man to prison for domestic violence, we are placing him in an environment that must be one of the least conducive in the world to rethinking misogynist attitudes and destructive notions of masculinity; then we release him back into the community. And all of these conditions and outcomes disproportionately affect people of color.

Restorative Justice

There are many victims for whom arrest and prosecution are critical to their safety and their sense of justice achieved. But not all victims of domestic abuse want their partners criminally punished or want to separate from them. Many anti-violence advocates, especially those from communities of color, are looking at alternatives to arrest and incarceration, particularly for people who are not (or not yet) repeat violent abusers and who may respond to other forms of intervention.

Restorative justice generally retains links to the criminal and legal system, often functioning as a form of diversion from prosecution and incarceration, with the threat of law enforcement interventions when offenders fail to comply with any agreements made. The process is victim-focused. The victim decides whether a restorative approach is appropriate, and defines what justice would look like and what steps are necessary for the harm to be made right. Those may involve a public (or private) apology, financial reparations, commitments to certain aspects of parenting or to substance abuse treatment, and so on. Unlike traditional carceral punishment, which doesn't require an abuser to take any steps to repair harm done or even acknowledge that harm, restorative justice requires that person to take responsibility.

Restorative justice has so far been used on only a very limited basis for domestic violence. The process is difficult, and may involve face-to-face encounters between abusers and survivors; it must therefore be facilitated with care by people trained in trauma and educated in the dynamics of domestic violence, and who understand how to assess risk and develop a safety plan for the survivor as the process unfolds.

With these new approaches to justice and accountability, we should proceed with caution. But we should proceed. The criminal justice response hasn't kept women safe and often doesn't change abusers' behavior. (Currently, less than 1 percent of men who batter their female partners are found guilty or plead guilty to domestic violence.) We have millions of abused women in this country who, despite wanting the abuse to stop, will not call the police. We need to keep an open mind about alternative approaches—*if* they have the potential to bring about justice for survivors and meet their safety needs, and hold abusers accountable in ways that support behavior change.

Coordinated Community Response

People who abuse don't just hurt their victims. Their behavior affects many aspects of our society—the hospitals and mental health systems that treat victims; the employers whose staff must take sick days because of abuse; the police, courts, and social services that are already overburdened and under-resourced. Given that the effects of domestic violence are multidimensional, it makes sense for the response to it to involve the coordination of many different agencies. Moreover, a survivor of domestic violence who chooses to engage with law enforcement or the courts must navigate multiple systems (childcare, legal aid, food assistance, and so on), and the better those systems are at cooperating with one another, the easier and more helpful for the survivor.

The "coordinated community response" (CCR) approach is a violence intervention and prevention model that integrates the activities of the criminal justice system, civil and family courts, and community-based organizations and social services. Numerous programs and services can come under its umbrella: shelters, batterer intervention programs, court staff, medical services, victim advocates, law enforcement, prosecutors, and probation and parole officers. It can also include faith leaders and schools as well as judges. One of the challenges for CCRs is getting everybody to the table. It is often the domestic violence service provider who is trying to do that, and they may not have a lot of power or leverage to make it happen. Judges can be helpful for encouraging other agencies to participate.

In the past—and sometimes too often now—there was a clear division between domestic violence service providers and law enforcement. The first program in the country to formally bridge this gap was in Duluth, Minnesota. Organizers from the Domestic Abuse Intervention Programs, started in 1980 by activists in the battered women's movement, set out to better understand the laws and procedures of the criminal justice system, along with the cultures of individual agencies involved in domestic violence cases. They established relationships with different actors, and eventually several agencies agreed to work together to improve how the criminal justice system responded to domestic violence. The "Duluth Model," which has evolved over the decades, has become one of the main community models in the field and has been replicated in many other places.

CCR initiatives aren't cookie-cutter approaches. Each one should be built around the resources, characteristics, needs, and culture of local communities. But they should all be built on a foundation of agencies mutually educating one another and sharing information. Between judges' orders, probation, rotating court personnel, and overburdened services, monitoring of abusers can be erratic. People and information slip through the cracks; lapses can have lethal consequences. Accountability within a coordinated system has to be structural as well as personal.

In rural Pulaski County, Virginia, the Juvenile and Domestic Relations District Court has committed itself to strong collaboration with other agencies and victim services. In addition to close monitoring of people on probation and those enrolled in batterer intervention programs, the court has made adjustments in practice that have cost virtually nothing but have made a difference. The court created an educational video on protection orders that both the victim and the abuser must watch. In the past, when survivors requested revocation of a PO, the judge routinely granted it, working off little more than a hunch about a survivor's safety. But then he developed a detailed questionnaire, which he goes through with survivors, and which makes them both think carefully about whether lifting the PO will really be safe. When the court learned from victim advocates that survivors felt very intimidated by their proximity to abusers in court, they responded by changing how survivors and perpetrators enter and exit the courtroom. They also created a video-monitored "safe exchange zone" for child custody exchanges.

It is estimated that in up to 83 percent of cases of domestic homicide, victims, perpetrators, or both had contact with the criminal justice system, victim services, or health-care agencies in the twelve months before the homicide. We know that, based on an analysis of risk factors, many domestic violence homicides are predictable. The Domestic Violence High Risk Team Model, a type of risk-informed collaborative intervention based on the work of Jacquelyn Campbell, is an approach to coordination that focuses on the most potentially lethal cases. A multidisciplinary team (led by a domestic violence agency and including social service and criminal justice organizations) uses evidence-based risk assessments to identify these cases, then monitors them and develops coordinated intervention plans to reduce danger.

Coordination around risk and safety can also involve a victim's informal networks. In High Point, North Carolina, the police developed a method called "cocooning," in which victims form a security network of people who know about the abuse and the identity of the abuser and whom the police can contact if they cannot reach the victim; the network also includes a "proximity informant" who knows the victim's daily schedule and will notice and contact police if something seems unusual or troubling.

Members of a coordinated response team in Winnebago County, Wisconsin, recall a time when defendants would be sent home with a form for victims to sign saying they didn't wish to pursue charges. Back then, there was no compliance monitoring of POs. And when the police weren't sure who the aggressor was at a domestic violence incident, they would arrest both people. Because various judges might be involved in a single case, lawyers often tried to delay hearings in hopes of a more sympathetic judge.

Winnebago County is a case study in going from worst to best practice. As a first component in building a coordinated system, an advocate set up an on-site domestic violence assistance office in the courthouse. A single judge now stays with a case throughout multiple hearings and petitions, saving the survivor from having to repeat her story, and enabling the judge to track an offender over time and, if needed, impose progressively more serious penalties. As the judge learns a family's particular dynamics, it becomes easier to craft remedies that fit that family rather than falling back on a one-size-fits-all model. In the past, victims had often dropped cases because they couldn't afford a lawyer, so the court established a pro bono attorney project. Everyone in the domestic violence court system in Winnebago County has been through specialized training. Bailiffs keep victims and abusers away from each other. A safe visitation exchange center features staggered arrival times and on-site security. A docket coordinator pulls together all relevant information on a case for the judge so nothing falls through the cracks.

The court is also linked with a twenty-six-week partner abuse prevention program, and most offenders who are put on probation must attend a domestic violence impact panel, where they listen to victims and survivors speak about their experience of being abused. Judges monitor offenders closely and apply sanctions if they fail to comply with the terms of the court's orders. Victim advocates are always in the courtroom, and accompany the victim at every stage of the judicial process.

Pursuing legal and judicial accountability is never going to be easy or comfortable for survivors of domestic abuse. But at least when they move forward within a coordinated network, so much confusion, frustration, and actual danger can be mitigated or avoided completely.

————

If I didn't believe change was possible, I couldn't do what I do every day. In order to effect change, though, we need coordinated, evidence-based early intervention that addresses risk factors as soon as possible. At the same time, we need to work on changing the centuries-old attitudes that degrade girls and women and encourage men to assert themselves through violence, power, and domination. We need to teach, first and foremost, a belief in equality and respect for other human beings, which is a much more profound undertaking than teaching conflict resolution or anger management. We have to stop accepting that domestic violence is something we just have to live with, and stop shying away from conversations about why it happens. I challenge us to listen to the stories of those who've been abused, to hold their abusers accountable in appropriate ways, and to give victims and survivors whatever they need to rebuild their lives. And we need to remember that men who do *not* abuse are key to ending domestic violence. They can and should join us as allies in building a world where any one person's most natural place of refuge—the home—never becomes the place they most fear.

We have examples we can look to of behavior that was once socially acceptable and is now readily condemned. Strange as it is to recall, there was a time when drunk driving wasn't considered a "real" crime; people laughed it off. Then came Mothers Against Drunk Driving, founded in 1980 by a mother whose daughter had been killed by a drunk driver. The campaign changed the way we think about alcohol and driving. Since 1982, deaths related to drunk driving have fallen more than 50 percent; for people under twenty-one, fatalities have decreased 83 percent. The concept of a designated driver is now embedded as a norm in our social culture.

If a group of mothers can kick-start a revolution on our roads—one that has saved an estimated four hundred thousand lives—then surely we can change cultural attitudes and behaviors around domestic violence. We need education, collaboration, and infinite persistence. Domestic violence is a solvable problem, but we have to *want* to solve it.

Epilogue

This was my story. Each victim and survivor has *their* own story. I can only share what I have experienced in my life and what I've learned from almost three decades in this field— volunteering, speaking, advocating, and doing the day-in, day-out work. Domestic violence impacts individuals and populations in different ways. I write here in support of all victims and survivors, but I know that each of us faces different obstacles, terrors, forms of abuse, and degrees of stigma and discrimination—and that we each take a different path to safety and autonomy. So I offer these final thoughts humbly—one thing I wish I'd known as a young woman, and another I've come to understand in the years since.

Trust yourself. Again and again, I go back to my instincts. The voice that told me when I first met Cedric: *Something isn't right.* I wonder why I didn't listen to that, when there were other ways I did trust myself. There was always a drive in me, something that said nothing was going to beat me down. And yet when it came to that niggling feeling that something wasn't right with this man, I didn't pay sufficient heed. This isn't victim-blaming. I'm just wondering how it was that a young woman might know herself and still not feel it was her right to say, "I've had our child but I won't live with you because I don't feel safe." If I could instill one certainty in young people, and especially young women, it would be that: You have the right to walk away. You deserve a life free of abuse and fear.

What I've learned as a survivor is that domestic violence doesn't define me. I don't want to minimize what happened—it changed my life—but I have not succumbed to it. It doesn't rule me and it doesn't prevent me from finding happiness. Survival is work, especially survival from trauma and violence. Victims can escape violence, we can survive and remake our lives. But we're just ordinary humans. We need support, and we need to be able to make mistakes. My memoir tells some difficult stories, but it is also a celebration of the work of survival and of the many people who have helped me do it, from my childhood to this very day.

I will never erase from my history the events of the past. I will never forget the sound, the smell, the experience of being shot. But as many times as I've spoken about violence, I will *not* be defined by it. It's part of the fabric of my life—but *I* determine the weave of that fabric. That's what I want to convey to anyone who is suffering or has suffered at the hands of someone who claims to love them: This is not the sum total of who you are. There are good people out there. Find your people, and let them help you.

I was once asked in an interview what gives me hope. You'd wonder. I've listened to countless women and men tell stories of violence and abuse. I read the news. There are days hope doesn't come easy. But what really sustains me is the people who are still out there striving for a world free of domestic abuse. Women my age who say, "I'm not tired yet because not enough has changed, and until it changes I'm going to keep going." Young women, energized and full of life, saying, "We won't take this." Young men who are working for a less violent and more equal society. All these people saying, "This isn't *just the way things are*," and saying it out loud, backing those words up with courageous action.

That's what gives me hope.

Acknowledgments

I wish I could name everyone I would like to thank, but it just isn't possible in the space I have.

My mom, Bobbie. I wish I'd had more time with her to express how wonderful and powerful she was. She was everything she needed to be.

My mother-in-law, Albretta, who demonstrated how you can move on from pain, and love again.

My six brothers: Ric, Will, Brady, Ronald, Wayne, and Gary. We keep going, and though we do not spend enough time together, I want you to know that there is a part of each of you in this book.

Mrs. Malcolm, who let me read in peace and showed me love.

Pam, my rock, my alarm clock, and the person I most look to for reality checks.

Regi, who never let me feel sorry for myself and always had faith that I would be okay.

Pat(ty) and Connie, my survivor angels.

Jacque, thank you for your consistent laughter over the many years.

The Usual Suspects—Adrienne, Cindy, Gretchen, Joscelyn, Kendall, Mary, Regi, Roz, Susan, and all those who have passed through this wonderful, strong, loving, fun, and supportive group of women. Many times, my lifeline.

The NCADV team: Gretchen, Jacquie, Lynn, and Rachel. And our Board of Directors: Cheryl, David, Katherine, Kristi, Melody, Tracy, and Vicky—along with all the others who've served over the years. What remarkable and tenacious people. They are hardly aware of the impact they've made, which makes them even more special.

The members of the National Task Force, wise and strong folks from whom I constantly get an education.

The women at the White House who always understood the importance of a survivor's voice on the front lines: Lynn Rosenthal, Carrie Bettinger-López, and Rosie Hidalgo.

Presidents Biden and Obama for listening to survivors and taking action on the issues of domestic violence and violence against women in general.

My biological father's family in South Carolina, thank you for welcoming me with open arms and love.

Others who have remained friends through different parts of my journey: Lisa D., Cheryl R., Rose M., Sherida A., Sethe T., and so many more who are in my life or have passed through and left their love on me.

Molly McCloskey, for her editorial guidance and help shaping my story. She was gentle and steady as we laughed and cried. Now my friend for life.

The whole team at Atria/Simon & Schuster; my agent, Gail Ross; and especially Amar Deol, who called me to say, "You should write your story."

All the victims and survivors, those I know and those whose names I will never know. To those who have not survived, and the loved ones left behind, we keep working on your behalf.

Love and hugs to all!

Notes

CHAPTER 1: SOMEBODY

11 *In the 1980s, those working*: Judith Herman, *Trauma and Recovery: The Aftermath of Violence—From Domestic Abuse to Political Terror* (New York: Basic Books, 1992), 32.

13 *They were preparing to address*: Dayna Straehley, "RIVERSIDE: School Desegregation Chronicled in New Book," *Press-Enterprise* (Riverside, CA), November 10, 2014, https://www.pe.com/2014/11/10/riverside-school-desegregation-chronicled-in-new-book/; David Downney, "Lowell Elementary Students Reunite 53 Years After a Desegregation Battle Burned Down Their School," *Press-Enterprise* (Riverside, CA), August 15, 2018, https://www.pe.com/2018/08/15/lowell-elementary-students-reunite-53-years-after-a-desegregation-battle-burned-down-their-school/.

13 *The fire was almost certainly*: Straehley, "RIVERSIDE: School Desegregation Chronicled in New Book."

CHAPTER 3: BELOW MYSELF

25 *Years later, having worked*: https://metoomvmt.org/get-to-know-us/history-inception/.

27 *She had just filed*: Katie Benner and Melena Ryzik, "FKA twigs Sues Shia LaBeouf, Citing 'Relentless' Abusive Relationship," *New York Times*, December 11, 2020 (updated January 22, 2021), https://www.nytimes.com/2020/12/11/arts/music/fka-twigs-shia-labeouf-abuse.html.

27   *At a gas station*: Marjon Carlos, "It's a Miracle I Came Out Alive," *Elle*, February 17, 2021, https://www.elle.com/culture/celebrities/a35460385/fka-twigs-shia-la-beouf-abuse/.

27   *In emails to the* New York Times: Katie Benner and Melena Ryzik, "FKA twigs Sues Shia LaBeouf, Citing 'Relentless' Abusive Relationship."

28   *It's very subtle, she said*: Interview with Gayle King, *CBS This Morning*, February 18, 2021, https://www.facebook.com/CBSMornings/videos/fka-twigs-speaks-out-against-shia-labeouf/181325336728059/.

28   *I know that when victims*: http://dvhrt.org/about.

31   *The physical violence is real*: https://ncadv.org/STATISTICS.

32   *Author, professor, and activist*: Beth Richie, *Compelled to Crime: The Gender Entrapment of Battered Black Women* (New York: Routledge, 1996), 70.

CHAPTER 4: LEAVING

37   *On March 3, 2021*: Press Association, "Body of Sarah Everard Was Found in a Builder's Bag and Identified Using Dental Records," *Scotsman*, March 13, 2021, https://www.scotsman.com/news/crime/body-of-sarah-everard-was-found-in-a-builders-bag-and-identified-using-dental-records-3164850.

37   *receive a life sentence*: Megan Specia, "Police Officer Sentenced to Life in Prison for Murder of Sarah Everard," *New York Times*, September 30, 2021, updated October 1, 2021, https://www.nytimes.com/2021/09/30/world/europe/sarah-everard-wayne-couzens-sentencing.html.

37   *Another officer, who was*: Chris Kitching, "Sarah Everard Police Officer 'Sent Sick Meme to Colleagues on WhatsApp,'" *Mirror*, March 16, 2021, https://www.mirror.co.uk/news/uk-news/sarah-everard-police-officer-sent-23733734.

37   *In a sick twist*: Julie Bindel, "Why Are London Police Telling Women to Stay at Home?," *Spectator*, March 10, 2021, https://www.spectator.co.uk/article/why-are-london-police-telling-women-to-stay-at-home-.

37   *nighttime curfew*: Laura Smith-Spark, "Sarah Everard Case Prompts Outpouring from Women Sharing Stories of Abuse and Harassment,"

CTV News, March 13, 2021, https://www.ctvnews.ca/world/sarah
-everard-case-prompts-outpouring-from-women-sharing-stories-of-abuse
-and-harassment-1.5346082.

38 *They were making the point*: Helen Lewis, "It's Time to Lift the Female
Lockdown," *Atlantic*, March 18, 2021, https://www.theatlantic.com
/international/archive/2021/03/sarah-everard-and-female-lockdown
/618321/.

38 *While defending the rollback*: Russell Falcon and Jala Washington, "Gov.
Abbott: Abortion Bill Won't Force Rape Victims to Have Babies, Texas
Will 'Eliminate' Rapists," KXAN News, September 8, 2021, https://
www.kxan.com/news/texas/gov-abbott-abortion-bill-wont-force-rape
-victims-to-have-babies-texas-will-eliminate-rapists/?utm_medium=
referral&utm_campaign=socialflow&utm_source=t.co.

38 *The belief that women are only raped*: Rape, Abuse & Incest National
Network, https://www.rainn.org/statistics/perpetrators-sexual-vio
lence.

39 *One recent study of*: Sharon G. Smith, Katherine A. Fowler, and Phyllis
H. Niolon, "Intimate Partner Homicide and Corollary Victims in 16
States: National Violent Death Reporting System, 2003–2009," *American
Journal of Public Health* 104 (2014): 461–466, https://doi.org/10.2105
/AJPH.2013.301582.

39 *Maybe you come from a religious*: https://ncadv.org/why-do-victims
-stay.

39 *Judith Herman, whose book*: Herman, *Trauma and Recovery*, 116–117.

40 *Cedric was already in custody*: Details of Cedric's arrest and charges: *Rocky
Mountain News* staff, "Auroran Held in Kidnapping," *Rocky Mountain
News*, March 30, 1992; General Offense Report, Aurora Police Depart-
ment, March 28, 1992.

CHAPTER 5: WOMAN, 32, SHOT IN HEAD . . .

55 *He raised it to my eye level and pulled the trigger twice*: Details of shooting,
police actions, and Cedric's death: Stacey Baca, "Woman, 32, Shot in
Head, Drives 200 Yards to Gas Station for Help," *Denver Post*, June 19,
1992; Natalie Soto, "Aurora Man Kills Self in Ohio as Police Close In,"
Rocky Mountain News, October 12, 1992.

CHAPTER 6: PICKING UP THE PIECES

67   *Here are a few statistics*: Majority Staff Report, Committee on the Judiciary, United States Senate, *Violence Against Women: A Week in the Life of America* (Washington: U.S. Government Printing Office, 1992), https://niwaplibrary.wcl.american.edu/wp-content/uploads/2015/VAWA-Lghist-SenateJudiciary-10.92.pdf.

74   *Judith Herman writes*: Herman, *Trauma and Recovery*, 33–37.

75   *Abuse within an intimate relationship*: Carol A. Lambert, "Abused Women Are Not Codependent and Here's Why," *Psychology Today*, September 11, 2018, https://www.psychologytoday.com/us/blog/mind-games/201809/abused-women-are-not-codependent-and-heres-why.

75   *Hamish Sinclair, who works*: Rachel Louise Snyder, *No Visible Bruises: What We Don't Know About Domestic Violence Can Kill Us* (New York: Bloomsbury, 2019), 115.

CHAPTER 7: THE WORLD WOULD CEASE TO FUNCTION

79   *There are many such programs*: Genesis Women's Shelter & Support, "Four Ways to Help End Domestic Violence in Corporate America," February 19, 2018, https://www.genesisshelter.org/four-ways-to-help-end-domestic-violence-in-corporate-america/.

81   *She photographed it*: Feifei Sun, "I Am Unbeatable: Donna Ferrato's Commitment to Abused Women," *TIME*, June 27, 2012, https://time.com/3789753/i-am-unbeatable-donna-ferratos-commitment-to-abused-women/.

81   *Then she tried to intervene*: Dennis Romero, "The Ugly Truth: Quest to Photograph Love Turns into Passion to Save Women," *Los Angeles Times*, July 27, 1994, https://www.latimes.com/archives/la-xpm-1994-07-27-ls-20396-story.html.

81   *Donna wasn't a stranger*: Ibid.

82   *In July 1994*: *TIME*, July 4, 1994.

82   *Ron was tragically in*: Smith, Fowler, and Niolon, "Intimate Partner Homicide and Corollary Victims in 16 States."

83   *In a 911 tape from 1993*: 911 transcript, *Washington Post*, June 23, 1994, https://www.washingtonpost.com/archive/politics/1994/06/23/transcript-of-911-phone-calls/89596579-c431-40d0-a1d2-49efb88f4a55/.

83 *Simpson would be acquitted*: Ezra Edelman, director, *O.J.: Made in America*, ESPN, 2016.

85 *The clothesline project had started in 1990*:Details on history of Clothesline Project: Cheryl L. Sattler, *Teaching to Transcend: Educating Women Against Violence* (Albany: SUNY Press, 2000), 68–72; University of New Hampshire, "The Clothesline Project at UNH," UNH Tales, November 9, 2015, https://www.unh.edu/unhtales/the-clothesline-project-at-unh/.

85 *More recently, 3,200 members* Snyder, *No Visible Bruises*, 6.

85 *Gratitude is due* Herman, *Trauma and Recovery*, 29.

CHAPTER 8: EDUCATED

90 *"I feel for once in my life"*: Pam Noonan, graduate thesis, University of Colorado, 1994, 68–71.

92 *As Roxane Gay wrote*: Roxane Gay, *Hunger: A Memoir of (My) Body* (New York: HarperCollins, 2017), 40.

92 *Judith Herman speaks of*: Herman, *Trauma and Recovery*, 196–97.

CHAPTER 9: FINDING MY COMMUNITIES

94 *In her searing and beautiful memoir*: Natasha Trethewey, *Memorial Drive: A Daughter's Memoir* (New York: Ecco, 2020); interview with Michel Martin, "Natasha Trethewey Reckons with Her Mom's Domestic Abuse," *Amanpour & Company*, PBS, October 13, 2020, https://www.pbs.org /wnet/amanpour-and-company/video/natasha-trethewey-reckons -with-her-moms-domestic-abuse/.

95 *As horrific as the murder*: NCADV conference video.

96 *NET is a PTSD treatment*: Details on narrative exposure therapy: "Narrative Exposure Therapy (NET)," Clinical Practice Guideline for the Treatment of Post-traumatic Stress Disorder, American Psychological Association, 2017. https://www.apa.org/ptsd-guideline/treatments /narrative-exposure-therapy; Katy Robjant and Mina Fazel, "The Emerging Evidence for Narrative Exposure Therapy: A Review," *Clinical Psychology Review*, no. 8 (December 30, 2010): 1030–39.

100 *It was the only program*: University of Colorado Denver, Center on Domestic Violence, https://www.ucdenver.edu/centers/domestic-violence /about-us/our-work/history-mission#ac-1996-0.

CHAPTER 10: TIME FOR ADVOCACY

115 *Lynn was the emcee*: Event: "Domestic Violence Reduction," The White House, October 27, 2010, https://www.c-span.org/video/?296250-1 /domestic-violence-reduction.

116 *"I love these guys"*: Ibid., minute 29.40.

116 *He mentioned the case of Dorothy Cotter*: The Associated Press, "Man Shoots Wife Days After Release," *Cape Cod Times*, March 28, 2002 (updated January 5, 2011), https://www.capecodtimes.com/article /20020328/NEWS01/303289976; Rachel Louise Snyder, "A Raised Hand: Can a New Approach Curb Domestic Homicide?," *New Yorker*, July 15, 2013, https://www.newyorker.com/magazine/2013/07/22/a -raised-hand.

117 *He cited studies*: Thomas R. Simon, Shari Miller, Deborah Gorman-Smith, Pamela Orpinas, and Terri Sullivan, "Physical Dating Violence Norms and Behavior Among Sixth-Grade Students from Four U.S. Sites," *Journal of Early Adolescence* 30, no. 3 (2010): 395–409; "Teen Dating Violence in the United States: A Fact Sheet for Schools," Office of Safe and Healthy Students, U.S. Department of Education, 2015, https:// www2.ed.gov/about/offices/list/oese/oshs/teendatingviolence-fact sheet.html.

117 *"If there's one group"*: Ibid.; https://www.c-span.org/video/?296250-1 /domestic-violence-reduction, minute 49.30.

CHAPTER 11: SHELTER

124 *The first official shelter for battered women*: Details on early women's shelters: Women's Advocates, Our History, https://www.wadvocates .org/about/legacy/; Elizabeth Llorente, "Strengthening Her Sisters," *AARP*, October 2009, https://www.aarp.org/giving-back/volunteer ing/info-10-2009/strengthening_her_sisters.html; Larissa MacFarquhar, "The Radical Transformations of a Battered Women's Shelter," *New Yorker*, August 12, 2019, https://www.newyorker.com/magazine /2019/08/19/the-radical-transformations-of-a-battered-womens -shelter.

125 *In January 1978*: Rita Smith, "History and Purpose of Domestic Vio-

lence Coalitions," domesticshelters.org, March 10, 2020, https://www
.domesticshelters.org/articles/domestic-violence-op-ed-column/history
-and-purpose-of-domestic-violence-coalitions; NCADV internal doc-
uments.

CHAPTER 12: DRIVING THE BUS

129   *They were staging an event at the National Archives*: Event: Violence Against
Women Act 20th Anniversary Commemoration, The National Archives,
September 9, 2014, https://www.c-span.org/video/?321382-1/vice-pres
ident-biden-remarks-violence-women-act.

CHAPTER 14: WHY WE DO WHAT WE DO

144   *She later changed "rape"*: Janell Ross, "Trump's Lawyer Defended Him
by Saying You Can't Rape a Spouse. That's Not True," *Washington
Post*, July 28, 2015, https://www.washingtonpost.com/news/the-fix
/wp/2015/07/28/trumps-lawyer-defended-him-by-saying-you-cant
-rape-a-spouse-thats-not-true/.

144   *As the owner of Miss USA and Miss Teen USA*: Eliza Relman, "The
26 Women Who Have Accused Trump of Sexual Misconduct," *Business Insider*, September 17, 2020, https://www.businessinsider.com
/women-accused-trump-sexual-misconduct-list-2017-12#mariah-billado
-and-victoria-hughes-6; Kendall Taggart, Jessica Garrison, and Jessica
Testa, "Teen Beauty Queens Say Trump Walked In on Them Changing,"
BuzzFeed News, October 13, 2016, https://www.buzzfeednews.com/article
/kendalltaggart/teen-beauty-queens-say-trump-walked-in-on-them
-changing#.etg6xVmzB; Allan Smith and Rebecca Harrington, "Multiple Women Say Donald Trump Made Unwanted, Inappropriate Sexual
Advances on Them," *Business Insider*, October 12, 2016, https://www
.businessinsider.com/two-women-new-york-times-donald-trump-2016
-10.

144   *In a* New York *magazine*: Julie Baumgold, "Fighting Back: Trump Scram-
bles off the Canvas," *New York*, November 9, 1992, https://books.google
.com/books?id=BeUCAAAAMBAJ&printsec=frontcover&source=gbs
_ge_summary_r&cad=0#v=onepage&q=like%20s***&f=false.

144 *A* Guardian *columnist looking*: Arwa Mahdawi, "This Is What Rape Culture Looks Like—In the Words of Donald Trump," *Guardian*, October 15, 2016, https://www.theguardian.com/us-news/2016/oct/15/donald-trump-words-what-rape-culture-looks-like.

145 *Chelsea Clinton called misogyny*: Decca Aitkenhead, "Chelsea Clinton: 'I've Had Vitriol Flung at Me For as Long as I Can Remember,'" *Guardian*, May 26, 2018, https://www.theguardian.com/us-news/2018/may/26/chelsea-clinton-vitriol-flung-at-me.

145 *Senate colleagues said*: Bennett Marcus, "Read Joe Biden's Powerful Speech About Combating Violence Against Women," *New York*, December 14, 2014, https://nymag.com/intelligencer/2014/12/bidens-speech-on-combatting-domestic-violence.html.

145 *The idea that there*: Snyder, *No Visible Bruises*, 12.

146 *The Puritans of the Massachusetts Bay*: Elizabeth Pleck, *Domestic Tyranny: The Making of American Social Policy Against Family* (Champaign: University of Illinois Press, 2004), 4–5.

146 *The so-called rule*: Eva Schlesinger Buzawa and Carl G. Buzawa, *Domestic Violence: The Criminal Justice Response* (Washington, D.C.: Sage Publications, 2003), 61.

146 *One eighteenth-century French*: Tonya McCormick, "Convicting Domestic Violence Abusers When the Victim Remains Silent," *Brigham Young University Journal of Public Law* 13, no. 2 (2013), https://digitalcommons.law.byu.edu/jpl/vol13/iss2/8.

146 *A ruling by North Carolina's*: State v. A.B. Rhodes, Supreme Court of North Carolina, 61 N.C. 453, (N.C. 1868), https://la.utexas.edu/users/jmciver/357L/61NC453.html.

146 *Finally, in 1871*: Reva B. Siegel, " 'The Rule of Love': Wife Beating as Prerogative and Privacy," *Yale Law Journal* 105 (1995–1996): 2117, https://law.yale.edu/sites/default/files/documents/pdf/Faculty/Siegel_TheRuleOfLove.pdf.

146 *By the start of the twentieth century*: Betsy Tsai, "The Trend Toward Specialized Domestic Violence Courts: Improvements on an Effective Innovation," *Fordham Law Review* 68 (2000): 4.

147 *Stalking eventually became*: "Stalking," Victim Connect Resource Center, https://victimconnect.org/learn/types-of-crime/stalking/.

147 *The President, meanwhile, continued*: Julia Carrie Wong, "Second White House Aide Resigns Amid Domestic Abuse Allegations," *Guardian*,

February 9, 2018, https://www.theguardian.com/us-news/2018/feb/09 /david-sorensen-white-house-domestic-abuse-allegations.

147 *From a policy perspective*: NCADV blog post, "Why Increasing Federal Funding to Domestic Violence Programs Matters," January 17, 2017.

148 *We also got very involved in the Fix NICS Act*: U.S. Department of Justice Office of Public Affairs press release, "Attorney General William P. Barr Releases First-Ever Semiannual Report on the Fix NICS Act," November 14, 2019, https://www.justice.gov/opa/pr/attorney-gen eral-william-p-barr-releases-first-ever-semiannual-report-fix-nics-act; NCADV blog post, "NCADV Applauds Introduction of Fix NICS Act," November 16, 2017, https://ncadv.org/blog/posts/ncadv-applauds -introduction-of-fix-nics-act-; U.S. Department of Justice Office of Justice Programs, FY 2021 NICS Act Record Improvement Program (NARIP), December 15, 2020, https://bjs.ojp.gov/sites/g/files/xyckuh236/files /media/document/narip21_sol.pdf.

149 *Before the Equal Credit*: Jessica Hill, "Fact Check: Post Detailing 9 Things Women Couldn't Do Before 1971 Is Mostly Right," *USA Today*, October 28, 2020, https://www.usatoday.com/story/news/fact check/2020/10/28/fact-check-9-things-women-couldnt-do-1971-mostly -right/3677101001/.

150 *For Domestic Violence Awareness*: Karen Kroll, "Walking 'In Someone Else's Shoes,'" *ABA Banking Journal*, February 20, 2020, https://bank ingjournal.aba.com/2020/02/walking-in-someone-elses-shoes/.

152 *We run on donations*: NCADV blog post, "How You Can Help NCADV and Our Work," October 28, 2021, https://ncadv.org/blog/posts/how -you-can-help-ncadv-and-our-work.

152 *But in 1986, NCADV*: Paige Sweet, *The Politics of Surviving: How Women Navigate Domestic Violence and Its Aftermath* (Oakland: University of California Press, 2021), 51–52.

154 *Anti-violence activist Gretta Gardner*: International Association of Chiefs of Police, *The Crime of Domestic Violence Training Video*, minute 21.30, https://www.youtube.com/watch?v=c5dVPVqOTDI.

CHAPTER 15: MAKING PEACE

157 *Darryl, his son and Cedric's half brother*: Joey Bunch, "Darryl Glenn Issues Explanation of 1983 Assault Charge Involving His Father,"

Denver Post, July 27, 2016, https://www.denverpost.com/2016/07/27
/darryl-glenn-responds-1983-assault-charge-father/; Megan Schrader,
"Colorado Springs Senate Candidate Darryl Glenn Opens Up About
Growing Up in Abusive Home," *Gazette,* July 30, 2016, https://gazette
.com/government/colorado-springs-senate-candidate-darryl-glenn
-opens-up-about-growing-up-in-abusive-home/article_261a3b43-cc
61-5aa8-996e-faedc7ccc1d4.html; Letters to the Editor, "No Surprise
That Darryl Glenn Didn't Recall Memory of Violent Incident," *Denver Post,* July 31, 2016, https://www.denverpost.com/2016/07/31
/no-surprise-that-darryl-glenn-didnt-recall-memory-of-violent-inci
dent-2-letters/.

CHAPTER 16: SOLIDARITY AMONG SURVIVORS

163   *In mid-September 2021*: Details of gymnasts' Senate testimony and
Larry Nassar case: Juliet Macur, "Biles and Her Teammates Rip the
F.B.I. for Botching Nassar Abuse Case," *New York Times,* September 15, 2021, https://www.nytimes.com/2021/09/15/sports/olympics
/fbi-hearing-larry-nassar-biles-maroney.html?action=click&module
=RelatedLinks&pgtype=Article; Juliet Macur, "In Larry Nassar's Case,
a Single Voice Eventually Raised an Army," *New York Times,* January 24, 2018, https://www.nytimes.com/2018/01/24/sports/rachael
-denhollander-nassar-gymnastics.html; Juliet Macur, "Nassar Abuse
Survivors Reach a $380 Million Settlement," *New York Times,* Decem-
ber 13, 2021, https://www.nytimes.com/2021/12/13/sports/olympics
/nassar-abuse-gymnasts-settlement.html.

163   *"Because it's terrifying to"*: Bryan Armen Graham, "Simone Biles and
Aly Raisman Testify Before Senate on Nassar Investigation," September 15, 2021, https://www.theguardian.com/sport/live/2021/sep/15
/simone-biles-and-aly-raisman-testify-before-senate-on-nassar-inves
tigation-live-updates.

164   *One of those provisions*: Nancy Armour, "USA Gymnastics, Abuse Survivors Have Deal For $380 Million In 'Full Settlement,'" *USA Today,*
December 13, 2021, https://www.usatoday.com/story/sports/2021/12
/13/usa-gymnastics-abuse-survivors-legal-wranglings-deal/6494590
001/.

164 *In 2006 Tarana*: Tarana Burke, *Unbound: My Story of Liberation and the Birth of the Me Too Movement* (New York: Flatiron Books, 2021), 145–153, https://metoomvmt.org/get-to-know-us/history-inception/.

166 *In November 2021*: NCADV webinar, "Flipping the Script on Why Victims Don't Leave," November 23, 2021, https://www.youtube.com/watch?v=MPv1qdckN7w&t=1s.

166 *I remember a* Vanity Fair: Lili Anolik, "How O. J. Simpson Killed Popular Culture," *Vanity Fair*, June 2014 (her throat "slit so deeply her head was attached to her body by the merest thread"), https://www.vanityfaircom/style/society/2014/06/oj-simpson-trial-reality-tv-pop-culture.

166 *When a seventeen-year-old boy*: Brittney McNamara, "People Call Out Headlines Saying Maryland School Shooter Was Lovesick," *Teen Vogue*, March 22, 2018, https://www.teenvogue.com/story/people-call-out-headlines-saying-maryland-school-shooter-was-lovesick.

169 *The lockdowns had led to a predictable rise*: Caroline Newman, "The Pandemic Is Increasing Intimate Partner Violence. Here Is How Health Care Providers Can Help," *UAB News*, October 26, 2021, https://www.uab.edu/news/health/item/12390-the-pandemic-is-increasing-intimate-partner-violence-here-is-how-health-care-providers-can-help; Brad Boserup, Mark McKenney, and Adel Elkbuli, "Alarming Trends in US Domestic Violence During the COVID-19 Pandemic," *American Journal of Emergency Medicine* 38, no. 12 (April 28, 2020), https://www.ajemjournal.com/article/S0735-6757(20)30307-7/fulltext; Jeffrey Kluger, "Domestic Violence Is a Pandemic Within the COVID-19 Pandemic," *TIME*, February 3, 2021, https://time.com/5928539/domestic-violence-covid-19/.

170 *Antivirus companies reported*: Melissa Godin, "How Domestic Abusers Have Exploited Technology During the Pandemic," *TIME*, December 31, 2020, https://time.com/5922566/technology-domestic-abuse-coronavirus-pandemic/.

170 *A study conducted at Brigham*: Babina Gosangi, Hyesun Park, et al., "Exacerbation of Physical Intimate Partner Violence During COVID-19 Pandemic," *Radiology* 298, no. 1 (August 13, 2020), https://pubs.rsna.org/doi/full/10.1148/radiol.2020202866.

170 *One particularly harrowing scene*: Hannah Knowles, "A Zoom Hearing

for Her Domestic Violence Case Went Viral. Now People Are Blaming Her, She Says," *Washington Post*, March 12, 2021, https://www.washingtonpost.com/dc-md-va/2021/03/12/mary-lindsey-coby-harris-zoom-hearing/.

171 *Money for the Fund comes*: NCADV blog post, "Why Increasing Federal Funding to Domestic Violence Programs Matters, January 17, 2017, https://ncadv.org/blog/posts/why-increasing-federal-funding-to-domestic-violence-programs-matters; U.S. Department of Justice Office of Justice Programs, "FY 2007–FY 2022 Crime Victims Fund Annual Receipts," February 28, 2022, https://ovc.ojp.gov/about/crime-victims-fund/fy-2007-2022-cvf-annual-receipts.pdf.

171 *Along with our partners*: Office of Senator Diane Feinstein press release, "Senate Passes Critical Legislation to Strengthen Victims of Crime Act," July 20, 2021, https://www.feinstein.senate.gov/public/index.cfm/press-releases?ID=5E94443D-5C7D-4F53-BB5B-4B6949EED67E.

172 *I traveled to Washington*: Event: "President Biden on Reauthorization of Violence Against Women Act," March 16, 2022, https://www.c-span.org/video/?518741-1/president-biden-reauthorization-violence-women-act.

172 *The reauthorization enhances*: S.3623—Violence Against Women Act Reauthorization Act of 2022, 117th Congress (2021–2022), https://www.congress.gov/bill/117th-congress/senate-bill/3623/text?r=1&s=1.

172 *All four of the bill's*: "Senators Announce a Deal to Reauthorize the Violence Against Women Act," NPR, February 9, 2022, https://www.npr.org/2022/02/09/1079717258/senators-announce-a-deal-to-reauthorize-the-violence-against-women-act.

172 *Half of female homicide*: Emiko Petrosky et al., "Racial and Ethnic Differences in Homicides of Adult Women and the Role of Intimate Partner Violence—United States, 2003–2014," *Morbidity and Mortality Weekly Report* 66: 28 (July 21, 2017), 741–746, https://www.cdc.gov/mmwr/volumes/66/wr/mm6628a1.htm?s_cid=mm6628a1_w; Chelsea M. Spencer and Sandra M. Stith, "Risk Factors for Male Perpetration and Female Victimization of Intimate Partner Homicide: A Meta-Analysis," *Trauma, Violence, & Abuse* 21, no. 3 (2020): 527–40, https://pubmed.ncbi.nlm.nih.gov/29888652/; "Who Can Have a Gun: Domestic Violence

and Firearms," Giffords Law Center to Prevent Gun Violence, https://
giffords.org/lawcenter/gun-laws/policy-areas/who-can-have-a-gun
/domestic-violence-firearms/.

CHAPTER 17: CAUSES AND PREVENTION

179 *Men in the U.S.*: Statistica Research Department, "Number of murder offenders in the U.S. 2020, by gender," October 7, 2021, https://www.statista.com/statistics/251886/murder-offenders-in-the-us-by-gender/; James Alan Fox and Emma E. Fridel, "Gender Differences in Patterns and Trends in U.S. Homicide, 1976–2015," Violence and Gender 4, no. 2 (June 2017), https://crimeandjusticeresearchalliance.org/rsrch/gender-and-homicide/Violence and Gender.

179 *Of the murder-suicides*: "American Roulette: Murder-Suicide in the United States," Violence Policy Center, July 2020, https://vpc.org/studies/amroul2020.pdf.

179 *Approximately 80 percent*: Fact sheet, Emory University School of Medicine, 2019, https://psychiatry.emory.edu/niaproject/resources/dv-facts.html; Shannan Catalano, "Special Report: Intimate Partner Violence, 1993–2010," U.S. Department of Justice Office of Justice Programs Bureau of Justice Statistics, November 2012, https://bjs.ojp.gov/content/pub/pdf/ipv9310.pdf.

179 *Hamish Sinclair, who has*: Snyder, *No Visible Bruises*, 114.

180 *Household income is one*: Leigh Goodmark, *Decriminalizing Domestic Violence: A Balanced Policy Approach to Intimate Partner Violence* (Oakland: University of California Press, 2018), 90.

180 *Some research has shown*: Edward W. Gondolf, "Evaluating Batterer Counseling Programs: A Difficult Task Showing Some Effects and Implications," *Aggression and Violent Behavior* 9 (2004): 605–31, https://www.biscmi.org/wp-content/uploads/2014/12/Evaluating-Batterer-Programs-CDC-summary-fin.pdf; Holly Johnson, "The Role of Alcohol in Male Partners' Assaults on Wives," *Journal of Drug Issues* 30, no. 4, (2000): 725–40, https://journals.sagepub.com/doi/10.1177/002204260003000404.

180 *We know that if an abuser*: Spencer and Stith, "Risk Factors for Male Perpetration and Female Victimization of Intimate Partner Homicide."

180 *In 2019, Black females*: Press release, "Study Finds Black Women Murdered by Men Are Nearly Always Killed by Someone They Know, Most Commonly with a Gun," Violence Policy Center, September 29, 2021, https://vpc.org/press/study-finds-black-women-murdered-by-men -are-nearly-always-killed-by-someone-they-know-most-commonly -with-a-gun-7/.

180 *Femicide is actually*: J. Campbell et al., "Risk Factors for Femicide in Abusive Relationships: Results From a Multisite Case Control Study," *American Journal of Public Health*, 93, no. 7 (July 2003), https://www .ncbi.nlm.nih.gov/pmc/articles/PMC1447915/.

180 *Perhaps one of the most*: Goodmark, *Decriminalizing Domestic Violence*, 132–33.

181 *Psychiatrist James Gilligan*: James Gilligan, *Preventing Violence* (New York: Thames and Hudson, 2001), 35.

181 *Domestic violence is not*: Snyder, *No Visible Bruises*, 154.

181 *Bancroft, who works with*: Lundy Bancroft, *Why Does He Do That?: Inside the Minds of Angry and Controlling Men* (New York: Berkley, 2002), 35.

182 *Another myth is that*: Ibid., 67.

183 *In 2018, the* Washington Post *reported*: Kyle Swenson and Samantha Schmidt, "Charlie Rose: The Rise and Plummet of a Man Who Preached 'Character' and 'Integrity,'" *Washington Post*, November 21, 2017, https:// www.washingtonpost.com/news/morning-mix/wp/2017/11/21/i-am -by-nature-civil-the-rise-of-charlie-rose/.

183 *One of the thirty-five women*: Amy Brittain and Irin Carmon, "Charlie Rose's Misconduct Was Widespread at CBS and Three Managers Were Warned, Investigation Finds," *Washington Post*, May 3, 2018, https://www.washingtonpost.com/charlie-roses-misconduct-was-wide spread-at-cbs-and-three-managers-were-warned-investigation-finds /2018/05/02/80613d24-3228-11e8-94fa-32d48460b955_story.html.

184 *In the police recording*: Trethewey, *Memorial Drive*, 168–69.

184 *We can define sexism*: Brian Nichols, "Why Do Men Batter?," Men Stopping Violence, 2016, https://vawnet.org/sites/default/files/materials /files/2016-09/WhyDoMenBatter.pdf.

184 *The promotional campaign included*: Rick Rojas and Kristin Hussey, "Is Remington's $33 Million Offer Enough to End Sandy Hook Massacre Case?," *New York Times*, July 29, 2021, https://www.nytimes.com/2021/07/29 /nyregion/sandy-hook-shooting-remington-settlement.html.

184 *Not every gun owner*: Emilee Green, "Mental Illness and Violence: Is There a Link?," Illinois Criminal Justice Information Authority, May 4, 2020, https://icjia.illinois.gov/researchhub/articles/mental-illness-and-vio lence-is-there-a-link.

187 *In 2018, the National Domestic Violence*: Sarah Mervosh, "Domestic Violence Awareness Hasn't Caught Up With #MeToo. Here's Why," *New York Times*, October 16, 2018, https://www.nytimes.com/2018/10/16 /us/domestic-violence-hotline-me-too.html.

187 *Aaron noticed early on*: Karen Garcia, "Owner of Meathead Movers Brings Leaders of Organizations Against Domestic Violence Together," *New Times*, May 17, 2018, https://www.newtimesslo.com/sanluisobispo /owner-of-meathead-movers-brings-leaders-of-organizations-against -domestic-violence-togetherfast-fact/Content?oid=5115340.

187 *Another great supporter*: "Drive Against Domestic Violence," Beverly Hills Center for Plastic & Laser Surgery, 2014, https://www.beverlyhillscenter .com/driveagainstdomesticviolence/.

187 *One day in 2019*: Nicki Jhabvala, "After Hearing a Survivor's Story, This NFL Player Joined Her Efforts Against Sexual Violence," *Washington Post*, November 24, 2021, https://www.washingtonpost.com/sports/2021/11 /24/james-smith-williams-brenda-tracy-domestic-violence/.

188 *The NFL fined the team*: Will Hobson, Mark Maske, Liz Clarke, Beth Reinhard, "NFL Fines Washington Football Team $10 million; Tanya Snyder to Run Operations for Now," *Washington Post*, July 2, 2021, https://www.washingtonpost.com/sports/2021/07/01/daniel-snyder -nfl-fine-sexual-harassment-investigation/.

188 *Brenda has talked about*: Ibid.

189 *Charlie Stoops, cofounder*: Charlie Stoops, "Mandatory Prosecutions Wouldn't Change Violent Behavior," *New York Times*, September 10, 2014, https://www.nytimes.com/roomfordebate/2014/09/10/going -after-abusers-like-nfl-player-ray-rice/mandatory-prosecutions-wouldnt -change-violent-behavior.

189 *Author Leslie Morgan*: *Steiner* Kate Torgovnick May, "How We Can Help End Domestic Violence," IDEAS.TED.COM, September 12, 2014, https://ideas.ted.com/on-whyistayed-and-the-violence-against-women -act-20-years-later/.

190 *One area we could expand*: "Preventing Intimate Partner Violence Across the Lifespan: A Technical Package of Programs, Policies, and Practices,"

Centers for Disease Control and Prevention, 2017, https://www.cdc
.gov/violenceprevention/pdf/ipv-technicalpackages.pdf.

191   *The vast majority of young people*: Peggy Orenstein, "If You Ignore Porn,
You Aren't Teaching Sex Ed," *New York Times*, June 14, 2021, https://
www.nytimes.com/2021/06/14/opinion/sex-ed-curriculum-pornog
raphy.html; Pornography Statistics, Covenant Eyes, https://www.cov
enanteyes.com/pornstats/.

191   *A study in 2020*: Niki Fritz, Vinny Malic, Bryant Paul, and Yanyan Zhou,
"A Descriptive Analysis of the Types, Targets, and Relative Frequency
of Aggression in Mainstream Pornography," *Archives of Sexual Behavior*
49 (2020), https://doi.org/10.1007/s10508-020-01773-0.

191   *Research is showing that*: Emily A. Vogels, "The State of Online Harassment," Pew Research Center, January 13, 2021, https://www.pewresearch
.org/internet/2021/01/13/the-state-of-online-harassment/; Paul J.
Wright, Bryant Paul, and Debby Herbenick, "Preliminary Insights from
a U.S. Probability Sample on Adolescents' Pornography Exposure, Media
Psychology, and Sexual Aggression," *Journal of Health Communication*
26, no. 1, (2021): 39–46, https://pubmed.ncbi.nlm.nih.gov/33625313/.

192   *As Jackson Katz has written*: Jackson Katz, *The Macho Paradox* (Naperville,
IL: Sourcebooks, 2006), 4.

192   *There is growing evidence*: "Preventing Intimate Partner Violence Across the
Lifespan," Centers for Disease Control and Prevention; Vangie A. Foshee
et al., "Assessing the Effects of Families for Safe Dates, A Family-Based
Teen Dating Abuse Prevention Program," *Journal of Adolescent Health*
51, no. 4 (2012): 349–56, https://pubmed.ncbi.nlm.nih.gov/22999835/;
"Safe Dates," Violence Prevention Works, 2016, https://www.violence
preventionworks.org/public/safe_dates.page.

192   *A study published in 2019*: Elizabeth Miller, Kelley A. Jones, Lisa Ripper,
et al., "An Athletic Coach–Delivered Middle School Gender Violence
Prevention Program: A Cluster Randomized Clinical Trial," *JAMA
Pediatrics* 174, no. 3 (2020): 241–49, https://jamanetwork.com/journals
/jamapediatrics/fullarticle/2758662; Melissa Jeltsen, "How to Stop Boys
from Becoming 'Me Too' Perpetrators," *Huffington Post*, January 13,
2020, https://www.huffpost.com/entry/stop-boys-me-too-perpetrators
_n_5e1caca7c5b6640ec3d8c8df.

192 *Evidence on community-level*: "Preventing Intimate Partner Violence Across the Lifespan," Centers for Disease Control and Prevention.

CHAPTER 18: INTERVENTION

194 *In January 2022, the FBI*: Associated Press, "Brian Laundrie Wrote That He Killed Gabby Petito, the FBI Says," NPR, January 22, 2022, https://www.npr.org/2022/01/22/1075058668/fbi-gabby-petito-brian-laundrie.

194 *Gwen Ifill once called*: Clarence Spigner, "Gwen Ifill (1955–2016)," School of Public Health, University of Washington, https://depts.washington.edu/hservmph/articles/2057.

194 *Indigenous women experience*: Alia E. Dastagir, "Everyone's Talking About Gabby Petito, But They're Having the Wrong Conversation, Experts Say," *USA Today*, September 21, 2021, https://www.usatoday.com/story/life/health-wellness/2021/09/21/gabby-petito-brian-laundrie-and-tragedy-domestic-violence/5792811001/; Ben Kesslen, "All-Out Search, Media Attention for Gabby Petito Reveals Glaring Disparity for Wyoming's Indigenous People," NBC News, September 24, 2021, https://www.nbcnews.com/news/us-news/all-out-search-media-attention-gabby-petito-reveals-glaring-disparity-n1279980.

195 *There was a female Park Service*: Kyle Dunphey, "'I Can Still Hear Her Voice': Arches Park Ranger Warned Gabby Petito Her Relationship Seemed 'Toxic,'" *Deseret News*, September 20, 2021, https://www.deseret.com/utah/2021/9/20/22684359/i-can-still-hear-her-voice-arches-park-ranger-warned-gabby-petito-relationship-seemed-toxic-brian.

196 *A statement was never obtained*: Aleksandra Bush, "Gabby Petito Case: Review Reveals 'Mistakes' by Utah Police," WGNO ABC, January 17, 2022, https://wgno.com/news/crime/gabby-petito-case-review-reveals-mistakes-by-utah-police/.

197 *In addition to the psychological trauma*: Jonathan Lifshitz, Sonya Crabtree-Nelson, and Dorothy A. Kozlowski, "Traumatic Brain Injury in Victims of Domestic Violence," *Journal of Aggression, Maltreatment & Trauma* 28, no. 6 (2019): 655–59, 10.1080/10926771.2019.1644693.

197 *Evidence-gathering techniques*: Russell Strand, "The Forensic Experiential Trauma Interview (FETI), An Exciting New Interviewing Method, Uses

Information About the Parts of the Brain That Experience Trauma," Battered Women's Justice Project, March 2014, https://www.bwjp.org/resource-center/resource-results/shifting-the-paradigm-for-investigating-trauma-victimization.html; M. Bennett and J. E. Hess, "Cognitive Interviewing," *FBI Law Enforcement Bulletin* 60, no. 3 (1991): 8–12, https://www.ojp.gov/ncjrs/virtual-library/abstracts/cognitive-interviewing.

198 *Emergency orders last*: Julia Saladino and Patty Branco, "How Can Protective Orders Support Survivors' Safety?," VAWnet, September 9, 2019, https://vawnet.org/news/how-can-protective-orders-support-survivors-safety.

198 *Some studies have shown*: "Preventing Intimate Partner Violence Across the Lifespan," Centers for Disease Control and Prevention.

198 *It is believed that around*: Patricia Tjaden and Nancy Thoennes, *Extent, Nature, and Consequences of Intimate Partner Violence: Findings From the National Violence Against Women Survey* (U.S. Department of Justice Office of Justice Programs, July 2000), http://www.ncjrs.gov/pdffiles1/nij/181867.pdf; Christopher T. Benitez, Dale E. McNiel, and Renée L. Binder, "Do Protection Orders Protect?," *Journal of the American Academy of Psychiatry and the Law* 38, no. 3 (2010): 376–85, http://jaapl.org/content/38/3/376.abstract.

198 *The risk of violation*: K. A. Vittes and S. B. Sorenson, "Restraining Orders Among Victims of Intimate Partner Homicide," *Injury Prevention* 14, no. 3 (2008): 191–95, https://injuryprevention.bmj.com/content/14/3/191.

198 *But because there is ample*: Victoria L. Holt, "Civil Protection Orders and Subsequent Intimate Partner Violence and Injury," U.S. Department of Justice National Institute of Justice, 2004, https://www.ojp.gov/pdffiles1/nij/199722.pdf; Judith McFarlane, Ann Malecha, et al., "Protection Orders and Intimate Partner Violence: An 18-Month Study of 150 Black, Hispanic, and White Women," *American Journal of Public Health* 94, no. 4 (2004): 613–18, https://www.ncbi.nlm.nih.gov/pmc/articles/PMC1448307/.

199 *Inconsistent enforcement raises*: Saladino and Branco, "How can protective orders support survivors' safety?"

199 *One study out of Johns Hopkins*: Vittes and Sorenson, "Restraining Orders Among Victims of Intimate Partner Homicide."

199 *We also have evidence*: Christopher D. Maxwell, Joel H. Garner, and Jeffrey A. Fagan, "The Effects of Arrest on Intimate Partner Violence: New Evidence from the Spouse Assault Replication Program," *National Institute of Justice Research in Brief*, July 2001, http://www.ncjrs.gov /pdffiles1/nij/188199.pdf.

199 *A 2015 study found*: Erin Grinshteyn and David Hemenway, "Violent Death Rates in the US Compared to Those of the Other High-Income Countries, 2015," *Preventive Medicine* (2019), https://www.science direct.com/science/article/abs/pii/S0091743519300659?via%3Dihub; Everytown Research & Policy, "Guns and Violence Against Women: America's Uniquely Lethal Intimate Partner Violence Problem," Everytown for Gun Safety, October 17, 2019, https://everytownresearch.org /report/guns-and-violence-against-women-americas-uniquely-lethal -intimate-partner-violence-problem/.

199 *More than half of domestic violence*: Grinshteyn and Hemenway, "Violent Death Rates," 20–26, https://www.sciencedirect.com/science/article /abs/pii/S0091743519300659?via%3Dihub; Spencer and Stith, "Risk Factors for Male Perpetration and Female Victimization of Intimate Partner Homicide."

199 *Domestic homicides rose*: Laura M. Holson, "Murders by Intimate Partners Are on the Rise, Study Finds," *New York Times*, April 12, 2019, https:// www.nytimes.com/2019/04/12/us/domestic-violence-victims.html ?action=click&module=RelatedLinks&pgtype=Article.

199 *States with the highest rates*: Aaron J. Kivisto et al., "Firearm Ownership and Domestic Versus Nondomestic Homicide in the US," *American Journal of Preventive Medicine* 57, no. 3 (2019): 311–20, https://www.ajpmonline .org/article/S0749-3797(19)30197-7/fulltext; Everytown Research & Policy, "Guns and Violence Against Women."

199 *In the mid-1990s*: U.S. Department of Justice Archives, "Restrictions on the Possession of Firearms by Individuals Convicted of a Misdemeanor Crime of Domestic Violence," *Criminal Resource Manual*, 1101–99, https:// www.justice.gov/archives/jm/criminal-resource-manual-1117-restric tions-possession-firearms-individuals-convicted.

200 *Studies have shown that limiting*: "Preventing Intimate Partner Violence Across the Lifespan," Centers for Disease Control and Prevention; Holson, "Murders by Intimate Partners Are on the Rise, Study Finds."

200 *Unfortunately, prohibitions are often* "Protection Orders," Battered Women's

Justice Project, https://www.bwjp.org/our-work/topics/protection
-orders-topic.html; Saladino and Branco, "How Can Protective Orders
Support Survivors' Safety?"

200   *We could go further*: Goodmark, *Decriminalizing Domestic Violence*, 261.

200   *In 2016, a bill passed*: Graham Moomaw, "House Passes Bill to Grant
Concealed Carry Rights with Restraining Orders," *Richmond Times-
Dispatch*, February 3, 2016, https://richmond.com/news/virginia
/government-politics/article_f7aeae02-73f5-59e3-8304-0dbf7d29c801
.html.

201   *The owner of a firearms store*: Jennifer Mascia, "Advocates Warn of New
Dangers as Sheriff Urges Domestic Violence Victims to Arm Themselves," *Trace*, August 17, 2015, https://www.thetrace.org/2015/08
/louisiana-domestic-violence-murder-gun/.

201   *Guns don't make us safer*: Garen Wintemute et al., "Increased Risk of
Intimate Partner Homicide Among California Women Who Purchased
Handguns," *Annals of Emergency Medicine* 41, no. 2 (2003), 282, https://
www.annemergmed.com/article/S0196-0644(03)70107-3/pdf; Douglas
Wiebe, "Homicide and Suicide Risks Associated with Firearms in the
Home: A National Case-Control Study," *Annals of Emergency Medicine*
41, no. 6 (2003): 775, https://www.annemergmed.com/article/S0196
-0644(03)00256-7/fulltext; K. M. Grassel et al., "Association Between
Handgun Purchase and Mortality from Firearm Injury," *Injury Prevention* 9 (2003): 50, https://injuryprevention.bmj.com/content/9
/1/48.

202   *A few steps have been taken*: Suraji R. Wagage, "When the Consequences
are Life and Death: Pretrial Detention for Domestic Violence Offenders," *Drexel Law Review* 7 (2014): 195–236, https://drexel.edu/~
/media/Files/law/law%20review/Spring2015/Wagage_Drexel%
20Website.ashx; Melissa Hanson, "A Rise in Dangerousness Hearings,
Which Can Hold a Defendant 180 Days Before Trial, Could Limit Pre-
sumption of Innocence," *MassLive*, November 24, 2019, https://www
.masslive.com/boston/2019/11/a-rise-in-dangerousness-hearings
-which-can-hold-a-defendant-180-days-before-trial-could-limit-pre
sumption-of-innocence.html; G. J. Wintemute et al., "Mortality Among
Recent Purchasers of Handguns," *New England Journal of Medicine* 341,
no. 21 (1999): 1583–89, https://psycnet.apa.org/record/1999-15073
-002.

202 *Police unable to tell*: MacFarquhar, "The Radical Transformations of a Battered Women's Shelter"; Goodmark, *Decriminali\zing Domestic Violence*, 50–52.

202 *Arrests of women increased dramatically*: Leigh Goodmark, "Stop Treating Domestic Violence Differently from Other Crimes," *New York Times*, July 23, 2019, https://www.nytimes.com/2019/07/23/opinion/domestic -violence-criminal-justice-reform-too.html; Alesha Durfee, "Situational Ambiguity and Gendered Patterns of Arrest for Intimate Partner Violence," *Violence Against Women* 18, no. 1 (2012): 64–84, https://journals .sagepub.com/doi/10.1177/1077801212437017.

203 *Danger assessments can identify*: Nicole Fauteux, "Jackie Campbell: Creator of the Danger Assessment," *American Journal of Nursing* 121, no. 10 (October 2021): 68–70, https://journals.lww.com/ajnonline /Fulltext/2021/10000/Jackie_Campbell__Creator_of_the_Danger _Assessment.29.aspx; Dave Sargent, "Maryland's Lethality Assessment Program: From Research into Practice," Battered Women's Justice Project, December 2009, https://www.bwjp.org/resource-center/re source-results/maryland-s-lethality-assessment-programs.html; Program description, "Danger Assessment: An Instrument to Help Abused Women Assess Their Risk of Homicide," American Academy of Nursing, https:// www.aannet.org/initiatives/edge-runners/profiles/edge-runners-- profiles-danger-assessment.

203 *Non-fatal strangulation*: Nancy Glass et al., "Non-fatal Strangulation Is an Important Risk Factor for Homicide of Women," *Journal of Emergency Medicine* 35, no. 3 (October 2008): 329–35, https://www.jem-journal .com/article/S0736-4679(07)00414-3/fulltext.

203 *The Lethality Assessment Program*: Lethality assessment program overview, Maryland Network Against Domestic Violence, https://www.mnadv .org/lethality-assessment-program/lap-program-overview/.

204 *But where there is strong*: "Pretrial Release New Hampshire," National Conference of State Legislatures, March 13, 2013, https://www.ncsl .org/research/civil-and-criminal-justice/pretrial-release-new-hamp shire.aspx.

205 *In 2011 law enforcement*: Goodmark, *Decriminali\zing Domestic Violence*, 292–95.

206 *High Point's trip-wire*: John Buntin, "How High Point, N.C., Solved Its Domestic Violence Problem," *Governing: The Future of States and*

Localities, February 25, 2016, https://www.governing.com/archive/gov-domestic-violence-focused-deterrence.html.

206   *The first batterer intervention*: Etiony Aldarondo, "Assessing the Efficacy of Batterer Intervention Programs in Context," discussion paper presented at *Batterer Intervention: Doing the Work and Measuring the Progress,* National Institute of Justice and the Family Violence Prevention Fund, 2009, https://www.ojp.gov/pdffiles1/nij/232426%2520Paper%25202.pdf; "Batterer Intervention," Futures Without Violence, https://www.futureswithoutviolence.org/batterer-intervention/.

206   *Although BIPs have become*: Patricia Cluss and Alina Bodea, "The Effectiveness of Batterer Intervention Programs: A Literature Review and Recommendations for Next Steps," University of Pittsburgh, March 2011, http://fisafoundation.org/wp-content/uploads/2011/10/BIPs Effectiveness.pdf.

207   *Edward Gondolf, who has*: Edward W. Gondolf, "Evaluating Batterer Counseling Programs"; Edward W. Gondolf, "The Survival of Batterer Programs? Responding to 'Evidence-Based Practice' and Improving Program Operation," position paper presented at the policy symposium *Batterer Intervention: Doing the Work and Measuring the Progress,* National Institute of Justice and the Family Violence Prevention Fund, 2009, https://www.ojp.gov/pdffiles1/nij/232426%2520Paper%25203.pdf.

207   *As I was writing this*: Ron Dicker, "Zac Stacy Makes Jaw-Dropping Claim About Alleged Beating of Ex-Girlfriend," *Huffington Post,* December 14, 2021, https://www.huffpost.com/entry/zac-stacy-excuse-attack-kristin-evans_n_61b89f7ce4b0f7962d815a41.

208   *Juan Carlos Areán, who directs*: Juan Carlos Areán speaks with Ed Heisler, Chris Godsey, and Kourou Pich, *Restorative Justice and Intimate Partner Violence,* Center for Court Innovation podcast, May 2021, https://www.courtinnovation.org/publications/APIP-Podcast-Restorative-Justice-Intimate-Partner-Violence.

208   *"There is a lot of fear that"*: Ibid.

209   *In 2021, the 10 to 10 Helpline*: Elizabeth Román, "Western Massachusetts Hotline for Domestic Abusers Is 1st of Its Kind in US," *MassLive,* April 15, 2021, https://www.masslive.com/news/2021/04/western-massachusetts-hotline-for-domestic-abusers-is-1st-of-its-kind-in-us.html.

209   *A project to create*: https://violencepreventionhotline.org/.

CHAPTER 19: SERVING VICTIMS AND SURVIVORS

210 *Evaluating victim service programs*: Min Xie and James P. Lynch, "The Effects of Arrest, Reporting to Police, and Victim Services on Intimate Partner Violence," *Journal of Research in Crime and Delinquency* (November 20, 2016), https://journals.sagepub.com/doi/abs/10.1177/0022427816678035.

211 *Domestic violence homicides*: *began* Fox and Fridel, "Gender Differences in Patterns and Trends in U.S. Homicide, 1976–2015"; Spencer and Stith, "Risk Factors for Male Perpetration and Female Victimization of Intimate Partner Homicide."

211 *Domestic violence is one of*: https://nnedv.org/content/housing/.

211 *between 22 and 57 percent*: Laura L. Rogers, "Transitional Housing Programs and Empowering Survivors of Domestic Violence," U.S. Department of Justice Archives, Office on Violence Against Women (OVW), November 1, 2019, https://www.justice.gov/archives/ovw/blog/transitional-housing-programs-and-empowering-survivors-domestic-violence.

211 *A shortage of both emergency*: "15th Annual Domestic Violence Counts Report," National Network to End Domestic Violence (NNEDV), 2021, https://nnedv.org/content/domestic-violence-counts-15th-annual/.

212 *it can take ten months*: "11th Annual Domestic Violence Counts Report," NNEDV, 2016, https://nnedv.org/wpcontent/uploads/2019/07/Library_Census_2016_Report.pdf.

212 *Transitional housing is one*: "16 Things You May Not Know About Housing for Survivors," NNEDV, November 24, 2017, https://nnedv.org/latest_update/16-things-may-not-know-housing-survivors/; Amy Correia and Anna Melbin, "Transitional Housing Services for Victims of Domestic Violence: A Report from the Housing Committee of the National Task Force to End Sexual and Domestic Violence," Housing Committee Transitional housing paper, November 2005, https://safehousingpartnerships.org/sites/default/files/2017-01/TransHousingServices.pdf.

212 *The U.S. Interagency Council*: "A Guide to Reviewing Domestic Violence Transitional Housing Projects Within the CoC Competition," United States Interagency Council on Homelessness, July 25, 2016, https://www.usich.gov/resources/uploads/asset_library/Guide_To_Reviewing_DVTH_Projects_July_2016.pdf.

213   *However, rapid rehousing can*: Lyungai Mbilinyi, "The Washington State
      Domestic Violence Housing First Program Cohort 2 Agencies, Final
      Evaluation Report, September 2011–September 2014," February 2015,
      http://wscadv.org/wp-content/uploads/2015/05/DVHF_FinalEv
      aluation.pdf; "Can Rapid Re-housing Work for Domestic Violence Sur-
      vivors?" National Alliance to End Homelessness, May 9, 2016, https://
      endhomelessness.org/can-rapid-re-housing-work-for-domestic-vio
      lence-survivors/.

213   *Property owners are often*: "Local Laws That Punish Tenants and Landlords
      for Calls to the Police or Criminal Activity Occurring at the Property,"
      ACLU, https://action.aclu.org/legal-intake/nuisancesurvey.

214   *VAWA reauthorizations have included*: "16 Things You May Not Know
      About Housing for Survivors," NNEDV.

214   *Since the mid-1980s*: "Housing," National Alliance to End Homelessness,
      January 2020, https://endhomelessness.org/homelessness-in-america
      /what-causes-homelessness/housing/.

214   *One nationwide study found*: "Getting Started: A Handbook to Address
      Economic Security for Survivors," Wider Opportunities for Women
      (WOW), 2012, https://safehousingpartnerships.org/sites/default/files
      /2017-01/Getting-Started-A-Handbook-to-Address-Economic-Security
      -for-Survivors-2012.pdf.

215   *We should ensure that*: H.R.2465—Healthy Families Act, 117th Congress
      (2021–2022), https://www.congress.gov/bill/117th-congress/house
      -bill/2465.

215   *The critical areas of focus*: "Paid Safe and Sick Leave Law: Frequently Asked
      Questions, NYC Consumer and Worker Protection, November 2, 2020,
      https://www1.nyc.gov/assets/dca/downloads/pdf/about/PaidSick
      Leave-FAQs.pdf; "Economic Security for Survivors," NNEDV, July 2019,
      https://nnedv.org/resources-library/h_economic-security-survivors/;
      "Preventing Intimate Partner Violence Across the Lifespan," Centers for
      Disease Control and Prevention; "NNEDV's Legislative Priorities for
      the 117th Congress," NNEDV, June 2021, https://nnedv.org/resources
      -library/nnedvs-legislative-priorities-117th-congress/.

216   *A survey by the Institute*: "Domestic and Sexual Violence Fact Sheet,"
      NNEDV, July 2020, https://nnedv.org/wp-content/uploads/2020/07
      /DVSA-Fact-Sheet-July-2020.pdf; Cynthia Hess and Alona Del Rosario,

"Dreams Deferred: A Survey on the Impact of Intimate Partner Violence on Survivors' Education, Careers, and Economic Security," Institute for Women's Policy Research, Washington, D.C., 2018, https://iwpr.org /iwpr-publications/report/dreams-deferred-a-survey-on-the-impact -of-intimate-partner-violence-on-survivors-education-careers-and-eco nomic-security/.

216 *All services need to be*: Victoria D. Green and Larisa Kofman, "Every Door Is the Right Door: Skills and Tools for Working with Domestic Violence Survivors," District Alliance for Safe Housing, February 2011, https:// safehousingpartnerships.org/sites/default/files/2017-01/Community -Based%20Advocates%20Trauma%20Informed%20Lens%20%26%20 Legal%20Protections_2016.pdf; Heather Phillips, Eleanor Lyon, Mary Fabri, and Carole Warshaw, "Promising Practices and Model Programs: Trauma-Informed Approaches to Working with Survivors of Domestic and Sexual Violence and Other Trauma," National Center on Domestic Violence, Trauma & Mental Health, September 2015, http://www .nationalcenterdvtraumamh.org/wp-content/uploads/2016/01/NCD VTMH_PromisingPracticesReport_2015.pdf.

217 *From the outset, VAWA*: H.R.1133—Violence Against Women Act of 1993, 103rd Congress (1993–1994), Subtitle D: Protection for Immigrant Women, https://www.congress.gov/bill/103rd-congress/house -bill/1133.

217 *But recently anti-immigrant*: "AIS Priority Principles Addressing Immigrant Survivors in Federal Legislation," Alliance for Immigrant Survivors, March 2021, https://static1.squarespace.com/static/5b9f1d48da02b c44473c36f1/t/604c115363949d1dc6f58086/1615597911103/AIS-Legis lative-Priorities_Brief.pdf.

217 *A U visa is for*: "Know Your Rights: New U Visa Bona Fide Determination Procedure," National Immigrant Justice Center, https://immigrantjustice .org/know-your-rights/know-your-rights-new-u-visa-bona-fide-deter mination-procedure.

217 *About 85 percent*: Marc Levy, "Immigrant Victims of Crime Hope Congress Eases Visa Hurdles," *AP News*, March 14, 2021, https://apnews.com /article/us-news-philadelphia-immigration-crime-united-states-01d1ce d7adb9772d11a90dd0ad73629f.

217 *But more than thirty thousand*: "Humanitarian Petitions: U Visa Process-

ing Times," U.S. Citizenship and Immigration Services, U.S. Department of Homeland Security, August 12, 2021, https://www.uscis.gov /sites/default/files/document/reports/USCIS-Humanitarian-Petitions .pdf.

217 *Applicants who have applied*: Jacob Sapochnick, "Breaking Policy Update: U Visa Victims of Crime Now Eligible to Receive Four Year EADs and Deferred Action," Sapochnick law firm, June 21, 2021, https://www .visalawyerblog.com/breaking-policy-update-u-visa-victims-of-crime -now-eligible-to-receive-four-year-eads-and-deferred-action/.

217 *Abusers will often use*: Phillips, Lyon, Fabri, and Warshaw, "Promising Practices and Model Programs."

218 *This is the situation*: Editorial Board, "The Stakes in Domestic Abuse Cases Are Dire and Often Dangerous," *Washington Post*, June 13, 2021, https://www.washingtonpost.com/opinions/2021/06/13/stakes-do mestic-abuse-cases-are-dire-often-dangerous/.

218 *In a recent case*: Ibid.

219 *But many studies have*: Ibid.; "Key Studies and Data About How Legal Aid Assists Domestic Violence Survivors," Justice in Government Project, March 2021, https://legalaidresourcesdotorg.files.wordpress .com/2021/04/domestic-violence.pdf; Jane C. Murphy, "Engaging with the State: The Growing Reliance on Lawyers and Judges to Protect Battered Women," American University *Journal of Gender Social Policy and Law* 11, no. 2 (2003), 499–521, https://digitalcommons .wcl.american.edu/cgi/viewcontent.cgi?referer=https://www.google .com/&httpsredir=1&article=1404&context=jgspl.

220 *I once read that when*: Phil Klay, "After War, a Failure of the Imagination," *New York Times*, February 8, 2014, https://www.nytimes .com/2014/02/09/opinion/sunday/after-war-a-failure-of-the-imagi nation.html.

CHAPTER 20: ACCOUNTABILITY

223 *"the dangers of alcohol"*: Victor Xu, "The Full Letter Read by Brock Turner's Father at His Sentencing Hearing," *Stanford Daily*, June 8, 2016, https://www.stanforddaily.com/2016/06/08/the-full-letter-read-by -brock-turners-father-at-his-sentencing-hearing/.

223   *"an underlying deep frustration"*: "Judge in Stanford Sex Assault Case Breaks Silence Amid Sentencing Controversy, Recall Effort," CBS/AP, May 8, 2018, https://www.cbsnews.com/news/judge-persky-brock-turner -case-speaks-to-media-ahead-of-recall-vote-live-stream-today-2018-5-8/; Robert Salonga, "Judge Aaron Persky Breaks Silence, Speaks Out Against Recall Effort as Campaign Hits Stretch Run," *Mercury News*, April 19, 2018, https://www.mercurynews.com/2018/04/19/persky-speaks-out -against-recall-effort-as-campaign-hits-stretch-run/.

223   *As Suzanne Moore remarked*: Suzanne Moore, "Reeva Steenkamp Was a Victim of Male Violence. That Is the Real Story," *Guardian*, October 22, 2014, https://www.theguardian.com/commentisfree/2014/oct/22 /discussion-of-reeva-steenkamp-killing-has-sidelined-male-violence; Laurel Neme, "This 'Rhino Court' Had 100 Percent Poacher Convictions. Why Was It Closed?" *National Geographic*, August 18, 2020, https://www .nationalgeographic.com/animals/article/rhino-poaching-court-closed -south-africa.

224   *Many men who wind up*: Etiony Aldarondo, "Assessing the Efficacy of Batterer Intervention Programs in Context."

225   *Tondalao Hall was nineteen*: Aimee Ortiz, "Mother Is Freed After 15 Years in Prison for Father's Abuse," *New York Times*, November 8, 2019, https:// www.nytimes.com/2019/11/08/us/tondalao-hall-oklahoma-commuta tion.html.

226   *This young man had a history*: Jessica Valenti, "How Many Women Have to Die to End 'Temptation'?" *New York Times*, March 22, 2021, https:// www.nytimes.com/2021/03/22/opinion/atlanta-shooting-women-vi olence.html.

228   *The original idea*: "Domestic Violence Issues: An Introduction for Child Welfare Professionals," Pennsylvania Child Welfare Resource Center, http://www.pacwrc.pitt.edu/Curriculum/310DomesticVio lenceIssuesAnIntroductionforChildWelfareProfessionals/Handouts /HO3DomesticViolenceTimeline.pdf.

228   *Abusers often want custody*: Llorente, "Strengthening Her Sisters."

228   *Despite laws that require*: Monica Ghosh Driggers, Carrie Cuthbert, and Kim Slote, Battered Mothers' Testimony Project 2000–2004, Wellesley Centers for Women, https://www.wcwonline.org/Archived-Projects /battered-mothers-testimony-project.

228   *For one thing*: Bancroft, *Why Does He Do That?*, 266.

229   *If a mother*: Ibid., 47.

229   *The father may also be*: Ibid., 263.

230   *Author and sociologist*: "Evan Stark discusses coercive control," YouTube video, DomesticViolenceFilm channel, https://www.youtube.com /watch?v=NLlXXt6WNsM.

230   *A strictly enforced*: "National Domestic Violence Prosecution Best Practices Guide" (white paper), National District Attorneys Association, Women Prosecutors Section, July 17, 2017, https://ndaa.org/wp-content /uploads/NDAA-DV-White-Paper-FINAL-revised-July-17-2017-1 .pdf.

230   *Proponents of no-drop*: Angela Corsilles, "No-Drop Policies in the Prosecution of Domestic Violence Cases: Guarantee to Action or Dangerous Solution?" *Fordham Law Review* 63, no. 3 (1994): 853–81, https:// ir.lawnet.fordham.edu/flr/vol63/iss3/5/; Robert C. Davis, Barbara E. Smith, and Heather J. Davies, "Effects of No-Drop Prosecution of Domestic Violence Upon Conviction Rates," *Justice Research and Policy* 3, no. 2 (2001); 1–13, https://www.ojp.gov/ncjrs/virtual-library /abstracts/effects-no-drop-prosecution-domestic-violence-upon-con viction-rates.

231   *Early evidence suggested*: Ibid.

231   *One study released*: Ibid.

231   *Because dismissals and acquittals*: Ibid.

231   *Feazell had been in*: Ray Couture, "Some States Have 'No-Drop' Policies for Domestic Violence Charges. Should Indiana?" *Evansville Courier & Press*, December 7, 2021, https://www.courierpress.com/story /news/local/2021/12/07/should-indiana-have-no-drop-policies-do mestic-violence-charges/8820790002/; Ray Couture, "Evansville Woman Dropped Ex-Boyfriend's Domestic Battery Charges. Then He Killed Her," *Evansville Courier & Press*, November 30, 2021, https://www .courierpress.com/story/news/2021/11/30/domestic-violence-evans ville-woman-killed-rachael-feazell/8801275002/.

232   *It is estimated that*: Ellen Barry, "The Woman on the Bridge: Police and Prosecutors Spent Five Years Chasing a Domestic Violence Case. Would It Be Enough?," *New York Times*, November 28, 2021, https:// www.nytimes.com/2021/11/28/us/domestic-violence-law-enforcement .html.

232 *Rates of incarceration*: "Mass Incarceration," *Smart Justice*, ACLU, https://www.aclu.org/issues/smart-justice/mass-incarceration.

233 *A statistic often quoted*: Catalano, "Special Report: Intimate Partner Violence, 1993–2010"; Louis Jacobson, "How Much Have Domestic Violence Rates Fallen Since the Violence Against Women Act Passed?" PolitiFact, February 22, 2019, https://www.politifact.com/factchecks/2019/feb/22/joe-biden/how-much-have-domestic-violence-rates-fallen-viole/; Lynn Rosenthal, "The Violence Against Women Act, 23 Years Later," *Medium*, September 13, 2017, https://medium.com/@bidenfoundation/https-medium-com-bidenfoundation-vawa-23-years-later-4a7c1866a834; Melissa Jeltsen, "Domestic Violence Murders Are Suddenly on the Rise. The Culprit? Guns, According to One Researcher," *Huffington Post*, April 11, 2019, https://www.huffpost.com/entry/domestic-violence-murders-rising_n_5cae0d92e4b03ab9f24f2e6d?0kk.

233 *In the years since*: Rachel E. Morgan and Barbara A. Oudekerk, "Criminal Victimization, 2018," U.S. Department of Justice, Office of Justice Programs, Bureau of Justice Statistics, September 2019, https://bjs.ojp.gov/content/pub/pdf/cv18.pdf; Goodmark, "Stop Treating Domestic Violence Differently from Other Crimes."

234 *Arrest and incarceration make*: Ibid.

234 *Restorative justice generally retains*: Goodmark, "What Should Happen To Abusers If We Don't Lock Them Up?"; Goodmark, *Decriminalizing Domestic Violence: A Balanced Policy Approach to Intimate Partner Violence*, 178–202; Leigh Goodmark, "Healthy Alternatives to Prosecution Can Help Victims," *New York Times*, September 11, 2014, https://www.nytimes.com/roomfordebate/2014/09/10/going-after-abusers-like-nfl-player-ray-rice/healthy-alternatives-to-prosecution-can-help-victims.

235 *Currently, less than 1 percent*: Stoops, "Mandatory Prosecutions Wouldn't Change Violent Behavior."

236 *Organizers from the Domestic*: Domestic Abuse Intervention Programs, https://www.theduluthmodel.org/about-us/.

236 *In rural Pulaski County*: "Judge H. Lee Chitwood and Court Coordinator Jaime Clemmer discuss strategies they use for domestic violence cases in their rural Virginia county," Center for Court Innovation audio, https://www.courtinnovation.org/areas-of-focus/domestic-violence.

237 *It is estimated that in*: http://dvhrt.org/about.

237 *The Domestic Violence High Risk*: Ibid.

237   *In High Point*: Alayna Bridgett, "Mandatory-Arrest Laws and Domestic Violence: How Mandatory-Arrest Laws Hurt Survivors of Domestic Violence Rather Than Help Them," *Health Matrix: The Journal of Law-Medicine* 30, no. 1 (2020): 437–73, https://scholarlycommons.law .case.edu/healthmatrix/vol30/iss1/11.

237   *Winnebago County is a case*: "Winnebago County Domestic Violence Coordinated Courts: Working with the Community to Address Family Violence," Center for Court Innovation video, https://www.courtinno vation.org/publications/winnebago-county-domestic-violence-coordi nated-courts-working-community-address-family.

239   *Since 1982, deaths related*: "Drunk Driving Fatality Statistics," Respon sibility.org, https://www.responsibility.org/alcohol-statistics/drunk -driving-statistics/drunk-driving-fatality-statistics/.

About the Author

Ruth M. Glenn is currently the CEO and president of the National Coalition Against Domestic Violence. Previously, Glenn served in the Colorado Department of Human Services for twenty-eight years, the last nine as the director of the Domestic Violence Program. She has served on many domestic violence program and funding boards, given hundreds of presentations on domestic violence victimization and survival, testified before the Colorado State Legislature and the United States Congress, and provided consultation, training, and technical assistance at the local and national levels on domestic violence victim/survivor issues. Glenn has advocated—professionally and personally—for many policies, including reauthorizing the Violence Against Women Act and legislation involving the intersection of firearms and domestic violence. She lives in Denver, Colorado. You can follow her on Twitter @RuthGlenn.